March On!

A Fourth Wise Man in Singapore

March On!

A Fourth Wise Man in Singapore

Andrew J. Wong

Spiritual Editor

The Rev. Dr. Francis J. Leong, MM.

M.Div., D.Min., Ph.D., D.S.M.

Principal Editor

David Vaughan Marshall

Front cover photography by Giordano Aita – Italy, www.giordanoaita.com

Back cover photography by Morgan & Owens – U.S.A, http://www.morganowens.com

Front and back cover conceptualized by Daniel Tay
Book cover designed by Unauthorized Media & Susan Hood

ISBN: 978-981-09-2546-8

This book is dedicated to the late Rev. Fr. Alfred Chan, who encouraged me to seek the Word of God and got me involved with *The Return of The Prodigal Son.*

(March 29, 1941–June 1, 2013)

May the perpetual light shine on him and the late Brother Kevin Byrne. He'll always be a hero in my book for listening to a frightened boy.

Suaimhneas síoraí tabhair dó, a Thiarna,
agus go lonraí solas suthain air.

(May 24, 1931–September 26, 2014)

This book is also dedicated to the late David Vaughan Marshall, a peaceable unbeliever, an enemy of sorts, yet an uncommon friend in his final years. He was the only one who wrestled with me between the lines of this book and helped guide my writing. I'm grateful for his agape.

(October 14, 1947–August 17, 2015)

Contents

Preface

Why is this book needed now?

Pope Benedict (as he then was) detected what he called a crisis of faith in the Church. During his ministry, His Holiness called for a Year of Faith to encourage believers to rediscover their faith by undertaking a journey. (*Porta Fidei*, 2) Under his leadership, the Church also published the *Note with pastoral recommendations for the Year of Faith*. It made a number of recommendations, one of which struck me as particularly important:

> All of the faithful, called to renew the gift of faith, should try to communicate their own experience of faith and charity to their brothers and sisters of other religions, with those who don't believe, and with those who are just indifferent. In this way, it is hoped that the entire Christian people will begin a kind of mission toward those with whom they live and work, knowing that they "have welcomed the news of salvation which is meant for every man." (IV.10)

This spurred me into writing this book, the intention being to share the experience of my faith journey—how I got onto a good path to follow Jesus Christ in my daily life. My motivation to continue writing was reinforced by the initiative known as the New Evangelization, which is intended to re-evangelize every believer. What's the relationship between my faith experience and the New Evangelization? Moved by the crisis of faith in the Church, I ask and suggest answers to two important general questions:

1. Why's there a crisis of faith?
2. How can the Church address this crisis?

And the answers for your consideration:

1. Most Christians probably haven't received enough faith formation.
2. By helping every Christian embark on a journey of faith to encounter the love of God!

Who should read this book?

I hope everyone with an interest in Christianity will read this book. This would include not just active believers, but also the others whose beliefs are less strong: e.g. those who know Jesus Christ but do little about it, or who have drifted away from the Lord. This may seem presumptuous to the entire Christian world. After all, each of the many different formal denominations strongly believes they have the *truth* about God. Given the scale of these different beliefs, I need to break the ice and make my own position clear. I'm a Roman Catholic living in Singapore, but. . .

I don't believe I'm right, and you're wrong.

I'm not trying to change your beliefs. Only the Lord can convert you.

Truthfully, the little I know about my own faith humbles me.

All I'm doing in this book is writing honestly about what I've learned on my own journey, namely, that I shouldn't stay the person I am, i.e. my Christian life needs to increase.

I hope this account of my encounters with Jesus and the light I've received will inspire you and help overcome potential prejudices. I believe the message of this book is relevant to every believer and encourage you all to read through to the end. We should want to become better Christians, follow Jesus Christ and have our heart transformed, no matter what the formal denomination of our belief. In writing this, I don't think I'm being naive. I know that many brothers and sisters in other denominations hold different views. All I'm aiming for is the common ground of Christian unity, the same unity the ecumenical movement promotes because the spirit of Christ resides in every brother and sister. Perhaps this sounds too theoretical so, as a simple scriptural truth, all Christians should be united in mind and voice. That way, together, we may, ". . . with one voice glorify the God and Father of our Lord Jesus Christ." (Romans 15:6)

The starting point for this unity is that all Christians consider beginning a journey of faith. No one is excluded. Looking at how quickly the modern world is changing, we should all see benefits in expanding our knowledge and learning new things, even when those things may, at first sight, make us feel uncomfortable or appear threatening. No matter which denomination you belong to, believers should want to be formed by the same God—this is faith formation or the necessary education of the Christian heart. All believers need to follow Jesus Christ, which is why faith learning and practice are important to everyone! Naturally, I'd want this book to be inclusive: its message isn't limited to Catholics like me. In good conscience, I believe the Lord calls you and me to make this journey with Him.

I'm now going to borrow an idea first expressed by C. S. Lewis in his book, *Mere Christianity.* He was wondering how people chose their church. He concluded that the choice itself wasn't terribly relevant. What mattered was that individuals chose to follow Jesus Christ. That they entered through *different doors* didn't make them any less holy. In the battle between style of worship and conscientiousness of belief, it's sincere love that triumphs. The Lord tells those who follow Him that they're united in aspirations of hope, mission, and love. What C. S. Lewis said regarding the Lord's response in John 21:22-23 is applicable here as well: we ought to do what Jesus tells you and me.

Yes, the one thing that unites every believer "in mind and voice" is Jesus Christ and what He tells us to do—this is the other common ground to which all Christians may relate. What Jesus says is central to the essential message in this book: take up our cross and follow Him. Hence, there's no room in my book for anything that makes for division, disunity, or discord among Christians.

To illustrate this mission, the second part of the book discusses what makes a Christian. I suggest he or she should *get up and eat*, especially if this believer is experiencing despair or suffering a loss of faith. Why should he or she *get up*?

Christians need to eat for the long journey.

What does this mean?

The Bible commands every Christian to arise and allow the Lord to feed him or her with the Word. God will transform the heart within our lifetime, if only we let Him. This change can begin when believers hear and obey the call to leave their Egypt for a journey with the Lord into the spiritual desert.

With this thinking in mind, I hope you'll understand why I believe every Christian should read this book.

Is a Christian a *Christian*?

To suggest why every believer should start this journey, let me ask you a few questions:

- Why do many Christians have simply no time to announce the Good News?
- Are scores of believers reluctant to carry their cross?

- What numbers have stopped trying to do what Jesus said?

If we're right to presume every Christian has *welcomed the news of salvation* into his or her heart, why then are many finding it so hard to follow Jesus Christ? If the presumption has been misplaced and we know to be true that many Christians *are* suffering a crisis of faith, isn't faith formation the answer to the crisis? Put in another way: how can we expect believers to follow Jesus Christ and do the will of God, if their faith does *not* stand on a firm foundation?

For the record, this book's message about faith formation isn't new. It was most recently helped along by the writings of the late Pope John Paul II (now St. John Paul II). He's been emphasizing the need for a systematic catechesis of all who gather to worship the Lord, both young and old.

In *Catechesi Tradendae*, St. John Paul II began with a historical perspective. The first missionaries were sent to countries that weren't Christian. They spoke with people who hadn't heard of Jesus Christ and His great love for humankind. That type of missionary work is still needed, but it ignores the problem *back home*. Most children in Christian countries are taught the basics of the Christian Faith. However, unless the learning continues into adulthood, their grasp of the love of God remains undeveloped. St. John Paul II said in particular: "Among the adults who need catechesis . . . who have never been able to study deeply the Christian teaching . . . have never been educated in their faith and, as adults are really catechumens." *(Catechesi Tradendae,* 44)

St John Paul II's concerns for the believers *back home* may sound astonishing, even startling. Are many Christians still perched on the "threshold of faith" (*Catechesi Tradendae,* 19) and, if so, why haven't they passed through the "door of faith" (*Porta Fidei,* n1)? I believe the lack of adequate faith formation explains why many Christians aren't practicing, or producing the fruit of, their faith. Someone should speak to them, as somebody did for my benefit.

How will we know whether an individual's faith formation is adequate?

We could look for understanding, asking: does this person possess knowledge of the Faith? Alternatively, we could look for action, asking: does the believer pray and celebrate the sacraments regularly? The problem with such questions is the uncertainty of the answers: it's extremely difficult to scrutinize the heart's motives and loyalties. The fact a person may be able to quote from the Bible does *not* mean he or she will act consistently as a Christian. Similarly, there may be a routine of church activities, but physically attending church does *not* of itself make the person a follower of Jesus Christ.

So what should we be looking for? What's the evidence of a crisis of faith and how do we tell whether it's being addressed?

It comes down to the extent to which each individual loves God *in* his or her heart. Complacency means no faith formation is likely felt needed. But if we feel it's a struggle to keep the Word of God, we've taken the first step to address the problem. Obviously, there will be good days and bad days, meaning the strength of our faith is likely to fluctuate as circumstances change. Recognizing the need to develop and reinforce our belief will gradually lead to true and lasting faith. This may sound daunting. Indeed, we may be setting off on a journey to learn and do the will of God but, with dedication, we'll reap rewards. Jesus tells every believer that, ". . . most men's love will grow cold. But he who endures to the end will be saved." (Matthew 24:13)

Was the Lord referring to the love of nonbelievers or people who haven't heard of Him? No, of course not. This tells me that no believer can take his or her faith for granted; everyone has to struggle to obey the Word of God till his or her final breath. Believers may have been struggling to practice the faith on their own or in unbelieving surroundings. Hence, the mission of this book is to make the case for lasting faith to be formed gradually in a small community, on a journey that may well last a lifetime.

Why may a lifetime of spiritual learning and training be needed?

The old thinking was convenient because it required little effort by believers. People supposed they were becoming Christians simply by going through a short course of catechesis, participating in a few Christian activities, and/or by making a public commitment to give up sinful behavior. Even today, many still treat all the baptized as Christians who have renounced themselves both in word and action, are daily following Jesus Christ, and carrying their crosses. Not surprisingly, many of these believers struggle to bear fruit without the continuing education of the heart. Indeed, somewhat ironically, such believers often become confused or even scandalized if any of their fellow worshippers prove *not* to be paragons of virtue, charity, and love. Yet this confusion can be minimized, if we all become more aware of and love those around us. That is, we take a leaf out of St. John Paul II's writings, then steps to rediscover the love of God and neighbor in our heart.

In all of this, where's the heart of the Church?

It's found in the hearts of all Christians!

It surges the strongest when all believers turn their hearts together toward the Lord in trust, humility, and love. When fewer Christians desire to love in the way of the cross—to love beyond oneself, carry one's cross, and follow Jesus Christ—the hearts of Christians may soon turn into stones. We aren't there yet, but before it's too late, we need to find out how many have become lukewarm, tasteless, and hidden.

There's something else you should know: I'm convinced the heart is the hardest to educate.

Why am I so convinced? Because when I look into my own heart, I see a lifetime's experience of:

- an unwillingness to listen,
- willful blindness,
- judgmental behavior, and
- resentment that I was suffering.

How do we help a believer receive *the news of salvation* into his or her heart? The process of faith formation is like the red pill. Not only will it educate the heart, help nurture Christian life, and open eyes and ears to the heavenly reality, it can also shape new hearts to join the ranks of the faithful. But remember that faith formation may require a lifetime of the Lord working in us. Although some pharmaceutical companies tell us their pills can produce an instant cure, we can't expect the course of faith formation to be completed in a few short years. That said, once a sound foundation is in place, Christians can undertake the Lord's mission of love and charity. So take heart. There is a plan to push back the crisis and reclaim lost hearts, lost souls, and lost lands.

How's the exchange of ideas developed?

At the beginning of the second part of the book in Chapter 14, I identify three archetypal Christians who may benefit from the message in this book:

- the Christian who has strayed (let's call him or her Andy),
- the churchgoing Christian (he or she is referred to as Andre), and
- the lukewarm Christian (let's suppose he or she may be Andreas).

There was a bit of Andy, Andre, and Andreas in the initial stages of my faith journey. I hope no one actually called Andy, Andre, or Andreas will take offense: these are only variations of my name, Andrew, and used to show the different parts of my history. If you see Andy, Andre, or Andreas in your history, I hope you'll recognize where you are on your journey and seek the Lord's help to form your faith.

Thinking that other Christians failed to show him love or kindness, Andy could have been scandalized. As a Prodigal Son, he might have run away, abandoning the Faith because he couldn't accept the feuding in his church. Or he may have suffered and didn't feel he received enough help from God, or his brothers and sisters. Or he may be a Christian sinning repeatedly, tried to change, failed, and gave up. Andy should take courage because he just needs to be reacquainted with God's message of love.

Andre could be an earnest, churchgoing Christian. Even so, he may not be fully aware of what goes on in the celebrations, or the breadth and depth of the Faith. He's conscious of the strangers gathered beside him to worship, offering the peace that seems more symbolic than meaningful. He may not even know that he's a priest, prophet, and king. Even if he does, Andre hasn't begun or doesn't know how to begin his mission and service. Take courage, Andre may not have started practicing how to love yet.

Andreas could be a lukewarm Christian, celebrating the sacraments regularly, or occasionally if he's busy with other commitments. However, he doesn't bear any fruit. If challenged, Andreas might tell us he already knows everything he needs to know about the Faith. When asked for more details of what he believes, or to explain what gives him hope of eternal life, he offers little or no answer. He might just say he is, or has been, busy. He might also justify his Christian life and experience by pointing out his church attendance, or the *good deeds* he performs. This Andreas is likely to be offended by the idea he isn't doing enough as a Christian. Moreover, he might bristle at the suggestion that he has never developed his faith beyond the first lessons he received. Andreas should take courage, though he ought to take steps to learn how to love.

In the exchange of ideas, I'm not directing what Andy, Andre, and Andreas must do. I can't persuade anyone to convert if they have already rejected the idea of sin, suffering, or salvation. I can't make a skeptic welcome the themes in this book that require faith. Coming to the believer, how can I oblige him or her to deepen his or her faith, live according to the Gospel, or love as Jesus commanded? All I can do in this book is share my experience and present what I've learned from the Word of God and the teachings of the Church. As a priest, prophet, and king, it's my duty to communicate the hope I've received in my encounters with Jesus Christ. I've no expectations that you'll accept what I have to say.

Rather it's the Lord Himself who will speak to all believers, one by one. It's Jesus who offers to do the principal work of conversion and the necessary transformation of hearts. The question for you today, at this crossroad, is whether you'll consider saying, "Yes!", to a journey of faith, with the Lord leading all the faithful.

What prompted me to write this book?

When I began writing in May 2013, I was responding to an inner urging to give an account of my faith journey, which had been germinating for a few years. My story begins as a young man searching for Jesus Christ who evolves into a believer, setting off on a serious journey to follow the Lord. My first plan was to write an entirely personal chronicle. This was to be me *as is*. My life would be offered up as an example to others. However, as the words flowered on the page, I felt drawn to another mission. I'm still describing my life's experiences and traveling the same road, but the motive has become outward-looking.

Since my youth, I've cast myself in the role of the Fourth Wise Man. Now, who is this character? In late Victorian times, Henry Van Dyke wrote *The Story of the Other Wise Man*. It features Artaban as the fictional Fourth Wise Man, who was supposed to travel with the other Magi but missed the camel train. In seeing my early self as Artaban, I'm not somehow claiming wisdom—quite the reverse! While continuing a frustrating search for the Lord, the Fourth Wise Man did many good works. Like Artaban, I was searching for the Lord and had the same impulse to reach out to anyone in need. In this way, I'd embraced the spirit of Matthew 25:40. There's similarly no happy ending in my journey so far, not without the eyes of faith. The most-recent path traveled has taken a deeper turn. It goes beyond searching for the Lord because I now want to follow Jesus Christ.

When asked about his book, Henry Van Dyke shared he'd never felt the writing was his own: it was as though he'd been given the story. In a similar vein, the focus of my writing changed midstream. I sensed the Lord was prompting a less passive emphasis. This additional prompting is what I meant by developing an outward-looking mission that "travels the same road."

The heart of this book is now a positive proposition that every believer should undertake a spiritual journey. I'm aiming to exchange ideas with you, so you may consider heeding His call. If you accept, I believe you'll find your heart transformed on such a journey with the Lord. To be clear, I'm not claiming any part of what I write about this journey is original. I'm doing no more than describe the ideas of others and showing what happened to me when I acted on their advice. I anticipate that someone may come later offering a better exchange of ideas, but they shall be doing the will of God if all believers are encouraged to follow Jesus Christ.

Reading cues

This book is an account of events in my life. I didn't imagine or make up any part of the factual narrative, although I've taken artistic liberties that will hopefully make the reading experience more enjoyable. The text is divided into two distinct parts:

- Part 1 describes the stages of my meandering faith journey during which I found His path, and
- Part 2 explains why I believe a transformative journey of faith is needed.

I offer the first part as a moral tale. It poses questions and invites you to draw possible lessons for your spiritual reflection. Chapter 1 also introduces the all-important theme of God's love and its relevance to the journey of faith. The love of God was what prompted my search. This led to several encounters, then the present marching on a journey that follows Him. In this chronicle of a Fourth Wise Man in Singapore, I give an account of this journey in a more or less chronological order, highlighting the various themes in play at certain ages as my faith took its shape from the Potter's hands.

In the second part, I offer an understanding of the Lord's path that should address the following questions. How does a Christian:

- Encounter the Lord?
- Learn the faith that's been given to him or her?
- Discern and do the will of God?

This path is a journey of faith on which all believers should encounter Jesus Christ. I'm confident the Lord will teach us His ways thoroughly, if only we let Him.

How have I written this book?

I've aimed for a plain writing style that mostly delivers an everyday meaning. There are, however, a few exceptions which I need to explain. Some subjects require technical language. I couldn't avoid the jargon. When talking about the spiritual message, I was occasionally inspired to offer prose that grafted itself onto the rootstock of the Word of God—I'm hoping my literary cultivar will bear spiritual fruit. I also liked to have fun. In bouts of creative exuberance, I painted similes and metaphors to add more color and depth. Now, I address the readers who enjoy puzzles: there are precisely 153 hidden references, most of which are derived from scripture. Each reference counts as one, even though its use is repeated or different versions appear in several places throughout the text. For example, if you look again through an earlier page of this Preface, you should see the phrase, "eyes of faith," and a reference to a "Potter." The former draws its inspiration from John 20:29, 1 Peter 1:8-9 and 2 Corinthians 5:7. The latter is another way of referring to the Lord that we see in Romans 9:21, Jeremiah 18:6, and Isaiah 29:16. Now, why did I hide so many references? I didn't want this book to be flooded with citations in parentheses, especially when the expressions tended to be descriptive, embellishing or idiomatic. Happy hunting! If you don't catch any fish, fret not. At this point, however, you should realize I haven't succeeded in my quest for plain English throughout!

Grasping the plain message in this book—marching on a long journey of faith—doesn't require you to recognize any of these scriptural, literary, pop-cultural or historical flourishes. For those with the wit to see, these literary expressions are intended to add new levels of meaning and reveal a deeper love for the Word. To a lesser extent, they also relieve my art's ache. More generally, the use of biblical themes in this book isn't in any particular order. I've used them as figurative expressions when they matched the episodes or topics in this book.

The characters and places in this book are real, so I needed to be sensitive about privacy. Not surprisingly, my wife, parents, other family members, friends or acquaintances (or even my tormentors mentioned in Chapters 4 and 5) prefer their identity and personal life to remain private. To protect them, their names and other background details have been concealed and, wherever possible, I've only revealed details in a pleasing light.

We then come to the decision of the Church to mark 2013 as the Year of Faith. To help explain what the Church hoped to achieve, I shared my experience in this book and offered a plan that should contribute to the New Evangelization. To bolster my case, I've referred to a number of illuminating texts and extracted quotations from them where they illustrated or supported what I wished to say about rediscovering the Faith.

Two caveats

The first caveat is a simple disclaimer:

I'm not a theologian, nor am I pretending to be an expert on scripture, hermeneutics, dogmatic theology, or the history of the Church and the Faith.

Some readers might expect a qualification in at least one of the theological disciplines before writing a book about the faith journey. I beg to differ. If I may draw another instructive inspiration from C. S. Lewis in his book, *Mere Christianity*: the best service I can offer as a Christian is to share my faith experience and take a stand on my concern—that faith formation is needed for all. I know what I know. This is my experience, and you can judge the competence of my understanding by reading and checking what I write.

If Christians accept this message and leave their Egypt for a journey of faith with the Lord, I'd have done no more than my duty. This is why the second part contains a number of quotations and references. I want you to understand that I'm not saying anything new about the Faith or the spiritual journey. All I'm doing is sharing my understanding of the Word and the teachings of the Church: these speak of the need for a timeless journey of faith.

My experience is also drawn from the marching on my journey of faith. Even if I'm wrong about some details, it doesn't change the nature of the service I want to perform. I wish for all believers to understand the need of growing the precious faith each has been given. Only then can we develop the right level of spiritual knowledge and sense of mission.

Because I'm not an "instructor in the faith," it isn't my job to tell you what should be learned on the journey. The responsibility for leading the development of your faith falls on your church. All pastors of souls have the knowledge, skill sets, and experience in teaching the precepts that are fundamental to a flowering of every Christian's faith. When you knock on the door of your church, the program of faith formation your pastor will provide should educate your heart and help you on the journey. Yes, I'm hoping you *will* consult your pastor. Ask him if the message in this book is relevant to your Christian life.

The second caveat is this:

Are you free to pursue other paths that lead to eternal salvation?

This book proposes a journey of faith as the panacea. It should cure everything that isn't right in your spiritual life, including a crisis of faith.

Are there other paths?

There should be, but I don't know enough to talk about alternate routes. All I can say is that people should find what works for them. If another path helps you to follow Jesus Christ, carry your cross, and do the will of God, that's already a good thing. There's no need for you to change. If the other paths don't help you to love as a follower of Christ should, then consider the proposition in Part 2 of this book for the love of the Lord.

Why do I keep referring to the Church?

Alert readers will have noticed the references to *Church* with a capital C. I apologize. I need to make an intrusion into the theological sphere (among many in this book). As I explained earlier, I'm not an expert in either theology or ecclesiology—the study of the Church. Even so, I need to distinguish and use the term *Church* according to its context. I'm using *Church* in a general sense to mean everyone who comes together to praise and worship. In my context, this includes the People of God (that is everyone), followed by the religious, the priests, the Bishops, and the Pope (who is *servus servorum Dei*—the servant of servants to God). When referring to the local parish church, I've mostly used the term *parish* or *church* in lower-case. This capitalization distinguishes the few that meet in a local assembly from the many churches that combine to make up the Church worldwide.

For the sake of some brothers and sisters who haven't grasped the true magnificence of the word *Church*, let me risk a few more words. The most familiar usage refers to the entire assembly gathering to celebrate the Eucharist, as the Body of Christ, with Jesus as the head. In this context, the local church (in lower-case) is the Church (in upper-case). This thinking is consistent with paragraph 1329 of the *Catechism of the Catholic Church* (CCC), which says: ". . . the Eucharist is celebrated amid the assembly of the faithful, the visible expression of the Church." In paragraph 7 of *Sacrosanctum Concilium*, an important conciliar document produced by the Second Vatican Council, it says explicitly that: "From this it follows that every liturgical celebration, because it is an action of Christ the priest and of His Body which is the Church . . .". When Christians assemble to celebrate, they constitute the Church that belongs to our Lord.

The final point I want to make is that there *is* a Church, even when the faithful gather to celebrate the Word of God, or pray and sing, without a priest present. By this, I'm not saying that there's no need for a priest—far, far from it! I'm saying something more profound. The Church is capable of assembling to worship without a priest being present. Paragraph 7 of *Sacrosanctum Concilium* says: "He is present in His word, since it is He Himself who speaks when the holy scriptures are read in the Church. He is present, lastly, when the Church prays and sings, because He promised: 'Where two or three are gathered together in my name, there am I in the midst of them'. (Matt. 18:20)"

Yes, the Church is not just the leaders, the clergy, and the religious—it's also you and I—all of us together. With these explanations, I hope you'll appreciate how I use the term *Church*, whether in upper- or lower-case, or why I sometimes use the term *parish*. To begin grasping the message in this book, ask yourself: "Who or what *is* the Church for me?"

With all this ringing in your ears, let's proceed. The star has risen, and there's a long journey ahead of us.

Part One

THE MORAL TALE OF MY INITIAL JOURNEY

Then the righteous will answer him, "Lord, when did we see thee hungry and feed thee, or thirsty and give thee drink? And when did we see thee a stranger and welcome thee, or naked and clothe thee? And when did we see thee sick or in prison and visit thee?" And the King will answer them, "Truly, I say to you, as you did it to one of the least of these my brethren, you did it to me."

—Matthew 25:37–40

Section I

LOVE OF GOD

1. Haven't I Loved All This While?

1. Haven't I Loved All This While?

God loves us all as we are

God loves me as I am.

I know He loves you too. What's God's love got to do with this book?

Everything! For I've encountered His love in my journey of faith. For this reason alone, I need to share my experience with you. Now, how am I sure about this love of God?

Well, God sent His only Son to live His life on earth. By doing so Jesus became a *slave*, the condition all of us share as a suffering people. Why did the Son of God assume our condition of suffering?

It was God's plan for Jesus to come and give us the Good News—the Good News that our God loves us very much. He desires all mankind to reconcile with Him. He is offering to wipe our slate clean by taking every one of our sins upon Himself.

Each time I look at the cross, I'm reminded that our Lord Jesus suffered horrendously for all men and women, *even though we were His enemies*. This proves clearly that God loves all of us as we are, including all our sins, willful warts, and blameworthy blemishes because He loved us even before we made the decision to lead a new life in Christ. Why did He make this awesome sacrifice of dying on the cross for you and me? He took the place of all guilty sinners to help us realize that all men and women need to love!

It's our sins—our failure to love—that nails Him to the cross every day of our lives. We suffer because we fail to love. Yet our Lord obediently accepted the shame, pain, and suffering (inflicted by all sinners) to prove the Father's great agape—His sacrificial love for you and me. God didn't give us this love for us to just sit back, enjoy, and bask in His love. He yearns to unshackle our capacity to love. He loves us, so we can love Him and, through loving Him, we can begin responding with the Christian agape by loving, serving, and giving ourselves to, our neighbors.

Yes, God's love has everything to do with the necessary journey of faith. Faith formation is all about learning the agape, the love of God that saves. When more Christians have learned to love, the truth of God's love can grow brighter again in this world now filled with so much noise.

Indeed, God is waiting patiently for every Christian to announce His love to the whole world.

The active love of a Christian

I'm assuming you're a believer and accept God's love for all of us. If you were a Christian once, you should have heard something about this Good News.

Now, how does one encounter this love of God?

For starters, Christian love isn't passive. We don't simply sit inside a building or in a room, and feel God's love. Feelings are fleeting—fervor fading fast when flustered. Suppose you attend church assemblies on a regular basis. Do you think God looks down from heaven and shines the light of love on you because you've come into a church hall? The experience of Christian love should be something more than just receiving the feeling that God loves you.

Think about it. Ask yourself, "Why do you choose to avoid or meet other people?" If you shut yourself away and avoid all social contact, are you doing this to escape opportunities for love? Now turn the question around. Do you go out and meet other people to give yourself a chance to experience love? Does meeting other people reinforce the possibility of giving and receiving love?

So then, Christian love is active!

To prove this to ourselves, we should leave the safety of our rooms and love God by loving one another. More importantly, there should be no precondition concerning when and whom to love. The decision to love shouldn't be something we make only when it's convenient for us. No matter what the time and place, no matter what other duties and commitments we have, we should love every person we meet. Everyone includes the hungry, the thirsty, the stranger, the naked, the sick, and the prisoner.

That list isn't exhaustive of Christian love. There *is* much more. If I may ask you:

"Do you love the sinner (the adulteress in John 8:5, the younger son in Luke 15:30, or the woman with a bad name in Luke 7:37)?"

No?

Let's try again, "Do you love your enemy?" (Matthew 5:44)

You don't?

"Are you one of those people who blames yourself, your brothers and sisters, or even God for the suffering in your life?"

You do?

"Have you given up trying to change?"

You have?

Well, you aren't alone!

What should you do?

Gather your courage and turn to the Lord. Begin by considering the possibility that you have *not* met the obligation to love another as he or she is, or in the Christian sense. Remember a Christian doesn't have an option to love, nor is the process of change a solitary activity. You can't wrestle yourself to the ground and force yourself to give up all your unloving ways. To make that change, you need the grace of God. To learn how to love, you need His help. Even those who consider themselves staunch Christians need to cooperate with God who is working so hard to teach us how to love. Don't be surprised if we find ourselves running away from God. What He is asking of everyone will require the essential Christian struggle. Indeed, most of us may need our entire lifetime to become Christians who can love God and one another.

What if we can't love?

I tell you frankly, for all my efforts, I'm still not able to love as well as I should. Although I'm making some headway, I'm not yet a Christian who can love wholeheartedly. This has been a hard truth to accept. After all,

- I was baptized,
- received catechism in my teens,
- attended church faithfully,
- was an active participant in various church ministries, and
- attended numerous talks on the Bible.

However, none of these outward signs of faith and devotion helped me to love. From my experience, I found that love couldn't be learned in a one-time lesson or in a short series of lectures. Love requires constant practice in a proper community, especially with people who are hard to love (including myself). All I've done in my life up to this point is take the first stumbling steps to follow where my Lord leads me.

Reading this, some of you may be feeling a little disheartened. Here I am, a lifelong believer, telling you I'm not yet a spiritual success. Allow me to offer you consolation from my experience. The first step is always the most difficult. That *is* the need to admit the failures:

- the unwillingness to listen to God;
- the inability to follow Him; and

- the reluctance to love as He has told us to.

When we're finally willing to admit that we need God in everything we do or say, we'll have begun to look for the way to a better state of Christian being and doing.

Before I found the right path, it was as though I was living in a bubble, seemingly separated from God's love and not knowing what to do about it. I didn't have a book like this to read. No one supervised the growth or direction in my faith. Had God not intervened, I'd still be lost. Now I can measure the number of steps I've taken along the right path. I receive more consolation in my progress. I know I'll make progress because the Lord is leading me. Courage! Once you've taken the first step, God will be by your side and give you the strength to continue even if progress seems hard. Trust in the Lord, follow His lead, and you too will make precious progress.

Though I was given faith to recognize the love of God, I needed more. What I lacked was sufficient spiritual training of my heart. I had no real faith formation, so my heart couldn't love like the crucified and risen Lord—it was just too difficult on my own. Why must I learn the cross? Jesus made this clear in Matthew 10:38.

Given my encounters with God's love, I've been driven to share my faith experience. It's my hope that you'll benefit from my account and decide how you can follow Jesus Christ beyond this crossroad.

"Without love"

In my earlier days as a believer, my life was a paradox. I believed I loved my Lord. If you'd been able to hear me, my lips were uttering the words, "Lord, Lord, I love you." The reality was rather different. I was full of pride and other heavy sins. Worshipping the idols of money, career, and success, I'd been deceiving myself. Despite mouthing the words of adoration, I'd been showing scant love for my Lord when I:

- failed to cherish the Lord's help in my life;

- forgot that He built my career; and
- claimed the success that I hadn't toiled for.

I lost sight of the truth that my life was blessed with generous gifts from the Lord.

This brings me back to the Christmas story I read under the title, *The Fourth Wise Man*. At that time, I was just an innocent boy, working conscientiously through school. Questions about life and death, and thoughts of a heavenly destination weren't high on my list of priorities. Somehow, when I turned the pages of the story, they became transparent and, through the words, the Lord spoke to me. This was my first encounter with the Lord. He planted the seed of faith in me, and I went searching for Him.

Three encounters with the Lord

Like all humbled Christians who are able to look back with eyes of faith, I can see the Lord's blessings in my history. There's no doubt that I've encountered Jesus Christ, the living God! We've all come across stories of individuals receiving *unexpected* forgiveness. In a different context, others tell of their recovery from a near death, albeit *heavenly,* experience. Then there are the accounts of those who were terminally ill, ready to die, who then received an *inexplicable* healing. My story is similar with comparable, astounding events. I've had three amazing encounters with the Lord in which He intervened in my history.

Recognizing this truth helped me draw closer to the Lord. The earlier encounters made me feel much love for the Lord—I wanted to pitch tents for Him in those times.

When I think about those encounters, the Lord's help felt like rain poured on an arid, parched desert. The Lord's rain had overflowed my cup with feelings of joy but, at the time, I didn't appreciate the nature of the thirst He was working hard to quench.

I thought my thirst had been quenched by my search for the

Lord. Instead, my Savior had been leading me onto His path of life. Unfortunately, in those early years, I didn't understand the need to begin a faith journey nor why the Lord was generous to me.

Busy, but not a follower

My reaction to the second encounter was to identify some church ministries in which I could help. I felt spiritually happy when I was shedding blood, sweat, and tears in those church groups. I was very committed and always busy on Sundays and special Feast Days, with activities in the church producing a calculation I didn't recognize as ironic. The more I devoted myself to the parish, the more I felt free to pursue my secular life. For want of a better expression, I was investing in the spiritual to justify a worldly pursuit of career and ambition without being judged. I thought I could excuse my materialistic pursuits with *good deeds* in church.

The nuggets in the Bible about conversion and renouncing the world didn't register in my heart because I was only skimming the scriptural surface. For example, I did hear what Jesus said in Matthew 16:24: "If any man would come after me, let him deny himself and take up his cross and follow me." Not wanting to see beyond the words and grasp the real meaning of this call, I chose not to ask what self-denial would involve. I just assumed that, in any given week, spending a few hours of my time in church or doing charitable works was enough. There was no basis for this wrong thinking. I simply supposed the idea of giving up everything only applied to the clergy and the religious, that they were the *followers* who should be obliged to accept this duty. *Ordinary* Christians like me were exempt. Indeed, in my pride, I claimed self-righteously that it shouldn't apply to me because I was a diligent parishioner who went further than *ordinary* believers by being so active in church. Consequently, I ignored the personal invitation from Jesus to become His follower.

I'd say I've spent the first forty years of my life squandering my Lord's patience.

Faith learning on my own

Because I was quite active in church, I became friendly with many priests. This should have helped me understand what the Lord was trying to teach me but, yet again, I didn't see a chance for learning. One such friendship was with the late Fr. Alfred Chan. He was close to my father, and naturally I befriended him as well. Like many churchgoers who looked forward to sermons given by their favorite priests, I enjoyed Fr. Alfred's many profound homilies. In private, he often encouraged me to read the Bible but, in my teens, I lacked humility. I didn't think I needed a priest for a spiritual guide.

This doesn't mean I ignored his advice completely. I did try studying the Bible, but it was tough thumbing through the tome on my own. So I did the next best thing when I got the chance, rare as it was: I attended occasional lectures given by priests in other parishes or in the well-regarded Pastoral Institute. I ended up hop-scotching among popular priests as they taught specific, but random topics. One week, I might listen to an exploration of The Sermon on the Mount and, in the next, whichever biblical theme piqued my interest, e.g. Salvation History. The result was an unstructured patchwork of occasional learning that left me unsatisfied and less clear on what the Lord wanted from me.

These early attempts to learn about God's love didn't penetrate my heart much. Saying *no* to a priest as a guide had become a problem—I'd denied myself a spiritual instructor who could regularly monitor the formation of my faith.

Until the scales fell from my eyes

Without any doubt, the Lord visited me and gave me an impulse of love to see the hungry, the needy, and those without safe harbor. Then accepting charity as part of the Christian role, I gave my time and money to the poor and needy beginning from my days as a schoolboy. This simplistic cause and effect comforted me. If a Christian was always generous and helpful, I thought I was being a good Christian. For as St. Cyprian counsels: ". . . he who gives to the least, gives to God."

I believed I was spiritually alright in those early days because I felt I loved my Lord Jesus, my family, the people I befriended in church, and the less fortunate the Lord put on my path. Considering my commitment and enthusiasm in the parish, and more general charitable works, I thought I was doing reasonably well in forming my own faith.

Above, I said I was like a man in a parched desert. Unfortunately, this made me the foolish man who built his house on sand (Matthew 7:26) because my life wasn't truly and completely centered on the Lord.

Despite receiving help from the Lord, I continued my own ways that were at odds with the Lord's will.

Dark suffering

Against stark odds, I became an attorney, educated in Singapore and trained in England. I've had many years of rewarding practice in Singapore, Thailand, and New York. My work required me to fight like a strong warrior for my clients. I thought nothing of engaging *Goliaths* and slaying those in my way, making *justice* my guiding principle, and aiming to redress all injustice suffered by the weak who engaged my services. Unfortunately, the victories and favorable outcomes reinforced my pride.

In the midst of my life, He also gave me unsurpassed joy in a beautiful partner, who also believed in the Lord. We fell in love and made a decision to build a life together, with the Lord as the cornerstone. I've no doubt that the Lord was present at our wedding. Yet tragically, as quickly as the sun shone and the rain poured, the Devil entered our marriage. My wife hastily slipped through my fingers, rock-solid one moment, fine grains of sand the next. She left our marriage and, after that, the Faith as well. No one could have prepared me for the glacial collision that sank my marriage.

My hope for a life to be filled with love and children touched the bottom in cold despair.

When my marriage fell apart, I felt as if a limb, or perhaps my rib, had been severed and discarded. I didn't merely suffer heartache, as some supposed. At the nadir, it felt as though a sharp sword had pierced my heart. Devastated, I awoke alone, outside the garden, on the cold hill's side. I experienced a dark, inconsolable grief—wondering if God still cared. Since 2007, I've been blinded, shamed, and brought ignominiously to my knees. Not surprisingly, my strength and skills as a man of justice couldn't save me.

If the Lord hadn't been by my side, I'd have gladly hung from a tree to arrest my grief, exclaiming to the whole world: *This is my suffering.* If the Lord hadn't given me the Word in Psalm 22, I'd have lost the will to continue living through this bitter strife—this bleak and dreary life. If the Lord hadn't been with me in my suffering, I wouldn't have had this favorable time today to learn the deeper, uncommon love.

In my third encounter with the Lord, He guided me onto His path that enabled me to learn the Word and His ways. As a result, my feet tread steadily on a better path that must replace my earlier self-serving itinerary.

Now motivating me is the unequivocal meaning of 1 Corinthians 13:3: ". . . haven't love, I gain nothing." If I want to be a faithful Christian—a follower of Christ, what love must I learn? In the language of the cross and resurrection, God's agape beckons a radical change in my life. On my forward journey, I must allow Jesus Christ to replace my heart of stone. With a new heart of flesh that my Lord may give me along the path of life, I hope to love as He did.

His path of life

A journey to learn the real meaning of love

At the age of twelve, I began my journey as a Fourth Wise Man, but only in recent years have I had the privilege to go further and deeper. The Church has given me the Word to forge a transformative relationship with the Lord. There's more faith formation to come, and more stripping of the *old man* in me. As I enter my middle years, the account of my life has moved on from the simple interpretation of the Fourth Wise Man. I'm still following in Artaban's footsteps, i.e. I'm still moving along the path to reach wherever Jesus happens to be. But instead of traveling onward as Andrew in the role of Artaban, I'm now marching on as a follower of Christ. This means I've embarked on a better journey to learn the radical love: the love of God that invites me to renounce myself, so I can love my Lord and neighbor.

To echo the Word I've received, I must do at least two things:

- write this book, because only when I've committed my beliefs to paper, will I make them clear to myself; and
- share the experiences which have led me to this junction and so benefit you.

Why must I echo the Word in my life? The Lord has said plainly that *the word that goes forth from His mouth shall not return to Him empty, but it shall accomplish that which He purposes, and prospers in the thing for which He sent it.* (Isaiah 55:11) It's the Lord's will that I believe in Jesus Christ and, through following Him, I can learn all His ways. More importantly, I need to learn how to love as He loves me. The Word has acted in my life, so what then is my response? How can I not share my experience or resound the hope I now have in me?

I also need to rediscover my first love for Jesus, which St. John spoke about in the Book of Revelation. (2:4) The encounters with the Lord had made me believe in Him in my heart. In the same way as a mother loves her newborn or the young man experiences his first love, I began to search and do many things for the Lord, i.e. this was my first love for Jesus. Unfortunately, this first love waned, but I'm being given the chance to reacquire this first love for my Lord by allowing His Word to reenter my heart and bear fruit.

Looking into the future, I don't know where the Lord's path will take me. Fortunately, there's no need to know. I trust my Savior and believe He will shape me by His love. The destination has already been picked out for me, which means the Lord should take me where I can best serve Him. This makes the journey holy. I'm still a sinner, who once thought it was hopeless to change, or pointless to love a difficult person. I don't deserve to be holy and can't earn my salvation, but it's the Lord who tirelessly wipes my slate clean. By this, I know He is forming me into His holy likeness. How can I be sure of this? I'm confident because He has promised His saving help, which I've embraced and accepted. With this confidence, I can take courage to carry my cross and follow Him.

Why does carrying one's cross and following Jesus Christ require courage? When the Lord engages with me, *He tells me what to do.* I always have a choice whether to obey or do something else that pleases me. On His path, the right choice of carrying my own cross is going to be hard. It'll sap my strength and test my resolve to do what the Lord says. I know hardship will come, but I can't run away—to do so would be to turn away from the love of God. This means I need my Savior's encouragement to make the right decisions and *accomplish that which He purposes.*

To help me stay on the right path, I've made my home in the Lord and invited Him to remain in me. This makes me shudder with expectation and trepidation for, as I move forward on my journey of faith, hope, and love, the Lord will give me lessons and experiences. Like any good gardener looking after his fruit tree, the Lord sometimes prunes, cutting away the dead wood. When the right action is taken, the next crop of fruit will grow in spiritual abundance and sweetness. As one of His branches, I can expect some of this cutting to be consoling; other times challenging.

For the love of my brothers and friends

Even writing this book is a challenge because it means you may be able to judge me. I'm sharing episodes that will shine a light on the skeletons so carefully locked away in my emotional closet. I fear some would be all too ready to shake their head at this narrative of suffering and shame at school, jeer at this tormented servant of the law, and sneer at this believer's broken marriage. Despite my anxiety, I know I can't expect your sympathy or ask for your understanding. Accepting the imminent judgment, the old man still in me winces in anticipation of the humiliation to follow publication.

There's just one consolation. It's the Lord softly prompting me to share my history with every brother and sister who does the will of God. Why do I think the Lord is prompting me?

So He can breathe life into all our dry bones and quench our thirst!

This account of my spiritual journey is also necessary for my recollection of the Lord's journeying with me—suffering alongside me—helping me to find His Way. By the light Jesus has shined in my darkness thus far, I risk sharing this precious memorial to thank Him for all the work He is doing in my history. This account is being given so that my light doesn't remain hidden and I can be salt to you. I thought my sign was broken, the beautiful sign of my marriage torn asunder, but I've been driven to place my lamp on the lamp-stand. My ego has to fall into the ground and die, thereby enabling every brother and sister to benefit from this testimony, and all may give thanks to the glory of our God. I can't be ashamed of what I've suffered or be embarrassed that I needed the Lord to work so hard to lead me in the right direction.

For this reason, I'm obliged to make this heartfelt plea to all pastors of souls everywhere to help form the faith of all Christians with the Word. Everyone *is* entitled to learn on a journey of faith, not unlike Abraham's. I can't in good conscience remain silent. I understand the essence of the Christian faith: that we believe in Jesus Christ in our heart and, through His saving power, we can all receive the divine redemption. My restatement of a timeless call for a spiritual journey doesn't differ from this essential message of hope. The Lord, however, has helped me appreciate that faith in Him is more than mere belief. Even adding in some charitable works or church activities isn't enough.

God's love in our life

The Lord offers the Good News that *is* the most profound message of love. To help us understand, He became a role model of what's required. Even when we were still sinners, He loved us by dying an undeserved death on the cross. Through this example of perfect obedience, the Lord shows us the immeasurable expanse of God's love for everyone. By this love, He invites us to do what He says: love as He loves us. The Lord unites His suffering with the unfortunate, unbearable suffering in our life. God's love and suffering will give meaning to our life in this world of suffering. So we should aim to learn this love of God, so terrible and yet beautiful as it was displayed on the cross.

I'm confident of the Lord speaking to all our hearts, then we'll say "Amen!" to His love. Yet the form of God's love is counterintuitive. It isn't love as most people understand this term. For we ought to:

- love even our enemies,
- forgive others repeatedly (and more still),
- carry our own crosses of tough love and difficult suffering, and
- allow suffering to transform us.

Only when we love in such ways, can we begin to love as Jesus loves us.

As soon as we have this Christian agape in our heart, the Lord obliges us with a mission to share the Good News with others who don't know about God's love for them.

How does a Christian practice this agape in his or her Christian life? To attain this Christian love, we might require a lifetime of learning from the Lord and prayer to deepen our relationship with Him. It's easy to say, "I believe," or "I love," but what does our heart really say? Some of us offer excuses not to love. Many more fudge their commitment to walk the walk. Indeed, too few persevere for the sake of the Lord's mission. So it's hard for our heart to learn humility and contrition. We all need His grace to become Christians ready and willing to love. It isn't easy to follow Jesus Christ, which is why He requires us to struggle.

Hence, it's very easy for all believers to take courage, despite any failure to follow the Lord in our life's journey thus far. All you need do is to begin a serious journey at this crossroad. No matter how well you think you know God, you can benefit by discovering faith, love and communion in small communities. In such a serious journey, you should experience the love of God and produce spiritual fruit pleasing to the Lord. You'll also have an opportunity to live a life according to the Good News that is Christ.

To give you the account of my journey as a Fourth Wise Man, I must start from the very beginning. I need to explain the significance of Henry Van Dyke's story and describe how my faith journey wandered left and right.

Have I loved my God with all my heart, soul, and strength? No, I haven't. I felt I'd been following my Lord but I didn't do what Jesus told me to do. In short, I haven't been a Christian. On the better faith journey I've begun, however, I'm sure the Lord is helping me learn the agape, the true meaning of *love.*

I'm convinced that He yearns to help you as well.

Section II

THE FIRST ENCOUNTER

2. The Story of the Fourth Wise Man
3. The Search for Jesus Begins
4. Fear
5. Mental Abuse

2. The Story of the Fourth Wise Man

The Lord intervenes

As you'll discover in the next Chapter, my life in the faith should have started on the best possible footing. I attended Catholic primary and secondary schools, and went through catechism in the church. Unfortunately, neither school nor parish advanced the training of my heart. When I was twelve-years-old, it took an intervention to kindle my spiritual love for the Lord. I read a *Reader's Digest* story called "The Fourth Wise Man," adapted from the original, *The Story of the Other Wise Man* by Henry Van Dyke. First published in 1895, the novel is much loved, but it never found its way to the recommended reading list for religious instruction. I believe the Lord wanted me to encounter Him and did so through this Christmas story.

Out of boredom behind my closed bedroom door, I'd turned to reading to escape the cheerless learning of my Chinese lessons. The reading habit then blossomed into a hunger for knowledge of all types. I began devouring the entire *New Book of Knowledge Encyclopedia* and *The Oxford Children's Encyclopedia of Science & Technology*. This gorging on knowledge then led to feasting on the Hardy Boys and Nancy Drew series. My appetite whetted; I rapidly graduated to the more mature titles and non-fiction books I could find on my family's bookshelves. They included *A Short History of the World* by H.G. Wells, military history titles, and books introducing the Greek and Roman mythologies.

Even though books surrounded me, I delighted when the postman delivered the latest edition of *Reader's Digest*. My first action was to turn to "Laughter the best medicine." I always enjoyed the humorous, rib-tickling jokes submitted by readers from around the world—laughing boisterously as only the young know how. I counted on *Reader's Digest* to publish thoughtful pieces and the occasional heartwarming story to comfort my soul. It offered other lessons that helped open my mind to our incredible world of fascinating personalities, compassion, and tenderness. Without my realizing it, the writers taught me about character, kindness, and hope as I was growing up. I'll always be grateful to the good writers for contributing their work. This all made *Reader's Digest* dependable as it offered good reads in each month's edition. The meatiest part was found in the last section: I could expect to find an original short story, or adaptations of the best of current and classic literature that were always enjoyable to read.

I supposed the Lord knew I was learning nothing from the catechism and must have reached out to touch me in my heart with the story of "The Fourth Wise Man." When I put the magazine down, my tears were flowing freely. From then on I wanted to dedicate my life to the same search for the Lord. This was more than a pleasant feeling or religious high. "The Fourth Wise Man" prompted me to search for the Lord among the hungry, the thirsty, the strangers, the naked, the sick, and the prisoners. I still have this yearning today—I still believe that Jesus is present in the poor, invisible, and forgotten.

What's this story?

"The Fourth Wise Man" is a fictional extension of Matthew's Gospel account of the "wise men . . . from the East." (Matthew 2:1) He was a physician, as well as an astrologer, who went by the name of Artaban. He too saw the signs in the heavens announcing the birth of the King of Kings and wished to make the journey with the other wise men. Artaban sold his beautiful home—imagine that. He used the money to buy three precious gifts, which he intended to give in homage to the Lord: a sapphire, a ruby, and a pearl of great price. The wise men agreed to meet each other at the appointed place and time of departure. Unlike the other wise men, Artaban always ran behind. On this occasion, he missed meeting the others because he'd been tending to an old, dying Hebrew man. The other wise men waited as long as they could and left without him. This forced Artaban to return to his hometown, where he sold the sapphire to buy supplies for the long journey on his own. Fortunately, his patient gave him directions to Bethlehem. A few days later, he set off in the direction of the star, carrying his remaining precious gifts, the ruby and the pearl.

By the time he arrived in Bethlehem, the birth of Jesus had already taken place. The Holy Family had fled the town and were reported escaping toward Egypt. While he was debating what to do, Herod's soldiers appeared, bent on massacring all the first-born male infants found in and nearby the little town of Bethlehem. Moved with compassion, Artaban gave up the second of his three precious gifts to rescue a mother and her newborn child.

In Egypt, Artaban searched for Jesus. He spent his time among the poor and lowly, and looked after the sick and needy. The Lord was nowhere in sight though there were many needing Artaban's help. After thirty-three years, he visited Jerusalem in the hope of finding the Lord. He was getting on in years and made this final journey with the ardent desire still of presenting his remaining precious gift to the Lord. He wasn't too late, and he certainly wasn't empty-handed.

When he arrived in Jerusalem, he learned a Jesus was to be executed. Despite doing great works, this man offended those in authority by claiming to be the Son of God. At this news, Artaban knew in his heart this was the King of Kings he'd been searching for all those years. Hastily, he made his way toward Golgotha, where the Lord was condemned to death by crucifixion, thinking he could buy the Lord's freedom (or at least try). At the gates, he chanced upon soldiers abusing a young girl. She pleaded for Artaban's help. This plea presented the same lifelong struggle between honoring the Lord in his journey and the impulse of love in his heart. Yet again, he allowed his heart to rule and used the pearl to buy the release of the girl. With the last treasure gone, he made his way to the Lord empty-handed.

Before he could reach the Lord, however, there was an earthquake and a piece of the roof from a nearby house fell on Artaban, gravely injuring him. As he felt his life draining away, he whispered his regret for failing to pay homage to the Lord. He apologized to the Lord for not arriving on time and having no gift with him. Then a voice from heaven spoke to Artaban in the words of Matthew 25:40:

> I tell you solemnly, in so far as you did this to one of the least of these brothers of mine, you did it to me.

Artaban then died a peaceful and joyful death, knowing the Lord had accepted his offerings of love.

Why was this story important to me?

"The Fourth Wise Man" became more than a story for me. Like Artaban, I'd also encountered the Lord, even though I'm just dust and ashes. As Psalm 8 says,

> . . . what is man that thou art mindful of him, and the son of man that thou dost care for him? (verse 4)

In another place, Psalm 90 tells me,

> For all our days pass away under thy wrath, our years come to an end like a sigh. The years of our life are threescore and ten, or even by reason of strength fourscore; yet their span is but toil and trouble; they are soon gone, and we fly away. (verses 9 and 10)

I'm no one. Why did my Lord see fit to visit and teach me?

He taught me to search for Him among the needy, the voiceless, and the neglected, with the same impulse of charity that the world thinks misguided, misplaced and misspent. They asked why I spent my money on the weak and poor who couldn't repay me? Why bother, when I should be lavishing all manner of indulgences on myself and my loved ones? Why spend time on the dying or the hopeless, when someone more important deserved my time and attention, someone who could further my interests or reward me? Such is the thinking of those who cling to the material world and all it promises.

He planted the seed of charity in my heart to help me recognize a need when it appeared and make the same love offerings to the Lord. Along with this impulse to love, the Lord gave me consolation because my soul would ache each time I came across a poor, homeless man—"Is that you, my Lord?" He also taught me to give without expecting any gratitude, return, or reward for these works—not in this life.

I hope we can be clear about how my young self understood the importance of the story. In Artaban's search for Jesus, he ended up practicing charity that was approved by the Lord. Artaban liquidated all his assets and bought three easily carried gifts. He wasn't reimbursed for the treasures he surrendered or spent on his journey. He ended up penniless because it was enough for Artaban that the Lord accepted his heavenly offerings.

In some ways, I wanted to accept this teaching from the Lord. Unfortunately, I only had the knowledge and understanding of a twelve-year-old, so I was barely able to tell my right hand from my left. Only the Lord knows what I've done. Remarkably, He taught me this journey of the Fourth Wise Man would be filled with seeming conflicts, disappointments, and of needs that never end. It was difficult to accept that the time and charity I would offer and the giving of myself would feel as if wasted, unacknowledged, and unappreciated. Looking back on this journey of *good deeds*, it's astonishing I retained any motivation given that I've had to confront similar, difficult questions to those faced by Artaban.

This was my first encounter with Jesus Christ. I made up my mind to look for the Lord, as Artaban did, when I was twelve-years-old.

Could this story be important to you?

My summary does little justice to Henry Van Dyke's beautiful prose, or that of the author (whose name I'm unable to recall) who produced the abridgment published in *Reader's Digest*. I hope you'll get a copy of either or both versions of this Christmas story, and read it yourself. Perhaps this will allow the Lord to begin a history with you.

Can you remember how faith was given to you? If you were a cradle Christian like me, was there an experience or a similar story that made your heart exclaim, "Yes, I need more of Jesus Christ!"? If you had such an experience and it prompted you to search for the Lord, then you've had an encounter with the Lord that's similar to my first. There's no logic to this. It's an experience of faith. What would prompt a person who didn't believe in God in one moment, then in the next cry out, "Abba, Father!"—unless faith has been given to this person? If I didn't receive faith, then what could have prompted me to begin a lifelong search for the Lord that's filled with difficulties and needs that never end?

What prompted you to believe in the Good News?

Some of you might protest and say you've had no such encounter with Jesus in your life. Let me ask you a few questions: Did your heart well up inside you when you saw pictures or heard accounts of Mother Teresa tending to the abandoned, hopeless, and dying? What about those of the late Pope John Paul II, who struggled with Parkinson's, but refused to stop serving and come down from his cross of poor health? What did your heart say when you saw Team Hoyt attesting an astounding ardor in endurance races all over America? How did you respond when you learned about the late Fr. John Tae-Suk Lee's zeal for the hapless children and lepers of Sudan? It's very likely that the Spirit moved you, but you might have forgotten or didn't know what to make of your experience. I hope you'll realize that the love of God is imprinted in your heart:

> The desire for God is written in the human heart, because man is created by God and for God; and God never ceases to draw man to himself. Only in God will he find the truth and happiness he never stops searching for. (CCC 27)

If, for some unknown reason, you haven't had an encounter with Jesus in your life thus far, I hope you won't rule out the possibility of one arising from the pages of this book. If having read this book, you are prompted to cry out in the manner described above, or search in any way for the Lord, then take note—the Spirit is moving you as a son, or daughter, of God.

3. The Search for Jesus Begins

Cradle Catholic

I was born in the old Sennett Estate, a few years after Singapore declared independence. It was the tradition then to baptize infants when they were just a few months old. So my parents took me a little way up St. Michael's Road for baptism in St. Michael's Catholic Church.

As I was growing up, they provided a loving environment, which made me aware of the faith given to me by the Church. As a family, we regularly attended Mass and novena prayer services. Everyone in the family celebrated the important feast days in Advent and Lent. When the time came around, we faithfully joined in the annual processions organized by St. Joseph's Church on Victoria Street and the *Novena Church* (Church of St. Alphonsus) on Thomson Road.

Up to the age of twelve, however, I remained indifferent to my Creator as the faith had yet to become significant to me. In part, this was because my family had neither learned the Faith nor prayed together at home or on a daily basis. So the extent of our Christian life was that we went to church regularly on weekends.

When the years added up to the right total, I began attending

Catholic High School for primary education and St. Joseph's Institution for secondary education. Catholic school education should have reinforced the little that my parents were teaching me. Strange to say, I don't remember any prayer or devotional life in my many years of Catholic school education. Perhaps I was a spiritual truant, stealthily slipping away in my head during all the prayers and Masses.

I do remember the Bible Knowledge classes in St. Joseph's. Michael Broughton, a De La Salle Brother, taught my class. Brother Michael belongs to an order of religious brothers that lives the faith through education in many countries, all around the world. He brought the Bible to life for me, unraveling the numerous symbols, e.g. the feeding of the 5,000 and the 4,000, or the contrast between the betrayals by Judas and Peter. Sadly, all momentum was lost when I moved to my junior college and discovered that Bible Knowledge wasn't offered as a G.C.E. 'A' Level subject.

The Teflon quality of religious knowledge continued in the parish, where I attended the catechism classes as a youth. I think this might have been a problem of teaching style, which presumed that I already had faith or that I knew the Lord. The Bible was taught as a series of stories. Notwithstanding the spiritual fog, I remember my first communion. It was built up as an event. It was given importance so that I would remember it. I couldn't, however, appreciate the significance of receiving the Lord at the time. It was only a matter of rote for me: "Remember, you are receiving the body and blood of Jesus Christ." I was required to believe this. So I did.

In the first part of my spiritual journey, I think it's important to share that my early faith foundation had little depth or direction. If you are or were a Christian with a faith that grew little or no roots, then take courage: I believe our experience is quite common.

My father's influence

I was born Julian Andrew Wong. These names appear on all my official identification documents. My father gave me the name Julian at birth, and Andrew when I was baptized a few months after. I've asked my parents about the unusual combination of my names but the mystery hasn't been satisfactorily put to rest. I'm guessing Julie Andrews and *The Sound of Music* (1965) had some influence on the choice of my names. My mother loved this movie so much that she watched it four times! I also recollect mom singing its tunes as I was growing up. My family and friends call me Julian, but my faith community has been reminding me to use Andrew in my onward faith journey. Hence, the name you see on the book jacket and title page is Andrew.

I attribute my English cultural leaning to my father, who is of Peranakan Chinese descent. This sub-ethnic group eagerly embraced English culture and traded with the British, with many in his generation also seeking employment in the colonial civil service.

My grandfather was a Chief Clerk in a city law firm.

The Second World War unfortunately disrupted my father's education. When the war ended in 1945, my father didn't have the luxury of continuing his studies, as he was obliged to help his family by entering the workforce prematurely. With his command of English, my father found work in the Singapore Police Force under the British colonial administration.

When I was young, my father often told me stories of his exploits as a policeman. There was the account of his service as the commanding officer in the wet jungles of Pulau Tekong, an island outpost off the Singapore coast where he met my mother and they fell in love. In the turbulent times of the Malayan Emergency and with only a few policemen working alongside my father, he carried out his duties faithfully.

In the 1955 Hock Lee Bus Riots, there was also the story of a dramatic encounter with a mob armed with parangs, knives, and metal pipes. His small detachment had been patrolling the streets, providing forward intelligence and was just turning into Telok Ayer Street from Cross Street when the jeep's engine abruptly stalled. Quite terrifyingly, his piddly party had run into an armed, angry assembly that was striding further along the narrow street and baying for blood. It would have been foolhardy for my father, a constable, and the driver to take them on. While encouraging the nervous driver to restart the vehicle, he calmly ordered the constable to alight and stand to with his Sten gun drawn. The mob hesitated to overrun this composed detachment when it realized the commander wasn't going to yield without a fierce fight; his furry, ferocious eyebrows might have helped a tad to terrify the mob. When the jeep restarted, an orderly retreat was made.

Had the War not intervened, my father would have realized his ambition to become a lawyer. Even though he was denied this career, he regularly appeared in court as a police prosecutor. In those days, senior officers prosecuted the majority of minor crimes in the Magistrates' Court. In that role, he had an inspiring encounter with the legendary lawyer, David Marshall. They clashed in a cheating case. Mr. Marshall's client had issued checks from an account without funds. With his reputation preceding him, Mr. Marshall insistently bellowed in the courtroom that my father was incorrectly prosecuting a civil matter. Despite their mismatched status, my father wouldn't be cowed. The Magistrate, however, preferred being cautious and urged my father to be sure of his case. Accepting the advice of the judicial officer, he visited the Attorney-General's office and persuaded the legal officer to back my father's stand on the law. The Magistrate then convicted, giving my father a heroic victory over a legal legend.

Through innumerable conversations, my father taught me the value of sincerity and hard work. In giving his lessons, he drew inspiration from the leaders and people of his generation who persevered and overcame bleak odds. The one faith lesson he did teach and kept reminding me about was the Christian's obligation to do good deeds: he felt that God would show mercy to any person showing kindness and compassion. My father still subscribes to this thinking.

As a tribute to my father, I embraced the English language, worked hard, and adopted his unrealized ambition to become a lawyer.

Mere charity

Inspired by the story of "The Fourth Wise Man," I began my journey looking earnestly for Jesus in the faces of the hungry, the thirsty, the needy, the sick and the prisoner. That didn't seem too difficult a task. I'd been given the impulse to love and was happy searching for Jesus. Fortunately, He is everywhere. When a man said he was hungry, my ears were open to Jesus' plea of having not: I knew what hunger felt like, and I helped as best I could. Then an old woman would tell me she was tired. I knew what fatigue felt like, and I did what I could to relieve the Lord's ache and loneliness. When a child was separated from his or her parent, I knew what fear and abandonment felt like, and I found help for my Savior as best I knew how.

My experience over the years proved to me that giving money wasn't the only way of offering to the Lord. An offering of my labor and time was equally, if not more, valid. In short, I've been viewing myself as a slightly Quixotic version of the Fourth Wise Man—see a person in need, and I'd tilt into action. In those early days, my grasp of Matthew 25 wasn't deep. I hadn't yet recognized that earth and everything it contains belong to the Lord. My failure to grasp this truth was similar to the incorrect thinking that man could decide the building of the temple or that it could contain the Creator; why, the Lord even uses Moab as His washbowl!

Looking back, I can see I didn't understand the true nature of charity. I also failed to grasp the meaning and practice of tithes. I thought this practice was outdated, but even though it isn't black letter law to give a fixed percentage of income or assets, the Church continues to view tithes as an obligation of conscience. So, just as the Lord has already blessed me with everything I've received, I should have been giving *as freely* to the poor or disadvantaged.

In those days of uneducated faith, I had no inkling that Christianity is all about the *agape*—love, service and self that are freely and unconditionally given. I didn't understand that this Christian love was, is, and will always be at the center of the New Commandments of Jesus Christ. I hadn't recognized that charity was giving my love to others, as I've received the same, undeserved abundance from my Lord.

The Bible teaches me this truth in the parable of the widow's two small coins. (Mark 12:41-44; Luke 21:1-4) At the celebration of every Mass, my hand would reach into my pocket readily to make an offering. Though I felt my charity was as painful as the old widow's offerings, truthfully, my contributions were a pittance. I didn't realize that my charity was limited and that I'd only gained the desire to love. Yes, I was inclined to offer some of my time and do some *good deeds.* That felt generous, but I was always holding back a big part of myself. My practice of charity may not have expected a return, but I certainly didn't give, help, or love as completely as I should. As a contrast in faith, the old widow was giving everything that she owned.

With a stone for my heart, I was giving only a small fraction of my money and time from my surplus. Yet, I couldn't have known what Christian charity entailed because I hadn't learned the full meaning of Christian love.

Though I'd desired to search for Jesus like the Fourth Wise Man, I tremble at the thought that my heart was no different from the rich young man's. I hadn't appreciated the need to depend totally on the Lord and His providence. That trust in the Lord also meant accepting suffering in my life, as Jesus did when He showed complete obedience to the Father by accepting suffering on the cross: for this is Christian love. I couldn't because I hadn't received the complete, spiritual training to understand charity, suffering, or love in those days.

In my teens, I slipped back to my unchristian ways. After my momentous encounter at the age of twelve, faith seemed to be on my lips, but I was simply going through the motions. One could say that I hardly knew the Lord. Thus, my understanding of His ways was consequently shallow, showing itself in hollow religious activity.

My teenage years were also marked by traumatic events.

QUESTIONS FOR REFLECTION ON CHAPTERS 1–3

1. Do you realize that God loves you very much—as you are—even though you may be a sinner?
2. Do you think that God will love you only when you stop being a sinner?
3. Have you stopped being a sinner? How do you stop being a sinner?
4. Have you encountered the Lord Jesus in your life? Have you had a faith experience that prompts you to learn more about Jesus Christ?
5. What kind of charity do you practice? Do you give everything like the widow, 50% of your assets like Zaccheus, or 10% of your income as prescribed in the Bible?

4. Fear

What's the topic of fear got to do with faith formation?

In Chapters 4 to 6, I've decided to write about the bullying I suffered during my teen years. You may think the decision to go public with this period of suffering a little controversial. There are two reasons for breaking my silence. Firstly, the suffering is relevant to my early journey of faith, as it led to an extraordinary second encounter with the Lord. Secondly, the fact I was abused gives me an insight into an aspect of the sex abuse crisis currently afflicting the Church. Namely that caregivers play a critical role both in reporting and bringing to justice anyone abusing a child under their care. From my experience, I believe proper faith formation can help caregivers respond better when harm is reported to them or identify better the symptoms of moral injury in their children. In this situation, true religion and basic morality teach us to protect the vulnerable and defenseless in our life. (James 1:27)

Traumatized by two boys

My first six years of primary education at Catholic High Primary

School were relatively idyllic and safe. I enjoyed my school life and cherished the occasional, carefree afternoons playing basketball or table tennis with my friends. I was also a good student with many of my classmates asking my help in spelling or pronunciation. I was happy to teach them my methods.

There was, however, a little blemish during this time. Catholic High teachers were well known for their strict approach to discipline, which was maintained by summary and painful corporal punishment. Talking in class or not paying attention resulted in disciplinary action. Worse, I had a squint-eyed condition and was punished once or twice when the teachers felt I wasn't giving them due attention. Thankfully, I had corrective eye treatment before my Primary School Leaving Examinations. In most incidents, the instant punishment for whatever behavior upset the teacher was striking my outstretched fingers with a thick wooden ruler. No errant student was spared this disciplinary regime. Fortunately, after the first demonstrations, we all learned discretion and the occasions for punishment were relatively few and far between.

Sadly, I was never able to master the written form of the Chinese language and fluency in the spoken form also eluded me. Thus, I couldn't continue my education in Catholic High. Looking forward, St. Joseph's offered a good choice for my secondary education. Whereas Catholic High excelled in the Chinese language, St. Joseph's taught mainly in English. Besides, the two schools were opposite each other on Queen Street, which meant another four years in familiar surroundings. With some optimism, I said my goodbyes to days of lively laughter, shooting hoops and tricky topspins.

The change, however, brought some sadness to my mother. She believed in the importance of the Chinese language. Mom also shares the name of a filial and patriotic daughter of Chinese folklore and was wont to fly the flag for all things Chinese. In my defense, I was keenly aware of the world in which I intended to excel expressing itself mainly in English. It's one of the official languages in Singapore. All the signs are in English, and nearly everyone speaks

English. What's more important, it's the language of the professions. Except for Chinese that was in the curriculum as a compulsory second language, all my other subjects were to be taught and written in English. Thus, my grasp of English would prosper at St. Joseph's. Everything was looking up.

Except the reality dashed my hopes. In my four years at St. Joseph's, I suffered both physical and mental bullying. This shouldn't have happened because, in theory, I was protected. A cousin was a teacher at the same school. A few friends from Catholic High Primary School had enrolled in St. Joseph's as well. My parents were also fully aware of the abuse. You may wonder why no one stepped in to help. Well, in those days, there were a number of criminal gangs who weren't afraid to inflict harm on ordinary folk. Instead of helping, my family and friends transmitted their fears that I might be further victimized outside the school. So I naturally grew afraid of the *long shadows* cast by boys who enjoyed intimidating, tormenting, and reviling me.

The first set of tormentors made their appearance in Secondary One. The two boys, Hume and Neil, were my classmates and known *gangsters*. Because my father was then the commanding officer of a police division, I was keenly aware of Singapore's criminal underbelly. He was involved in many criminal investigations and often worked late into the night. Occasionally he would share snippets about secret societies, turf killings, and drug pushers. By the early 1980s, Singapore had mostly thinned the ranks of organized criminal gangs and significantly reduced their influence. But small groups remained, carrying on the traditions of the scary, secret societies of yesteryear. They peddled drugs and prostitution, promoted illegal gambling, and ran extortionate money-lending syndicates. There were also youth gangs filled with restless, testosterone-charged and short-fused adolescents. Many gangsters even claimed affiliation with the infamous *sah-lak-kau*. In the Hokkien dialect, this means 3-6-9 and it's a symbol of the underworld's mythical secret societies. There had been incidences of youth violence with a few, isolated killings in recent years. It was common knowledge then and now that thugs and youth gangs found their way into schools: there were a few in my secondary school years.

Hume and Neil probably picked on me because I was new. Not, of course, that I was alone in being a newcomer. Many of the students had enrolled from feeder mission schools such as St. Stephen's, St. Gabriel's, and Maris Stella Primary School, but they shared a common history, which was different from mine. I also stood out for a different reason. At the age of thirteen, I was probably the tallest student in my cohort. Before I started secondary school, I was already five feet, five inches tall. I shot up another four inches in Secondary One. Perhaps that made me a challenge to these smaller thugs.

With the restlessness of puberty in the air, a victim is needed. When radio and television news reported youth gang violence, the commonest behavior claimed to be provocative was *staring*. It didn't matter that the victim wasn't looking at the assailant. This was the pretext for confrontation.

These two boys began their gambit by alleging my provocative staring. My reaction to the confrontation would reveal whether I was some prey or predator. Unfortunately, I showed my inexperience by explaining myself. Having risen to their bait, I played into their script of fear, intimidation, and extortion. If they bumped into me in the corridor, they would yell at me to get out of their way. On another day, they would pick a fight with me on whatever pretext amused them. If they squared up to me, it was an unspoken rule that I couldn't speak unless a reply was required. They were essentially training a *new boy* to learn obedience and his place.

These thugs then escalated their pattern of harassment by regularly extracting money from me. I can't remember the reasons they gave. They naturally expected their demands to be met.

I did try to get help from my father, but he advised giving in. To the rational mind, this predicament needed careful thinking. There was no telling how many other *gang* members they could enlist to amplify my troubles. As my father pointed out, their retaliation could end up taking place outside school, at the time of their choosing, with larger numbers summoned to inflict a painful or permanent lesson in a moment or place where he couldn't protect me.

Further demoralizing me, my cousin didn't take my complaints seriously.

It came down to a simple choice. I could quit St. Joseph's or stay. St. Joseph's was the school I wanted to be in. I had friends in school, and it was close to my home on Beach Road. However, I was quite alone in my suffering, with no other option than to endure. Given my circumstances, I *had* to pay the price for caution and safety. It was my decision to stay—better the devil you knew as some would say.

By then, fear had sunk its claws into my thinking. Like a leech caught in my flesh, it was draining my courage. In the sorry circumstances, I endured their bullying for almost the entire school year. Later on, my friends added to my fears with tales of an underage thug detained (indefinitely) at the President's pleasure for killing another student in a fight. I was trapped between a rock and a hard place. If I fought back, was I ready for an escalation of trouble?

Some friends did encourage me to fight back. To demonstrate their point that I should be positive and defend myself, they passed on an urban legend about a Korean student, who was ambushed outside school by eleven gang members. He proved well trained in *tae-kwon-do* and happily fought off his assailants. Even though I was tall, fighting didn't come naturally to me. With no knowledge of even simple fighting techniques, landing the second punch was going to be a bridge too far. Ironically, my mother often warned me to be careful around my fellow students. She was afraid I might not know my own strength and accidentally hurt or injure them in play. In a way, she was right. Even if I'd known how to fight, my conscience dominated on the right side of the law—it would have bothered me had I injured any boy in a fight.

In those days, I prayed to the Lord regularly, asking Him for help to rid me of my tormentors. He remained silent and made no effort to give me what I wanted. This should have helped me understand that I wasn't praying correctly. I thought all I needed to do was beseech my Lord for favors. As you can see, my religious awareness during my teen years was sorrowfully shallow. I put together a wish list for all the wants my heart desired. By the time I'd finished, there must have been hundreds of wishes on the list. Not surprisingly, the Lord ignored me. I found this confusing.

Adults I respected advised me to look to the Lord as a child looks to his parent for all needs and wants. The Word in Matthew 7:7 seemed to support this erroneous encouragement when the situation was urgent: "Ask, and it will be given to you . . . how much more will your Father in Heaven give good things to those who ask Him." So I asked the Lord to stop these thugs because their campaign of fear was robbing me of my dignity. Wasn't this a reasonable request? Well, not really. I was asking the Lord to interfere with the choices available to the boys. This fails to acknowledge the freedom that the Lord has given every man and woman to act or abstain, including the freedom to decide the big questions of life or death, good or evil, love or hate. He wasn't going to interfere with the boys' freedom to learn the consequences of their choices. My Lord certainly didn't interfere with my freedom either.

At the tail end of Secondary One, a good classmate of mine, Ian (we liked to think we were *half-brothers* because of our similar names) finally counseled me to end this distress. He strongly urged me to report the bullies to the principal. I appreciated his concern but still felt that, despite his good intentions, he didn't really fathom the depths of my accumulated fears. Then a final incident occurred during the school session. My class was between lessons, and no teacher was in the classroom. The usual class disorder erupted. Hume was probably bored and, for no apparent reason, started jabbing me with a thick wooden ruler. Ian looked intently at me—defend yourself—this is wrong! Something stirred within me to summon all my courage. Fears of gang violence and the shadows dissipated at that moment. I was quite strong and simply held on to Hume's instrument of torment, refusing to let go. I was finally able to stand my ground and look my tormentor in the eye. My push back only made him even more furious, since he wasn't expecting any resistance from me; after all, I'd been a doormat all this while.

The Lord must have given me additional courage and drove me running to the principal's office.

Heaven continued to smile on me. Brother Kevin Byrne was in his office and available to talk to me. I poured out the story of a year's abuse, extortion, and fear at the hands of these two boys. I finished by confessing how afraid I was going to be, for the shadows were waiting outside his office.

To this day, I can still remember his gentle response. He was full of reassurance and compassion. If the Lord would personally enter my life of suffering and give me some peace, He did so in the pleasing promise that Brother Kevin made. He promised he would take away their spirit of fear. He assured me that they would be obliged to look away from me and never darken my path again. True to his promise, even though we were in the same class, I had no further contact with the boys again. Brother Kevin's assurance also meant there were no shadows waiting to hurt me outside school. I was safe because of the Lord's help through Brother Kevin.

I now realize that, in my prayers, I didn't ask for the spirit of courage to speak plainly to the two boys or to any figure with authority over the tormentors. During that time, I lived foolishly in fear of shadows and negative consequences, but the Lord showed me how easy it was to deal with my Anakim.

Losing my self-esteem

I thanked the Lord for sending my *half-brother* to open my mind. I was also thankful for the kindness and gentleness He showed me through Brother Kevin, whose open door meant the suffering in Secondary One could end. If only I'd understood then how the Lord acts in this world of suffering, fear, and helplessness.

My failure to report the bullying that lasted almost a year had damaged me. The boys broke and enslaved my spirit. Fearing reprisals in the shadows after school, I froze and was trampled on. I may have been a physical giant, but I opened the door to the burglar and allowed myself to be tied up by bullies smaller than I was.

The resulting practice of *wise submission* gave free rein to my tormentors to take away my lunch money. This gnawed at my self-esteem. Losing more than a few coins, I lost much of my dignity.

For every abuser, there's a victim who suffers unjustly. To keep myself safe, I avoided conflict by walking away from anyone who posed a threat. I became a loner of sorts. Even today, this episode continues to affect the way I interact with people. I sometimes freeze when fight or flight is a better response.

A frightening incident in Secondary Two

Even with the two boys kept out of my sight, my troubles with abusive tormentors weren't over—they were just beginning. In Secondary Two, I crossed paths with Sealie, who became my patrol leader in the boy scouts. It isn't entirely accurate to call Sealie a bully. I remember him as an abusive person: a foul fellow, ferocious at fools and frightening for his short fuse. From the first moments, Sealie took a dislike to me. It seemed to be as instinctive as hating a color or a particular sound. Perhaps irrational is a better word to describe his behavior. Whatever the reason, he set out to make my scouting life hellish. I was dealt another bad hand. Thinking about it, the whole episode might well have been payback for the action against the two boys in Secondary One.

From my reading of *Scouting for Boys*, I was familiar with the Scouting movement. This book held out the promise of fieldcraft that made me look forward to the joy of the great outdoors, but there was no tradition of scouting in my family. This was a voluntary, extracurricular activity that taught discipline, with an emphasis on camp life and skills. Having had a horrid Secondary One enduring Hume and Neil, I was hoping to enjoy the promised adventure scouting offered and make new friends. I was wrong about the fun of scouting because I found myself amid the recurring fear of the shadows.

I was assigned to the patrol under Sealie's leadership. It was soon evident that the other boys were all wary of his temper. There was seldom a meeting without Sealie's abusive scolding or punishment. We found ourselves actively avoiding him or trying vainly to get on his better side. Many of the patrol members even questioned the need for this abuse, given that scouting wasn't compulsory. I struggled against quitting and consoled myself by thinking this an occasional commitment. I wasn't suffering every day and thought I could bear with Sealie's abusive leadership.

Without realizing my error, I was internalizing the abuse again as I'd done in Secondary One.

Then a frightening incident took place at an outdoors camp. I had a sinus condition that day, which gave me a stuffy nose and forced breathing through my mouth. Sealie decided my apparently gaping mouth was disrespectful to him. He kept yelling about a fly entering my mouth and choking me to death. I tried drawing his sympathy, but to no avail. Not getting the response he was expecting, Sealie pulled me away from the troop to the bushes behind our camp. I thought he was going to give me another explosive, expletive-filled rant. Instead, he brandished a long parang: a blade similar to a machete. This seemed dangerous and not a game. Sealie then told me how much he hated my open mouth and if I didn't shut it, he was going to shove his long parang down my throat. To make his point very clear, he gripped my arm and tried to place the tip of the parang on my lips. When Sealie promised to cut me open with his parang, it was the single, most terrifying experience in my young life.

Eventually, I left the scouts. This was disappointing for three reasons:

- having to give up the chance to learn from scouting and grow stronger from outdoor activities;
- internalizing much of the abuse, which further damaged the injury to my self-confidence; and
- failing to spend time with the Lord in prayer to seek His counsel on the ordeal I was suffering.

5. Mental Abuse

Crippling my self-confidence

I hoped for better classmates in Secondary Three and Four, but this wasn't to be. As the new academic year began, I judged my classmates smart and found many to possess interesting personalities. There were the quiet, bookish, intellectuals, sporting jocks, religious, and one classmate excelling in the Chinese language. Many in the class also showed an outsize penchant for boyish mischief-making. Then we come to the *muggers:* this is Singapore slang for students fiercely competitive in every academically advantageous assessment. These classmates had zero tolerance for any grade that was less than a distinction.

The tragedy that unfolded was compounded by the composition of this class remaining the same in both years. We were all on track for the 'O' Level examinations, which is a momentous milestone met in Secondary Four. The 'O' Levels decided every student's future in those days. Those awarded excellent grades qualified for entry to the better junior colleges or polytechnics. In turn, the top academic programs offered superior opportunities for a place in the sought-after universities, locally and abroad. I was full of expectation to be among smart students. What I didn't expect was the mental abuse a minority heaped on me during those critical years.

In this tiny island of Singapore, it was generally accepted that competition was not only desirable, but it was also critical to its survival and prosperity. Singapore was a young city-state in the 60's and 70's, and it had few, natural advantages or resources. This made the people the most important resource. There was a sense that Singapore could only succeed if we pulled ourselves up by our bootstraps. We had to study and work hard, be thrifty, and be prolifically productive. On billboards all over the island, "Teamy the Bee" was the productivity mascot cheering on the workers.

Why did we need the steady drumbeat of productivity? In 1965, the economy of Singapore was largely inward-looking. Many were unemployed, living in overcrowded conditions, and impermanent slums. There was a high level of poverty, and more than half the people were illiterate and unskilled. So the young had to be encouraged through competition for the better, but limited tuition classes, schools, and colleges. That way, we could fulfill our destiny to build a better future. As an incentive, we were told that only achievers with the top qualifications got the hot jobs.

Because of this social pressure to survive, strive, and succeed, there were stories of students so desperate to win they refused to share study notes and hid essential library books. Some even tore out useful pages to get a leg up on other students in the tightly competitive race. To express the apparent *no-choice, zero-sum* hothouse reality, Singaporeans coined two infamous slang expressions: *kiasu* and *kiasi*, meaning "afraid to lose," and "afraid to die," respectively. It would, however, be wrong to say every aspect of life in Singapore was an encounter with crazy, cutthroat challenges. The more virulent expressions of *kiasu* and *kiasi* behavior were the exception and not the rule. Nevertheless, whether people were prepared for the competition, this question seemed regrettably irrelevant. Society's main focus was on the long-term performance of the winners under pressure.

Some of us struggled in sometimes unforgiving and perhaps unruly rivalry. At that age, I was still naive. It didn't occur to me that I was in a fierce fight for future fulfillment. Inevitably, it was my misfortune to compete against a close-knit group, which gave no quarter. They were determined to win at any cost.

It began innocently enough. There was to be a school debate. Every class could field a team to participate in the competition. Unknown to me, the team had been formed and it just became known a boy called Hwan was the leader of the group for our class. There was neither a process of choosing candidates nor was the team selection transparent. I belatedly approached Hwan only to be told I didn't make the cut. He acted as if he was the sole arbiter of the skill sets and experience needed to qualify for membership, having decided I didn't qualify. When I tried to show him I had it in me to be a member of the team, he rejected my bid. The research I prepared for the debate topics didn't matter because the discussion about the selection was closed.

It wasn't long after that Hwan mounted a campaign to disparage me. He began calling me names intended to humiliate: "cretin," "idiot," and "moron." It didn't help that I froze in the maelstrom of those coordinated attacks. My defensive missteps intensified the name-calling and hectoring, which muzzled my voice. I was like an animal that had its chance to defend itself or flee, but froze, then became trapped in the crosshairs. This proved that when any prey freezes, it becomes an easier mark. The mischief-makers joined in the chorus because my *schadenfreude* served up irresistible laughs.

My voice was frequently drowned out when I needed to ask the teacher questions or generally participate in class. So effective was their raspberry racket that I was practically shut out of the class lessons. I could neither move nor find any space to score, thus degrading my learning opportunities and confidence. I was so frustrated with the harassment that I punched the wall and broke my hand, trying to redirect the resentment boiling inside me to no avail.

With each heckle, rattle, and rankle, I became drained and grew dejected—I wasn't learning as well as I should. I didn't try confiding in the teachers because they were also having a hard time reining in this class: it had a mind of its own.

I can't say I was the brightest student, but I was certainly creative, resourceful, and ambitious. I also have a knack for forward planning and thinking out of the box. At the early age of fourteen, I made up my mind to be a lawyer and planned my education road map on my own. The immediate problem was the knowledge that I was going to fail Chinese, which was a compulsory subject. Even if I passed the other 'O' Levels with flying colors, failing my Chinese subject would disqualify me from all junior colleges. Without consulting my parents or friends, I investigated and uncovered a dispensation in the academic rules. It allowed me to study a third language in substitution for Chinese as my second language.

French was my choice because, as a language, it appeared more familiar to me than the Chinese language. My attraction to French gave me the confidence to excel. This meant I had to organize my two-year crash course in French at the *Alliance Française de Singapour*, a learning option outside the school system. Fortunately, when I told my father, he gave his warm support for my ambitious plan—it helped to have family members with a love for foreign languages.

When streaming took place in Secondary Three for 'O' Level subjects, I was given the option to study the sciences or the humanities. I chose the humanities course to read history and literature because these were subjects relevant to my plan to read law at a prestigious university.

None of my planning and ingenuity could, however, save my academic performance from the mental battering I suffered. As I hobbled into the 'O' Level examination hall, I was already mentally defeated.

In hindsight, I don't believe it was Hwan's outright intention to wreck my future. He was probably competitive as boys were at that age. Whatever his motives, my young self was entangled.

I was so wracked with self-doubt that I was no longer looking at the Lord. I led myself to my own slaughter in those pivotal examinations, running away from the nations besieging my strength. If only someone had taught me Psalm 127:1, ". . . Unless the Lord watches over the city, the watchman stays awake in vain." Why did I not cling to the Lord, spend time with Him in daily prayer and seek His counsel? Even now, I can't explain my failure to turn to the Lord.

My results weren't good enough for any junior college, much less the prestigious junior college I was aiming for. I was fit only for the pre-university center.

Section III

THE SECOND ENCOUNTER

6. Exodus

Make us glad as many days as thou hast afflicted us, and as many years as we have seen evil. (Psalm 90:14-15)

Misfortune

I was assigned a place in the Siglap Pre-University Center. The sense of relief and safety was real. The teachers were competent and my classmates friendlier, resembling the classmates from my days at Catholic High. No one needed to be *kiasu*. There were no thugs lurking in the school and no long shadows waiting for me outside. For about a month, I found myself enjoying the general environment and the syllabus.

Unfortunately, society at that time had a somewhat dim view of the three-year 'A' Level curriculum. Many unkindly rated the pre-university centers as inferior to the junior colleges, which offered the two-year curriculum. In objective educational terms, the additional year could be beneficial. Students were given the chance to gain a more rounded view of the content at a comfortable pace, only focusing on examination preparation in the final year of the course. Some, however, saw this opportunity differently. They thought that only *dull* students were admitted and so required the *slower* pace of study.

I overheard a relative asking my brother whether I had the *smarts* to continue my studies. The question put me down, as though I'd been told I was studying in a *ghetto* school, a school not designed to offer adequate chances to those with aspirations. I began to doubt myself anew. Even if this school could produce good students, as I'm sure it did, I found despondency growing in power again. My wounds from secondary school, still fresh and raw, were being rubbed again to reveal new injuries. My mind was in disarray as the negative thinking dominated. I began to feel trapped in this school.

During this time, I lived as though in shameful exile in a foreign land. Like the Israelites in the desert, it seemed as though I too had turned away from the Promised Land. Thousands of years later, I was making the same mistake by not trusting my Lord to fight the nations, larger and stronger than me. I'd feared the Anak, which appeared in each of my four years in secondary school. My memory of the Lord's marvelous intervention through Brother Kevin had similarly grown faint. History was repeating itself. Humiliation got the better of me in secondary school. I was again allowing shame to reign over me in this pre-university center.

I found it best to avoid company, but if it was impossible, I endured the social encounter. In those distressing times, neither family nor friend was able to comfort me. Questions about my progress or future plans alarmed me, so great was the resentment that others were judging me. This distress led me into an emotional wasteland, where I savored the safety of solitude. The Lord allowed this time of suffering in my wilderness.

Help comes from the Lord

My physical wilderness was Singapore, a land clamoring for proof of competence. This is a land where people are measured not only by results—but also by the consistency of results. The route to a better school, job, and life is usually secured with predictable, superior results. People told me there can be no mishaps along the way. The mantras were:

- "Don't make a mistake!"
- "Don't drop the ball!"
- "Don't commit a foul, or it's *game over*!"

This forced me to realize how far off the well-trodden path I'd strayed. My family and friends couldn't help. They believed my future was sterile and stillborn. So I stopped talking about my ambition to become a lawyer.

Eventually, I concluded I couldn't make my father proud—not without help from the Lord. Feeling very much alone, I was utterly floored by shame, pessimism, and despondency. It felt as though the heavy hand of Haman's hostility was pressing down my head, intent on destroying me for not stooping. Like dry bones—only the Lord had the power to return the living breath to me—He alone could make my deadened hopes regain life.

With no more pride in my own strength, I got down on my knees and begged the Lord. From the depths of my soul, I cried to Him to extricate me from this entanglement. I admitted to the Lord that I was at my wit's end and had no strength to win this battle on my own. The Lord heard my cry and responded.

This was my second encounter with the Lord.

The Guardian of Israel bade me acknowledge that help comes to me from Him. And God's help did arrive.

Miraculously, my courage and confidence returned with strength that I made the audacious decision to retake my 'O' Level examinations. Aiming for a better set of grades, I hoped to qualify for the better junior colleges. The plan was risky because I was wasting this first year in a three-year curriculum. Second chances were very scarce in those days, but I went ahead anyway.

I trusted the help from the Lord!

Sex abuse crisis

Given my own experience of abuse, let's pause for a moment to examine an aspect of the clergy sex-abuse crisis. I believe this tragedy is connected to the crisis of faith and that proper faith formation can help produce better outcomes for the future. At the beginning of Chapter 4, I suggested that caregivers play a critical role when abuse is occurring.

Who are these caregivers?

They are parents, other family members, and guardians. Closely connected to them are the many people with roles to protect minors and promote their safety. They are parish administrators, teachers, health-care and child-care service providers, police officers, town leaders, and other individuals in positions of authority.

With so many cases of sex abuse coming to light around the world, it's increasingly evident that pastoral administrations often fell short. The silence of the caregivers and responsible community leaders is just as inscrutable. We should ask two questions:

- Why did many victims fail to complain at the earliest opportunity or exhibit signs of abuse when they were children?
- Did their caregivers and others interacting with these victims fail to see the signs of abuse?

If a small number of victims feared negative consequences from their abusers, it's understandable they were reluctant to report the abuse. Why then did the majority of victims apparently fail to report the offense at the time it occurred?

The John Jay Research Study of 2004 investigated child sex abuse by the clergy in America and explained why the cases were significantly underreported. In instances where victims did report the abuse, many factors contributed to the delay in disclosure. I found the role of the caregiver most telling. At page 85 of the Research Study, many scholarly studies were discussed: the study of DeVoe and Coulborn-Faller found that child subjects in their study required assistance with disclosure; in a study by Sorenson and Snow, the researchers found that 22% of the victims recanted their disclosures; the researchers, Lawson and Chaffin, found the belief of the caretaker to have played a significant role in the truthfulness of the complaint by the victims. Then, we come to Bradley and Wood's research. These researchers took a similar view that the role of the caregiver was significant, given that half the children who recanted did so under pressure from a caregiver; albeit this finding arose from a small sample.

In many of the complaints, the disclosures by the victims were not contemporaneously translated into actionable justice. My own hypothesis is that excessive clericalism and inadequate faith formation could be the reasons why the caregivers who doubted or didn't assist with the children's disclosures remained silent.

What is clericalism?

In his address to the Bishops of the Antilles on May 9, 2002, St. John Paul II warned against clericalism, a phenomenon that Vatican II aimed to eradicate.

Clericalism is the way in which church administrators use power to govern rather than to give service. Although the notion of pastoral service is at the heart of the Gospel, some of the clergy may have been ruling the laity with a heavy hand. This may lead some lay members to treat some of the clergy with excessive adulation or affection. The result is that a priest could be so well-respected or cherished that no one was willing to question his actions, words, or conduct.

What's the relevance of clericalism to the sex abuse crisis?

Whether it was a desire for quiet justice or a hesitation to accuse a well-loved priest, the acts or omissions of the caregivers or pastoral leaders neither served the moral and emotional welfare of the victim, nor the moral leadership of the pastoral administration in question. Internal and police investigations ended up being mishandled, which caused more harm. More importantly, Jesus gave every Christian a stern warning in advance not to cause the faith of the children to stumble (Matthew 18:6)—this advice was *not* heeded in many of the sex abuse cases.

It isn't just the caregivers—any one of us can get the wrong idea about our priests. Many believers have been scandalized, and the pendulum of respect and admiration for the clergy is threatening to swing too far the wrong way. It's true that there have been a small number of rogue clergy and religious doing heinous things, but they represent an abominable aberration that dioceses and parishes have been working to weed out. As evidence of this shift in America, the 2005 Charter for the Protection of Children and Young People shows steps in the right direction. Together with the annual reports on its implementation, these prove the right path of the American churches with their detailed analyses, guidance, and action.

Even though I've referred to what's been happening in the American churches, we should scrutinize the symptoms and malady, and ascertain if they could be the same for other churches struggling with the same crisis worldwide. I urge you to read the documents for yourself.

What do we get wrong about our priests?

The Second Vatican Council reminded us that, in the summit that is the Eucharist, the presiding priest isn't the only celebrant, but a minister acting in *persona Christi*. He acts on behalf of the true priest, Jesus Christ, because it's the assembled community (together with the priest), the Body of Christ united with the Lord, that celebrates. (CCC 1140-1142) Yet, I've come across parishioners telling me that the priest is the celebrant and he *is* Jesus Christ.

What other ideas could be wrong?

Now that we've learned about the crimes committed by the rogue clergy and religious, what *has* changed about our Faith? Did these serious wrongdoings result in any change to the promise and our hope in the Good News? Has the right hand of the Most High lost its strength? Have the wrongful acts of the wolves in sheep's clothing unraveled all the good work by the remaining thousands upon thousands of hardworking clergy and religious, and countless other faithful men and women everywhere? No! All of them continue to sacrifice their lives with love, compassion, and sometimes in harm's way, to do the work of God and His Church. It's also their work in healthcare, education, care of the poor, and other areas of charitable service that has shaped a lot of what we are and have today, all over the world, over the centuries and millennia. Their priceless works of faith, mercy, and love continue to contribute to our world.

The offenses in question were explicitly prohibited and condemned by our Lord. Yet, are the grave offenses capable of destroying the Church established by Jesus Christ, who remains its head, king, and the perpetual high priest?

All believers standing on the threshold of faith should ask ourselves:

- Can we find our own way to eternal salvation without the aid and communion of other Christians who are sinners like you and me? Our Lord Jesus has given Peter authority here on earth, and the Church remains charged with the same duties and responsibilities. (Matthew 16:18-20; 28:19-20) References to Peter include all priests, good or bad. When a priest acts badly, he fails Christ, His Church, and the lay members he serves.
- Are the betrayals by the rogue clergy and religious any different from those of Judas's, an original Apostle chosen by Jesus Himself?
- Do we suppose we know what Jesus is thinking, and are right to decide that His Church has lost its usefulness or moral authority?
- Have we forgotten that Peter was a proud man who

denied Christ three times or that nearly all the Apostles deserted the Lord at Calvary?

- Has any believer not deserted Jesus or hasn't nailed his or her sins to the cross of Christ? I know I have.

I'm no better than my ancestors. For my own part, I'm certain that faith formation in and by the Church will help me convert and keep my faith to the end. (Hebrews 3:13-14)

My motives here

Let me be clear about two important discussion points:

- What I say here isn't intended to excuse the rogue clergy and religious, or the inadequate action taken by the pastoral administrators to investigate the abuse cases. No one shall gloss over the terrible harm the victims suffered. The wolves in sheep's clothing will have to answer for their crimes.
- I don't present my thinking here as an unquestionable truth. All I'm doing here is offering my analysis so that we can consider this issue clearly, together, as involved members of the Church.

Action and healing are now needed. On the one hand, every diocese needs to offer pastoral healing to all victims who were wounded spiritually, physically, and emotionally. There's something that we believers should also do: we ought to consider our individual responsibility for having lifted our priests onto a pedestal. By this, I'm not suggesting we should start throwing our priests to the ground or disrespect their office as our shepherds. Doing this would be to flagrantly forget Peter's strong advice given in 1 Peter 5:1-5: ". . . be subject to the leaders," which was similarly echoed by St. Paul in his letter to the Hebrews. (13:17)

For starters, we should stop looking at our priests as holy men incapable of any wrongdoing. Our priests may do important works but, like the saints, they can also make mistakes. Just as some caregivers made mistakes when they doubted the complaints of the children in their care or took every action other than prosecuting the offenses. I also make mistakes. Every one of us is capable of making mistakes.

We also don't need to expect our priests to set the standard of good work and Christian conduct—our Savior has already done this on the cross for all men and women, for all time. Each of us should aspire to the only standard by learning and copying from the Lord in a faith journey.

In the second part of the book, I discuss the attributes we ought to have as followers of Jesus Christ. As a brief introduction, every lay member has a share in the ministry of our Lord Jesus Christ. This makes it urgent to address faith formation for all Christians. Everyone should be fluent in every teaching of Jesus Christ, which will help us to love. Only then can we begin serving the Lord in this life He has given us. The clergy and the religious may have taken holy vows, but they *are* men and women like us. However, they ought to heed St. Augustine's impassioned advice in the "Discourse on the shepherds." (Disc 46.9)

I take the simple, but sensible, stand that lay members well formed in the Faith will respond compassionately, conscientiously, and correctly to the future cries of the children and others who are defenseless. There must be no fear, folly, or deferring of justice, for the Lord was pointedly clear about hurting the little ones who have faith. Even if we aren't directly responsible for the harm, the Lord is also clear about everyone's responsibility to aid the weak and needy. Every Christian has a duty to save them from the clutches of the wicked. (Psalm 82:4)

Despite my plea for learning, involvement, and action by all Christians, the crisis may well continue to smolder. This may be the dreary way forward if only a few are able or willing to step forward as priests, prophets, and kings led by the Church.

Questions for Reflection on Chapters 4–6

1. Have you suffered any bullying, abuse or shame at the hands of tormentors? Did you cry out to the Lord from the depths of your soul?
2. Were you able to report or share this incident with anyone close to you?
3. Did anyone (especially a child or a vulnerable person under your care) report an incident of abuse to you? Have you seen symptoms of abuse in a child or other defenseless person?
4. What did you do about the abuse?
5. Have you shown excessive affection to your priest to the extent you won't question his obvious wrongdoing? Did you put anyone else on the pedestal such that they can do no wrong in your eyes?
6. Given the sex-abuse crisis, do you now distrust or disrespect the priest?

7. Song of Victory

What happens next?

In Chapters 7 to 9, my narrative reaches a heady pitch filled with great rejoicing. The Lord taught me that help comes from Him. Help not only was sent, but it arrived in a great downpour! I was like a pendulum, swinging from one extreme to the other. When in crisis, I had little or no hope—like the man in a desert without water. Following His answer, I was full of hope and optimism. The unthinkable happened, and I was then able to travel to London and secure what I needed to become a lawyer. I was also given the opportunity to experience reconciliation with my enemy.

That sounds good. Young people should always move forward in hope. Even so, there was a sign I should have noted: I continued to search for the Lord. This rambling search evidenced my failure to understand how to relate to Jesus Christ. If I trusted in Him to help me in my hour of need, why did I not feel as though I was walking with Him? This problem arose because there was no pastor supervising the flowering of my faith, and so I wasn't living my life according to the Gospel. For faith formation to stay on track, St. John Paul II urged the study of the Faith in a church group or ministry. No one is born wise. All Christians need pastoral supervision at every stage of their spiritual development until they're able to love. All I did was randomly pick spiritual topics or subjects for private study. There was no structure to my faith learning.

In the end, nothing I did on my own deepened my faith. I wandered about, became more confused, and asked more questions without waiting for the answers.

I'll tell you of my studies in London. As a true Singaporean, I was focused on academic success. What was the predictable result? There was precious little time for any learning from the Lord, which led to my faith lessons backsliding. A spiritual supervisor might have helped me with advice for a balance between studying and nurturing my relationship with the Lord.

The European travel episode also confirms the weak state of my faith. In an innocent and romantic way, I pursued a Slovakian girl. I thought she was *The One.* Instead, I should have been searching for the only One, who is true, faithful throughout time, and full of love for all mankind. A beautiful, perfect companion can neither offer me true happiness nor make my life complete—no person can.

How did I honor my Lord following this song of victory? Left to my own devices, I showed ingratitude to my ever patient Lord.

Happy days at Victoria

The Lord made my path straight and clear. The second time around, with French as my substituted language, I achieved the 'O' Level grades needed for entry into Victoria Junior College. During the two years I studied at Victoria, I was like a Mulberry shrub learning to yield to the gardener, thriving as a tree needed good ground and manure. The teachers were accomplished and nurturing—they always encouraged every student to engage in analytical thinking, and it was wonderful they included me. My classmates were also smart and supportive with none of the darkness I endured in secondary school. As a result, my confidence grew and I made great strides.

I joined the *Talentime* singing contest with a couple of college friends and had a swell time, even though we didn't win. As the sole participant from the faculty of humanities, I happily represented my class in the Decathlon event, finishing last!

I share these apparently humiliating failures with you to pose a question, "Does losing diminish our life experience?"

There was also a heroic battle in which we took on giants. A few classmates wanted to compete in the school badminton championships. My class had a few competent players, but was still one member short to form a team. I was asked to join just to make up the numbers, even though I couldn't play for nuts! To make matters worse, we had the misfortune of drawing the best of the best in the first round. My team leader became frantic about the talented and experienced school players we were facing. After a bit of thought, we chose a stratagem full of the fortitude displayed for D-Day. Our best player was obviously no match for theirs. Thus, my job was to be the sham sacrifice—to persuade the school captain to switch places for me, a newborn newbie. Come the day, my real game was to put on an illusory performance solely for the consumption of seasoned players. As the opposing teams gathered on cue, I deployed my smoke and mirrors. Appearing to warm up, I was swishing my racket with apparent aplomb, lunging with agile aggressiveness, slicing the air to amplify apprehension. As the seconds ticked away, my heart was thumping louder than the tell-tale's. The school team then made a last minute change as hoped for. The school champion then wasted his brilliant talent on me, with a priceless 21-0 score, only realizing the tactical misdirection after his second serve. My class of rank amateurs handsomely surprised the school team with a 2-3 loss: there were no doubts in all our minds that we fought the good fight that day, like the Greeks at Thermopylae.

Victoria Junior College was more than a great school for me in academic terms. She encouraged me to pick myself up, dust off, and carry on—who said there was no room for second chances in Singapore? For the only One who has real power didn't take away my opportunities, but desired to give me abundant life.

This second chance seemed like a dream: my mouth was filled

with laughter and my tongue with song. I was industrious in forming study groups made up of friendly, earnest students from different classes. It didn't matter to me that members weren't contributing evenly to the writing and research. All of us benefited from this collaborative study scheme.

A classmate once got me into happy trouble when she sought my help in the midst of a History tutorial. Annoyed by my talking, the tutor invited me to give that lesson in his stead—except I didn't react to his sarcasm quite as he'd expected. Rather I rose to the occasion and taught for the rest of the period. I must have struck a chord because my lecturer decided to cultivate my aptitude by inviting me to take the Special Paper for History. This opportunity was reserved only for the bright ones who were aiming for enrollment in the Oxbridge universities. Fortunately, I graduated with good enough grades to gain entry to the premier school of law in London.

All this time, there was an amazing irony. Hwan was enrolled in the same junior college! He was in a different class and a year ahead of me. Remarkably, we weren't unfriendly. It was likely that I was neither in his way nor he in mine. This wasn't to say there were no missteps during my time at Victoria but, all in all, I made the most of my two years in junior college. I reaped so abundantly from this opportunity that I wanted to sing praises to the Lord.

Philosophy of the doors

I loved reading English literature, both as a subject and for the beauty of English prose. My favorite poet is Philip Larkin. Of all his poems, *Triple Time* struck a deep chord in me such that I fashioned my own rule of life about opportunities.

Triple Time is divided into three stanzas, each reflecting on a different view of the same moment in time. The first stanza describes the present—dull, disagreeable, and disapproved. The second recalls the past looking forward to the future (that *is* the present)—full of the bright promises of adult life. The third is set in the future looking back, warning against squandering opportunities in the present.

Naturally, I was grateful to the Lord for the help He had given me, but I fell into error. Initially, I held the sensible view that industry and toil were needed for every undertaking. Then, I couldn't help supposing that the options and opportunities in my life were the product of my own merit and essential effort. I ended up deceiving myself into thinking I could decide my destiny. Over time, I borrowed the thinking in *Triple Time* and fashioned my own *Philosophy of the Doors.*

I told myself that, at any given moment, there could be doors in front of me to the left and right. The only requirement was to think about the possibilities behind each door. I had the option of walking through any door or even rejecting the new options. The worst I could do, which was the concern of my *Philosophy of the Doors* was doing nothing. Once the option expired, the doors disappeared—the opportunities were lost. That would lead only to regret. There was a subsidiary idea: for the thinking behind each option, there were no right or wrong answers. What really mattered was reaching a reasoned decision: turn left or right, or stay on course. I trained myself to think about options because there was no positive value in regrets.

While my *Philosophy of the Doors* helped me to think, act decisively, and seize the day, it was going to bear inedible figs. Such thinking began to foster my ungrateful rebellion against the God of love, mercy, and help in the favorable time.

Army days and my continued search for Jesus

At the age of eighteen, all Singaporean males are required to enlist for up to two-and-half-years of full-time national service. Some enlistees dread national service. They believe a precious chunk of their life will be wasted, when they could have been engaged in more personally productive pursuits. Having had surgery to correct my squint, I was ambitious for a stint as a sniper. Unfortunately, even though I considered myself a crack shot, this option wasn't offered to me. Instead, I was assigned to a combat unit as a radio signaler.

My unit seemed particularly active with the regular field training often encroaching on weekends. I found them so tiring that, for almost the whole time I was serving my country, I didn't read a single book! It was in this combat unit that I was given the opportunity to represent my Infantry formation in an inter-formation shooting competition. My eyesight may have been poor, but I had hands steady as a rock and calm breathing that were key to a natural shooting skill. It was an enjoyable experience, and my unit came in second behind the elite favorites! I also participated in an intra-formation boxing championship. Ignoring my poor vision again, I signed up as a light heavyweight. My unit wasn't well represented in certain weight classes, so I was elevated to the heavyweight division. I went up against a combat driver, who was half a head taller and at least ten kilograms heavier. Do you remember my mother's warning about my unknown strength? Despite being half-blind, I was able to land a solid punch squarely on my opponent's face in the second round. As precious seconds ticked by, I stood by curiously waiting for him to fall to the mat. He didn't. I eventually lost the match on points, but came in second with a consolation medal.

In the midst of these happy experiences, my sergeant acted as though it was his duty to give me tougher assignments and punishments. This may have been because I was a *White Horse*, the label given to the sons of families thought to be influential. On the other hand, it might have been caused by my failure to *give face* to (i.e. a colloquial slang similar to the idiom, "to play along with") my platoon mates and go on drinking jaunts with them. Even though my camp was just a stone's throw from the lively and loud Changi Village, I never once ventured out to savor its bacchanalian delights. Not needing to be cool, I also didn't give in to the other rite of passage of taking up smoking and binge drinking. Harry, my Indian buddy, and I were the odd ones out in a platoon of young men determined to act out the stereotype of cussing, smoking, and drinking. For them, this was a time of youthful independence. Free at last from family or social ties, they were going to be seen to put childhood behind them and embrace what they saw as an adult lifestyle.

Harry and I looked out for each other until my combat days unexpectedly ended. I was injured while serving and suffered a permanent tear in my left shoulder. This meant a medical downgrade to non-combat duties in the final months of service.

With only non-combat duties, I had free time over the weekends and decided to seek a closer relationship with my Savior and improve my knowledge of the Faith. I wanted to know my God better. He had, after all, helped me:

> . . . At the acceptable time I have listened to you, and helped you on the day of salvation. Behold, now is the acceptable time; behold, now is the day of salvation. (2 Corinthians 6:2)

Beginning my search at the bulletin board in my parish, I checked out a number of activities that I could sample. There were seminars on spiritual themes, lectures on the gospels, retreats, and various other programs. Fr. Alfred, of course, advised me to attend everything, confidently assuring me they were all good. Above all, he urged me not to neglect my study of the Bible. Always respecting the advice of a kind shepherd (and one who loved scripture), I attended a number of talks on the Bible. Remembering my days of Bible Knowledge classes, I focused on the gospels. I would nod my head or murmur in appreciation when I knew the theme well or had learned it before. In reality, though, this wasn't a serious learning exercise. I was only using these lectures to reassure myself that my limited grasp of sacred scripture was better than none.

The retreats I attended during the weekends supplied talks given either by priests or nuns, and opportunities to pray and reflect. I also got to experience my first all-night Easter Vigil. It was an eye-opener to learn a vigil meant the whole night and not a celebration that ended before, or about, midnight. There were devotional prayers, lectures, and even a slide show at this Easter Vigil. All these activities were educational, but I felt something was amiss. Participating in

Christian activities didn't help me feel I was becoming a spiritual person. An emptiness inside me was growing more apparent. There were two reasons:

- I should have been looking for a new depth of knowledge to complete the education of my heart. Instead, I overlooked the extent of my ignorance by seeking only to confirm what I already knew.
- There were no real connections with the people who attended. We might be sitting in the same room, but I didn't see myself as part of a community and remained detached.

Nevertheless, I was steadfast in wanting a connection with the Lord. Perseverance was and still is my calling card.

During my free-fall into the 'O' Level abyss, I became mildly addicted to the cinema. My elder brother introduced me to this medium of art, and I became hooked after watching the Machiavellian drama of *Godfather* (1972), the technical creativity of *Star Wars* (1977), and the music and dance of *Grease* (1978). Although the cinema experience was entertaining at times, there was only a small number of movie greats in the genres I like. I often went to the movie theaters, watching as many as two or three movies each week, but walked away at the credits accepting I'd yet again wasted my time, grumbling at the forgettable 99%. Nevertheless, I persisted in going to the cinema. Why? This was escapism, a distraction from the bleakness of my life. When I was sitting in the dark, I didn't have to interact with anyone socially—it was a wonderful place to hide. If there was a good reason for continuing, it was that one out of every hundred films proved to be a gem.

Over the years, many movies have delighted me including *The Elephant Man* (1980), *The Mission* (1986), *Au Revoir Les Enfants* (1987), *Driving Miss Daisy* (1989), *Dead Poets Society* (1989), *Shindler's List* (1993), *Life is Beautiful* (1997), *What Dreams May Come* (1998), *Hero* (2002), *The Passion* (2004), *Quill* (2004) and *Cinderella Man*

(2005). I loved these movies for the sublime art, the aching emotions they stirred in my heart, and some for the beautiful lessons they taught. For the sake of finding new gems, I persisted in sifting through the ninety-nine that weren't.

This observation translated itself into another extension of the *Philosophy of the Doors*. The length of time I stayed in each room depended on what I discovered behind the door I'd chosen. If I felt I'd entered a room without event or prospect, I *had* to move on, always hoping to find the one room in which the new gem would be discovered. As with movies, so within the Church, I kept opening and going through doors. I hoped to find the one gem in a room that would help me know my Lord and forge a closer relationship with Him as my Redeemer.

Forgiveness and reconciliation

While I was wandering from room to room in my parish, lo and behold, I ran into Hwan, the last person I expected to meet. By then he was a young man, changed by his experience in the military. I can't remember in which talk we bumped into each other. There was much surprise to see him in my parish and witness with my own eyes that he was attending a talk on spiritual themes too. I never got to the bottom of his story: I suppose his experience prompted him to search for the Lord as well. If the Lord permitted the occasion, we met for Mass.

After a few meetings, I knew in my heart that the Lord desired reconciliation between Hwan and I. The first meeting with my enemy was too much of a coincidence. So I suggested a quiet place to talk, mustered my courage, and poured out my grievances, like poison in the body that needed to be purged. Hwan learned how much I loathed what he'd done to me in secondary school—the heckling, jeering, and name-calling that had degraded my learning. I told him plainly that I'd lost a year as a result of this mental battering. Hwan was surprised by what I said and apologized. The

Lord helped me that day to defeat a belligerent nation that had oppressed me in secondary school. We reconciled that day.

I made peace with my enemy.

8. Entering His Church

He gave me a talent to sing

At the close of one Sunday evening Mass, the Marian Choir appealed to parishioners to join its ranks. The choir was the reason I preferred attending this Mass. It not only selected songs with great melody lines, but the singers always sang them beautifully in harmony. They could have been a secret assembly of angels in disguise! The leader was a small but vivacious woman, who projected presence and authority. She was always in control of the music and the singers' energy. I wanted to audition but was so intimidated that I didn't immediately respond. Sitting just behind the choir for a few Sundays, I observed them and eventually gathered my courage to step forward. At first, Hwan told me that he would join me in any spiritual venture, but he backed away at the last minute, leaving me to introduce myself on my own. When I told the leader I was responding to the recruitment exercise, she made me undergo a singing test on the spot. Much to my surprise, I passed the test! What a relief to be accepted by the angels.

At school, my self-confidence was low because of the fears I was carrying inside me. This reluctance to step forward, however, reflected a genuine lack of singing experience. I often sang in the shower and actively raised my voice as a member of the assembly, but that was the extent of my abilities. I wasn't sure of my vocal range and couldn't even sight-read music. Despite all these shortcomings, the leader pronounced me a baritone, a singer most comfortable in the middle range, with some agility to reach the low Tenor and high Bass notes. She then pressed me into the ranks. In the first few months, I really had no idea about what I was doing. Thus, I sang quietly and did my best to learn.

Given my range, I was asked to sing with the Basses. It seemed difficult to find an authentic male Bass because there were always just three or four of us at any given time, and none could really hit the deepest notes.

The choir was well organized. An administrative deputy assisted the leader, and there were four music section leaders (Soprano, Alto, Tenor, and Bass) helping in training.

I became quite worried when I realized this choir regularly sang with sheet music. Fortunately, there were a few rank amateurs like me, goats among the sheep, who neither sight-read nor possessed perfect pitch. I did recognize the dots flowing with the music in an *up* and *down* pattern. This helped me remember the general direction of the piece in question, and the rest was memorized. Over time, I learned the other important aspects of sight-singing sheet music: pitch, tempo, rhythm and dynamics.

Even though I had no prior music training or experience, I was able to project strong volume in my vocal range—I was like an amplifier, making up for the small numbers in my section. As I gained singing experience, I discovered my natural ear for music when I found myself singing along in any spontaneous two-part vocal harmony. I was also taught techniques such as smiling while singing because this opened up my vocal resonance.

Because of my strong voice, I had to be in precise unison with the rest of the choir. I was naturally obedient and kept my eyes on the leader when she conducted. The choir needed to sing in one voice; it didn't need a rogue soloist singing anything else. As a beginner, I paid close attention to the conductor and avoided looking too intently at my sheets during the singing. It was embarrassing when an errant member missed the cue. I wasn't going to be the one to throw everyone off.

After a few months, I realized I had a toehold in this heavenly choir.

In addition to the serious commitment to good, technical singing, the choir prayed together and occasionally had a priest to look in on us as spiritual director. Before we began each practice and when about to celebrate Mass, the leader led the intercessory prayers to petition the Lord to help us in our singing, praising, and worshipping. We prayed again at the conclusion of our meetings after Mass. We also had personal petitions for anyone in need or when a birthday was celebrated. Without fail, we spent one weekend in retreat every year.

It was in this choir that I learned a maxim about choral singing. Our leader shared with us an ancient Latin proverb, *bene cantat bis orat*, i.e. "He who sings well prays twice," to encourage us to sing with all our heart and give praise to God. I took this maxim seriously and, despite my limited ability, sang with all my heart. In my mind, participation in this choir meant I was finally serving both the Lord and His Church. I felt I was giving a lot of myself. Putting everything together, it was a significant commitment of time and effort learning new hymns and reaching for perfection. Thus, I didn't think twice about putting my study of the Faith on the back burner.

Looking back, *Regina Cæli* (Queen of Heaven) still echoes sweetly. It's an ancient Marian hymn that the choir typically sang on Easter Sunday. In this hymn, we rejoiced with the Mother of Christ in the Easter glory of her son. When we were introduced to the version of this hymn arranged by M. Labat, it felt tough in triplicate. We had to learn how to pronounce the Latin words, remember the four-part harmony and master the strict timing—this hymn is dynamic, yet solemn in parts. It was especially tough for the Basses because our part required a deep, sonorous Bass voice. Another beloved song for the Lenten season was *Via Dolorosa* (Way of Suffering) by Sprague and Borop, parts of which had to be sung in Spanish! I loved this song for helping me cherish the Lord's suffering, hurt, and humiliation on a street in Jerusalem—a street that bears this name after the fact.

The most challenging pieces for the choir to master were selections from Handel's *Messiah*, namely, *Hallelujah Chorus* and *For Unto Us A Child Is Born*. They required hours of effort over many a weekday and Sunday afternoon practice sessions. There was so much fatigue on everyone's face after the training sessions, but these are fond memories. We experienced much joy and consolation in the struggle learning these classical masterpieces, which acclaim the birth, death, and resurrection of our Lord.

There were also many delightful Christmas songs such as *What Child Is This* and *O Holy Night* given contemporary arrangements, and modern Christian songs such as Michael W. Smith's *All Is Well*. Caroling with the choir became a priceless experience of service during the Yuletide season, more meaningful than the season of merrymaking, parties, and gift exchange.

It is *I Love You, Lord* by Laurie Klein, a contemporary Christian song that remains my enduring favorite. It's a praise and worship song that's both deeply meditative and full of reverence. This hymn is especially relevant to the service given by any church singer because we all lift our voices to worship the Lord. In those days, I rejoiced that my Lord accepted the sweet sound of my worship in song. I may have learned these hymns and song arrangements in the service of my Lord and my parish, but I also treasured the music for the joyful consolation it gave me. This was a time when I felt my soul dancing and whirling in song for my Lord.

When Saul came into the picture, the choir experience became easier for me. Saul was twelve years older than I, and more talented than the rank and file. Even though he wasn't musically trained, Saul had a natural talent to learn, remember, and sing the notes beautifully. He also possessed a marvelous, mellow voice, which projected personal charisma and the love of God in every vocal—an equal to the leader's dramatic soprano voice. Saul's natural music sense was extraordinary, as he could master any given piece just by listening to it once. He could instantly serve up vocal harmonies for any given hymn, which were delightful because I could join in and sing along. With my natural ear for music and strong voice, I just needed to stand beside Saul. As long as we sang side by side, the Basses were strong vocally. More generally, Saul's regular participation allowed me to learn any hymn rapidly, raising my vocal talents to something from nothing. I often wondered if the Lord had sent him to loosen the ligaments in my singing and help lift my voice higher in praise to my Savior. As a result of our joyful time together, we remain good friends.

Halcyon days

There were no worries, and every day was a summer day in the company of Christian friends from the choir. My life was resplendent with harmony and the peace of God as, in full measure, pressed down, shaken together, and running over, many gifts from the Lord were poured into my lap. I was grateful to my Lord for all the mercy and kindness He showed me—above all, the Lord rescued me from my enemies. He pulled me out of the well and allowed me to serve Him. It was my Lord who taught me how to sing and praise my Father in heaven.

Despite my reverence for the Lord, I wasn't chosen for the celibate priesthood. Everywhere I looked, at every age, in every school or church locale, a girl caught my eye. In the Marian Choir, it was Sue. She was the archetype of the girl next door: fresh-faced, and friendly. We got on well, but having secured a place in London to read English law, I was going to be away for at least four years and remained just friends. Ironically, Hwan befriended a girl in the choir even though he never joined. I left him to his newfound love and prepared myself. The next door was opening in my life, soon to reveal a new room of fresh opportunity and promise.

When I left for London, my family and friends from the choir gave me a warm send-off at the airport. I was departing on a new leg of my journey and opening a new chapter. All my troubles from secondary school were so far away then. I thought I was looking for the Lord, but it was He who came to me, carried me as a man carried his child, all along the road I traveled on the way to this place.

> Take heed lest you forget the Lord your God, by not keeping his commandments and his ordinances and his statutes, which I command you this day: lest, when you have eaten and are full, and have built goodly houses and live in them, and when your herds and flocks multiply, and your silver and gold is multiplied, and all that you have is multiplied, then your heart be lifted up, and you forget the Lord your God, who brought you out of the land of Egypt, out of the house of bondage, who led you through the great and terrible wilderness, with its fiery serpents and scorpions and thirsty ground where there was no water, who brought you water out of the flinty rock, who fed you in the wilderness with manna which your fathers didn't know, that he might humble you and test you, to do you good in the end. Beware lest you say in your heart, 'My power and the might of my hand have gotten me this wealth. (Deuteronomy 8:11-17)

The Promised Land and its temptations

Looking back, I wish a shepherd had given me advice about pride and temptation. The Lord made me understand that help comes from Him. Despite this valuable knowledge, I began claiming each victory for myself in the days unfolding and told in the following Chapters. I did it! I made this! I deserved that! I even adopted and proselytized my own idolatry of *the Palm*. Yes, I saw His hand in my life, but how could I've displeased my Lord by fashioning the *Baal* in my own hand?

9. Land of Milk and Honey

Happier days in London

The university I attended had a claim to being the third oldest in England. It was established with royal patronage as a rival to the *godless one* on Gower Street. Many leaders, judges, Queen's Counsels, academics, poets, Nobel laureates, and other eminent men and women have enrolled in this place of higher learning. They breathed its rarefied air, debated, and whispered in its indiscernible cul-de-sacs. Every student desired to be sown with the seeds of learning, virtue, and religion. When I entered the School of Law, I was swept away by the sense of its august, accomplished academia.

I arrived expecting fierce competition. Achievers from many parts of the world were enrolled in the same class. There were the Brits, of course, from England and Wales, and a single Scottish lass. Courtesy of elite exchange student programs, a handful of serious intellectuals joined us from France and Germany. A single scholar from the United States defied isolationism and enrolled as well. From Asia, there were distinguished scholars from the Commonwealth nations of Hong Kong, Malaysia, Singapore, and Sri Lanka. I was among the few Asian exceptions without a scholarship. Yet, to my pleasant surprise, none of my classmates were aloof or mean.

Life in the faculty was quietly stern and stood in sharp contrast to the gregarious warmth of the Malaysian and Singaporean social communities. We had many convivial dinner parties and countless invigorating conversations. Speaking only for myself, I drank far too much poison of the distilled and brewed varieties when I was in good company, which was often the case in England and Europe. Nearly every Malaysian and Singaporean student was intent on having a tantalizing time savoring London's history and culture, relishing the opportunity to broaden mind and experience.

I had to check myself many times to recall the serious objective of my mission in London. On the first day in university, I broke away from the crowd to explore the library. It was beautifully old, with rows upon rows of shelves stocked with well-worn law reports, journals, and essential reference law books. There were neat rows of antique oak readers' desks, spaciously arranged, bathed in ample reading light. I pulled out a law report to read and found myself, like Miriam, unable to read past the first page. Gasping in my alarm, I realized then the effects of full-time military service: I'd lost the habit of study. Except, much as I would have liked to blame conscripted service, there was no one else to blame. I was responsible for the slack in my intellectual vigor. The candidate who enrolled for study in this venerable institution of higher learning wasn't the student who arrived.

The first step in solving any problem is acknowledging it exists. How does one recover the habit of study? On that first day, I resolved to work hard, spend long hours in the law library and persevere in disciplined study. I had to master my meager rigor. My resolution led to the earnest study of law from the opening hours of the library, until it shut its doors at nine in the evening, as many days as it was opened each given week.

Why should I be totally committed?

The Lord had unbolted this door for me, that's why!

I was without hope in the abyss one day; on another, I was enrolled in this fabulous place of learning. Having been gifted the phenomenal opportunity to make my father proud, I became a firebrand of hard work and eventually instigated many students to labor in the law library.

If you'd seen me in those days, I was like a fixture in the library, often not aware I'd missed the lunch hour. My reading desk was strewn with many opened law books. Yes, the study of law fascinated me a great deal.

I realized early on there was no end to the laws and rules that we were required to read in each subject for any given year—rote study couldn't help an aspiring law student. What motivated my serious study was the desire to grasp the rule of the laws. The long hours were dedicated to delving, dissecting, and discerning the *ratio decidendi, obiter dictum,* and the mind of the *Man on the Clapham Omnibus* in each legal precedent. Looking back, I'm quite sure that it was my scrupulous study of hundreds of law books, countless hours of research, and the inspiring tutors that shaped the legal mind I have today.

I didn't forget my Lord and the voice He gave me to sing praises to my Father in heaven. During the early weeks of orientation, I made inquiries and was elated to learn the university choir was recruiting. I attended the initial meeting in the gorgeous chapel and made up my mind, quite quickly, that I was out of my depth. Each member was likely a choral scholar, academically trained and certified in vocals, or a member of the music department. Most members of this choir would eventually go on to pursue postgraduate vocal studies at a conservatory, or professional careers as soloists or as members of an ensemble. It was the repertoire that was decisively daunting. They performed compositions such as Haydn's *Missa Sancti Johannes de Deo* (Little Organ Mass), Franck's *Panis Angelicus,* and Mozart's *Laudate Dominum*—all telling me I was very far away from home. I was humbled but not deterred, and quietly excused myself. I made inquiries at smaller choirs in the university and in my new parish. It was disappointing that I didn't even make the grade in these choirs as well. Regretfully, I resigned myself to the unhappy conclusion that there wasn't going to be any choir service for me during my time in London.

Without regular service to the Church through song, I felt I had to keep myself close to the Lord. So I attended a meeting of my college's Catholic Society. Sadly, I couldn't connect with the members and didn't return.

In the first academic year, I corresponded with a few friends from the Marian Choir. I missed the choir as my soul yearned to sing praises to the Lord with my friends. After a while, these letters also lost their direction and purpose.

One of my seniors and a former classmate from St. Joseph's, Sherman, suggested Sunday Mass in the Chelsea parish when he learned of my love for choral music. He was right about the choir. The singers in the Church of Our Most Holy Redeemer sang *a capella* regularly and were exquisitely ethereal. There were no more than twenty members serving in that choir, but their harmonious voices filled the church hall. It was as though the ceiling had opened to join heaven, and a host of angels was joyfully lending their voices. Kudos was due to the thrilling talents of the singers, who were aided in no small part by the amazing acoustics in the church hall. Needless to say, the credentials for membership in this choir were well beyond my reach, and I settled for listening to these celestial voices.

After Mass on Sundays at noon, I habitually adjourned to Wong Kei's, a budget Chinese Restaurant on Wardour Street, for a Sunday lunch of rice noodles with beef in black bean sauce. This delicious meal came with complimentary, comforting Chinese tea at the affordable price of £2.20.

Speaking of food, which I confess to liking, I attended a formal dinner on Maundy Thursday to recall and celebrate the Lord's Supper. This event was hosted by the London University Catholic Students' Society. There was a celebration of the Mass, followed by dinner. I fainted during the long prayer before the meal, which prompted my table companions to mischievously inquire if I'd already begun my fast!

The truth was that I never did fast faithfully. It wasn't as if I didn't know the fast began on Good Friday. As with all my fasts, the day would start earnestly but by lunch, after a cup of hot beverage, my good intentions invariably crumbled in my belly and I succumbed to the demand to feed the suffering in my stomach. As quickly as the disciples scattered after the arrest of Jesus, I disengaged from my Lord's Passion as well.

I didn't even appreciate the need to attend penitential services on a regular basis or for the solemn seasons such as Advent or Lent. *Ergo*, I didn't confess my sins for a very long time. In those spiritually uneducated days, I supposed the Lord would forgive me if I mouthed prayerful words that I felt were contrite.

There was a second event organized by the Catholic Students' Society, which was meaningful to me at the time. A group of us visited an orphanage that was home to autistic children. We sang songs and spent time with them. I lifted and carried a few of the children for fun and laughter. A faculty friend, chancing upon snapshots of my visit, remarked that I was good with children.

My studies got tougher and I eventually drifted away from the Catholic Students' Society.

Summers by InterRail

In the spring of my first year, Sherman encouraged me to visit Europe during the Summer Breaks, telling me this opportunity might not present itself again, once the studies are completed and I return home. He was right in some ways. The luxury to take off, visit any city or town, spend a day here or a week there, on a whim or two months at a go, was hard to come by again. After obtaining my English professional qualifications, I returned home for the Singapore Bar Finals. Once settled, I only managed one time-out for a two-month vacation for the sake of European romance and a final indulgence of my love for train travel in Europe. Twelve years later, I returned with my newlywed wife on our honeymoon to share a sentimental part of my memory.

What made the European vacations so alluring was the adventure of traveling by train. The locomotive and its railroad cars hark back to a bygone era in which heroes and heroines boarded the train for epic, life-changing journeys. Savoring the stunning scenery from large windows, sometimes framed by frilly curtains and vintage brass lamps on the cabin wall, every train was bound for exotic adventures.

With this dream in mind, the second-year student made a promise to visit Europe as the *air had become lambent with adult enterprise.* Spread out over three summers, my vacation travel took me practically all over Europe.

There was no plan. For my inaugural trip, I bought a single-month InterRail Pass at Victoria Station, a Thomas Cook train timetable, and a Let's Go travel guide. I got on a budget flight from London and arrived in Frankfurt to begin my adventure by rail. After spending two days wandering about the city, I was ready to use the InterRail Pass. I can still remember that summer evening: day one of my many train journeys. Inexperience made me blunder at the first hurdle. Without a seat on the train, I had to disembark the overnighter bound for Vienna and spent the first inglorious night of my misadventure on a bench.

The next day, not wanting to waste the daylight hours traveling long distances, I headed to West Berlin. This city appealed to me from my study of history. After the Second World War, Berlin was divided into the western sector under the joint administration of the western allies and East Berlin under the control of the Soviet Union. Immediately after the war, the Soviets restricted access to all military, passenger, and cargo traffic in and out of West Berlin: it was practically an island isolated in a *red sea*! What ensued was probably the greatest humanitarian assistance of our times—the Berlin Airlift or the *raisin bombers* christened by the German children.

The first place I wanted to visit was Checkpoint Charlie. The Berlin Wall was being dismantled when I visited; yet, surprisingly, there were still some border guards in place. This legacy from Germany's division gave extra fascination to the history of secret escapes and the Cold War intrigue played out in the earlier decades. I also visited the Brandenburg Gate and the famed *Unter den Linden* that used to be the grandest street in Europe. After spending the night in Berlin, I got on the train to Prague and found myself in the same cabin as a newlywed couple from North Carolina.

Half the fun in train journeys is striking up a conversation with complete strangers. Exchanging stories and sharing experiences on a long journey help break the monotony and foster fledgling friendships. So much so, we often ended up less stranger and more friend, exchanging contacts or agreeing to share accommodations at the same destination.

The newlyweds must have enjoyed my company or my melodrama about getting arrested (as I had no visa to enter the country). On arriving safely, we agreed to share a two-bedroom *pension* and spend time together in the city of Prague. We did very little sightseeing. It was just three days of beer hall and tavern hopping, beginning with the wildly popular U Fleků brewery founded in 1499. A half-liter of *pivo* (pilsner lager or dark ale) was quite affordable then in Prague at S$1.90 or 30 Koruna; though, the experienced backpackers told me that prices had risen dramatically after the fall of the Iron Curtain.

It seemed customary for backpackers to gather in a circle at each drinking hole. There were plenty of singing of national songs and dancing. It was a merry sight: the young travelers were all holding giant beer glasses and wearing happy grins. It was easy to greet everyone. I only had to say: "*Dobré pivo*!", "*Prost*!", or "Cheers!" After all that inebriated revelry, but not so wasted as to forget about my exorbitant and expiring three-day transit visa, I left Czechoslovakia abruptly.

When I look back at those journeys beyond Berlin and Prague, I'm truly grateful to my parents for their gifts. Had it not been for their generosity, my prodigious travel all over Europe would have been impossible: as far north as Stockholm; as far east as *Efes*; as far south as Seville; and as far west as Fatima.

Spiritual wandering

In addition to my wanderlust for new tastes and experiences, I went looking for Europe's rich treasures of sacred art and religious architecture that have amazed and inspired visitors from all over the world. From the veiled pilgrims in solemn prayer to tourists with a camera slung round their neck, and artists with their quiet canvas, I was never alone. Visitors delighted in the visual and spiritual beauty of the sacred spaces, where art and faith came together to pay homage to the Lord. Most visits disclosed a delectable dichotomy. The world on the streets outside was usually busy, bothered, and noisy with a scooter screeching or a car cranking; but inside the church building, visitor and worshipper were treated to a restful respite in spellbinding serenity.

In Rome, I was glad to visit the *Basilica di Santa Maria Maggiore.* This church building is a Constantinian Basilica still retaining its Roman roots from the early fifth century, with very antique Athenian columns still supporting the building. Very close by this gorgeous basilica is the unassuming Church of St. Alphonsus Liguori. It holds a fantastic treasure—the original icon of our Lady of Perpetual Help—dear to everyone all over the world who prays the Novena.

From the experience of enjoying these and other timeworn marvels, I came to appreciate the role of the Church as the custodian of Christian art. It's important to preserve this rich heritage for the benefit of all generations. Yet the early Romans didn't always strike the right note. When I was with my wife visiting a very ancient Egyptian tomb in the Valley of the Kings, we were astonished to come across less ancient Roman graffiti in Latin.

In Istanbul, Turkey, I encountered the stark, early Byzantine architectural style when I visited the *Hagia Sophia.* My visit to *Efes* (ancient Ephesus), also in Turkey, gave me a spiritually happy encounter with the Lord. I arrived too early and, without the aid of a tourist office, went looking for the House of the Virgin Mary from the bus station. After a considerable walk, I found a sign pointing up what seemed like a high hill (that was Mount Koressos or *Bülbüldağı* in Turkish). Acknowledging the test of my faith in the scorching sun, I accepted the Lord's beckoning. Before I could take another step, grace showed up in a car pulling alongside. An Aussie (with family in tow) greeted me, "G'day," and asked if I knew where Mary's house was. I did and pointed to the top of the hill. Plainly seeing the direction of my footsteps (or perhaps already possessing Christian charity in their hearts), Captain Ross and his wife, Lorrain Pearce, kindly offered me a ride. How could I say no—I accepted all gifts from my Lord! At the well, I offered grateful prayers to the Lord, noting the uncountable petitions stuck to the wall. I was also grateful to spend serendipitous time with this unimaginably hospitable family, who later became friends with my parents on their subsequent visits to Singapore. We visited the burial site of St. John, the Evangelist, and possibly that of St. Luke, the Divine and gave thanks in our prayers for these heroes of the Church.

The early Byzantine style is also found in *Sveta Sofia* in Sofia, Bulgaria. The Romanesque style in the Lisbon Cathedral and the St. Vitus Cathedral in Prague is similarly austere, but grand nonetheless. I was awed by the Gothic architecture displayed in the examples of *Cathédrale Notre-Dame* in Paris, *Kölner Dom* in Cologne, Germany, *Duomo* in Florence, Italy, Barcelona Cathedral in Spain and St. Mary's Basilica in *Kraków*, Poland. In Munich, I was overwhelmed by the ornamental Rococo style used in the church of St. Johann Nepomuk, also known as the *Asamkirche*.

These free visits to so many beautiful churches in Europe offered outstanding occasions to feast on divine art to my soul's content. Having visited countless churches, the Renaissance style emerged as my favorite, and the greatest example for me will always be St. Peter's Basilica in the Vatican City.

A visit to a church or sacred destination might be an occasion to bend my knee in prayer. It was habitual for me to just enter any church I chance upon, gaze and drink in its beauty. But when I discovered a serene and achingly contemplative church, the Lord would beckon me to spend some time in quiet prayer or sit awhile. I once visited a beautiful church in Prague but ended up attending Mass in the Czech language, not understanding a word that was being said. I found myself moved by the experience and doodled a silly poem about my poor faith overleaf a receipt. Otherwise, the

Lord knew I had abundant youthful energy. I would fill my days with miles of brisk walking all over the city or town I was visiting—so many attractions, so little time.

Even though I didn't plan a pilgrimage, a few churches or places of pilgrimage drew me, as a faint, delightful tune whispers its notes and draws a musician to its source.

In Dresden, the *Frauenkirche* or Church of Our Lady was, at the time of my visit, still substantially in ruins due to the bombing. Only the altar and a few pillars remained standing—its ruins stood to teach me the horrors of war and the endurance of faith. As a pilgrim of sorts, I offered a prayer to those who suffered and died.

In another memorial, my soul was moved to cry a prayer for the souls of millions of my Jewish brethren, prisoner 16670 (now Saint Maximilian), and the uncountable others who suffered senselessly. This multitude of innocents perished horrifically in Auschwitz (or *Oświęcim* in Polish), in other death camps in Poland, and elsewhere.

There were also the pilgrimages to Lourdes in France and Fatima in Portugal. In spite of being a Sunday Catholic in those days, I wanted to make a pilgrimage to these holy sanctuaries. It was my desire especially to see, hear, and understand for myself the source of so many inexplicable, miraculous healings. One of which was the incredible account of *Vittorio Micheli*'s pilgrimage that became the sixty-third documented miracle I'd read about as a young boy in *Reader's Digest*. I've since learned that the Church's investigation, scrutiny, and scrupulous approval of each miracle needed to be scientifically meticulous and theologically demanding as well. Not even the witness by a Nobel laureate of not one, but two, astonishing cures in Lourdes could qualify as miracles in the Church's books. I was also amazed by the incorrupt *corpus* of St. Bernadette, who had witnessed the appearance of the Immaculate Conception. With the Lord's providence, I was able to visit Lourdes three times, once on my own and twice with my mother. I drank the healing waters and was fortunate to immerse myself in the pools with prayers said over me.

When I arrived in Rome for the first time, my heart and soul leapt to visit the Vatican City and St. Peter's Basilica. I must have spent a whole day delighting in the sheer majesty of this heavenly city. I returned many times because the Sistine Chapel seemed coy and was always shut for repairs on each visit.

Many years later, together with my wife, I shared all the joys of my youthful adventures in Europe and my love for the Eternal City. Fortune finally smiled with the elusive *Cappella Sistina* revealing its treasures to us. I was captivated by the sublime ceiling artwork that Michelangelo had beheld and brought into being, as well as his magnificent *Last Judgment* painted on the sanctuary wall.

At a church in Vienna, my wife and I found a chapel dedicated to St. Jude where we lit a candle and offered a petition for Manna's father, then stricken with a grave illness.

The One

In the second year of traveling by InterRail, I focused on Central Europe. Why? Because this part of Europe was then affordable to a student backpacker on a shoestring. This trip began in Warsaw, Poland, in the North and ended with Sofia, Bulgaria, in the South. Yugoslavia's borders were shut as war had broken out in that year.

Czechoslovakia, as it was then known, fascinated me for three gorgeous reasons: picture-perfect places, pleasurable pilsners, and a pretty *priatel'ka.* On my second, sober visit to Prague, I found this to be the prettiest European city. Prague or *Praha* offered many starry-eyed attractions. *Staré Město,* in particular, provided a glimpse of a bygone, bohemian era: the Old City dates back to the ninth century and is still gorgeously paved with medieval cobblestones. Taking center stage (for me) was *Karlův Most* (or Charles Bridge), with its statues and statuaries still evoking dreamy visions of romance, intrigue, and the Old World. The *Orloj* (an astronomical clock), installed in 1410, is the world's oldest working clock, charmingly intricate with the hourly movement of the figurine of Christ marching ahead of the twelve Apostles. It also features four other figurines moving in tandem: Vanity, Greed, Death, and Gluttony. Then the Rooster crows and the bells chime the hour. Many of the country's cultural attractions thankfully survived the World Wars mostly unscathed. The Velvet Revolution in 1989 was also practically non-violent.

Besides the excellent pilsner and dark beer I enjoyed in Prague, I savored probably the best beer on my list of ultimate life experiences in České Budějovice, the capital of the southern Bohemian region. I set off on my beer adventure and arrived nonchalantly past seven in the evening. I was well aware that this was a small city, and its tourist office was probably shut (it was), which meant the possibility of not finding affordable digs. The alternative was the station hotel that offered rooms at 400 Koruna or S$24 a night—an arm and a leg for my student budget. My fallback was to take an overnight train to somewhere else. Walking along the wide boulevard from the train station, I caught sight of a busy, somewhat antiquated tavern and made a mental note of getting my dinner, as I was ravenous by that time. I didn't find a youth hostel at the end of that boulevard and decided to retreat.

Pushing past the swing doors of the tavern, I felt a hundred eyes staring at me in bewilderment, as though I'd stumbled into a Western saloon that didn't welcome out-of-towners. I was too hungry to be concerned and quickly moved to the rear, where a table was free. *Budvar* wasn't available, but everyone seemed to be enjoying the lager. I ordered a large glass of the house beer, my dinner of pork chops and *knedlíky,* or traditional potato dumplings. An old gentleman was seated at the next table, quite happy with ten empty glasses to show for it, chatting with the youths at another table. He then turned his attention to me. In no time, we were communicating in fragmented French, German and Czech. I then asked, "*Connaissez-vous Zimmer-Studentka*?" He went back to the students and consulted them. A while later, he smiled at me and motioned that he was going to show me the way to the youth hostel! After he'd quaffed his eleventh glass and I, my second, I offered to pick up his tab, all of which came up to the grand total of 180 Koruna or S$11. I could have been taken for a ride to the dark side, but I was open to the goodwill of this stranger.

The old gentleman kindly took a tram with me and walked me all the way into the lobby of the university dormitory: such was the remarkable hospitality of Czechoslovakia! As the students were away for their Summer Break, I was allocated a whole dorm at 25 Koruna for the bed and 2 Koruna for a clean towel, all for less than S$2 a night.

The next day, I made my way to the *Budweiser Budvar* brewery. A canteen close to the brewery was open so I promptly plonked myself down on a seat near the tap. It was dispensing freshly brewed *Budweiser Budvar* at the unbelievable price of 8 Koruna or about S$0.50 for a large half-liter glass! I knew that Czechoslovakia produced many original and delicious kinds of beer such as the Pilsner Lager created in the Czech town of *Plzeň* (or Pilsen in German). Thus, I found it perfectly natural to drink copious quantities of excellent Czech beer at lunch. The *Budweiser Budvar* was a crisp, enjoyable and luscious beer with a full body—I could even taste the delicious, natural spring water they used. I also saw a sign that hinted at the Budweiser wars. Note to self and the Lord willing, I should return to České Budějovice one day with my father who enjoys delicious beer.

It was in Bratislava that I found a pretty *priatel'ka*. Those who know the Czech language will realize I'm not referring to a Czech *přítelkyně*. I'm instead referring to the romantic pursuit of a Slovakian girl. After spending time in Prague with Sherman and other seniors from London, I headed toward Bratislava on my own. I had a later appointment to join another of the seniors in Budapest, which was a three-hour train ride away. I was keen to sample Slovakian spirits and the historical delights this city had to offer, as it'd been an important part of the Habsburg Kingdom for a few hundred years. Three days in Bratislava was more than sufficient on my backpacker's schedule or so I thought.

As was my SOP (i.e. standard operating procedure in Singapore soldier parlance), I would leave my large backpack in a public locker (or the attended left luggage office in the train stations). This facility enabled me to carry a smaller, day bag into the destination city.

After checking into a budget *pension*, I was kicking myself for missing a needed item and returned to the train station.

Upon retrieving what I needed from the locker, I spied a fruit cart. One thing I required for my diet in Central Europe was fruit. Quite unlike my father who can't subsist long on meals that don't include rice, I can dine on foreign cuisine and exotic fare for months on end because I live for the pleasure of new tastes. But the Slavic cuisine seemed starchy and didn't feature fresh vegetables then. So I needed fresh fruit in my diet.

I went up to the fruit cart single-mindedly. Pointing to a small bunch of bananas, I handed the vendor a large enough note and hoped to receive something in return. With the change in hand, I realized the bananas were cheap because they cost only 20 Koruna. This was a pleasant surprise because the same went for 50 in Prague. My surprise triggered a curious expression from Jana (or Jane in English).

It was then that I noticed her gorgeous, gray eyes looked like diamonds with a soft, tremulous gleam, well hidden behind large spectacle frames. The puzzled look on her face revealed more—a diminutive, lovely smile. An arrow must have struck me then because I spent the whole day thinking about her beauty, in the same way a new color, perspective, or image agitates a hapless artist, and he's then caught in a creative kaleidoscope. I couldn't find peace until I addressed the ache in my heart.

I returned to the train station the next day, pretending to buy more fruit from Jana's cart or perhaps to see what lay behind this door. Then, I shyly mentioned I was a stranger in her city and waffled about not knowing my way around. Surprisingly, she introduced herself and asked me plainly if I would like to date her: this was my cue! I was mindful that she wasn't entirely fluent in English, so I asked her again in a different way to be sure (about the date). This was how I communicated in every foreign land by rephrasing my questions or responses. I'm grateful for any opportunity to interact, particularly when the locals accommodate me by conversing in English, a tongue that isn't theirs.

We met at a *pivnice* (tavern) of her choice. Listening to her, I learned of her studies in social anthropology at a local university and her love for animals. She was also an unusual vegetarian; she had white meat for her main course. I was quite brash in those days. At the end of that first date, I asked if she had a boyfriend. When she said no, I offered myself, and she countered with a demure, "Maybe." Though the romantic feelings were bubbling like champagne within me, I didn't have any clue what offering myself entailed. We spent the following day exploring her city, and *rapturous* didn't quite capture what I felt because this is the stuff of love stories told in romance novels or unreeled on the big screen.

I went on to delight my friends in London and Singapore (over the following few years) repeatedly with accounts of how I'd found *The One.*

On a different visit in another summer, she took me to a bathing pond. What pleased me about the freshwater pond was its enormous size: I wanted to think it was a lake, but then everything in Singapore is tiny, and my perspective on its size isn't helpful. That day the beautiful, bright, balmy weather and sparkling water made me feel so happy to be in Jana's company.

One winter was especially memorable because I'd entered Czechoslovakia and departed from the Slovak Republic to enter the Czech Republic on January 1, 1993. On that visit, I missed the last train going into Bratislava and had to hike from the Austrian border to the Slovakian checkpoint because I wanted to keep my promised appointment. I was invited to her home, and Jana treated me to homemade strawberry *fizzo* she'd specially prepared for me. We spent a lovely evening sharing what was happening in our lives.

As in many other serendipitous encounters, the visit to the pond, being invited to a family dinner or spending time with a new friend in a foreign land, were all precious gifts from people (including Jana). Even if such time were for a day, a few weeks or a few years, they shared their life with me and this love that I've experienced could only be given freely. Even so, romance or goodwill among friends can wilt quite quickly. Love in the family or between spouses may be stronger, but it too can become brittle for lack of emotional nourishment, or crushed by the hidden weight of expectation or disappointment.

Back in those days when emails could only be found in science departments, and cell phones were as easy to find as righteous men, there was no way of contacting my friend to cancel or postpone our meeting. I'd already promised to meet him at the American Express outlet in central Budapest. If there's anything more valued than youthful passion, it would be my principle of keeping promises.

I expressed my regret in cutting short our first date, but it was Jana's idea that we keep in contact with regular letters, the snail mail's way. As a result of her request, we exchanged many letters over the years while I was in London and continuing even after my return to Singapore.

Just as my first visit to Prague was filled with abundant, unexpected drinking, my first visit to Bratislava overflowed with abundant, unexpected romance.

Even though I eventually lost this pretty *priatel'ka* in the fragile fabric of life, I consider this yarn about Jana one of the many precious gifts from my Lord. I believe He was teaching me to pursue the love of the faithful One.

Hey look, I've come through

As soon as I arrived in London to begin my first year, time accelerated. And before anyone could say, "Jack Robinson," I was ready to return home to begin my vocation. Having survived law school, I left thinking like a lawyer. I'd devoted myself to the disciplined reading of English laws and graduated with a *Legum Baccalaureus* (LL.B).

I spent the fourth and last year working flat out to pass the Bar Vocation Course, one of two prerequisites to obtaining the professional qualification of Barrister-at-law, England and Wales. In addition to five subjects from the LL.B curriculum, there were five new subjects requiring my study. Just when I thought I could take it easy in my final year, the new subjects obliged me to work even harder, particularly as the pass rate was reputedly low.

No sir, the first year isn't the hardest.

When I received my examination timetable, I was aghast at the backbreaking schedule of being examined in all ten papers over a consecutive stretch of five days, without a weekend intervening or a day's break. Undeterred, I devised a simple strategy of fitting flow charts of any given subject on a single sheet of paper. This forward thinking paid off. I was mentally exhausted by the time I arrived at the two-hour lunch break on the fifth and final day of my examinations, with a three-hour paper in the morning and a three-hour paper in the afternoon. I had only so much time to grab a bite and refresh my memory. Thankfully, I was able to answer the questions at hand and was very relieved to clear this final hurdle.

In honor of my father, I was called to the Bar at the Middle Temple, of which an elder statesman that he admired was also a member.

Questions for Reflection on Chapters 7–9

1. Has the Lord given the help you asked for? Were you grateful? What did you do next?
2. If you had been prompted to know the Lord and the Faith better, what did you do to receive spiritual training of your heart?
3. If you are actively serving in the church, have you sought faith formation? Do you have a community of faith? Do you study the Word of God with your brothers and sisters?
4. Do you announce the Good News?
5. Have you been given the opportunity to forgive, and reconcile with, your enemy?
6. Do you confess your sins regularly?
7. Are you focused in your academic, sporting, artistic, or career pursuits? Do you apply the same focus and determination in your Christian life?
8. Have you loved anyone romantically with all your heart? Do you love the Lord with all your heart, more than your father, mother, spouse, family, and friends?

10. The Waters of Meribah

Inadequate faith formation and growing blindness

In Chapters 10 to 12, you'll read about how my pride grew in strength and my spiritual folly led me further astray. It culminates in tremendous suffering—*a colossal collision and capsizing*—that's the story told in Chapter 13. You might be wondering, "What happened to the gratitude for the second encounter with Jesus Christ?" Yes, even though I possess an exceptional memory, the feelings of spiritual fervor waned without a Christian life 24/7. Like many men and women of faith before me, my memory of the Lord's mighty hand and outstretched arm conveniently faded during this part of my journey.

In this Chapter, I return home to Singapore. In addition to starting my legal career, I'll tell you about my stint as a teacher for two years. The positive teaching experience helped rebuild the self-esteem so badly damaged in secondary school. I rejoin the choir, albeit my experience of different cultures introduced a more combative streak in my behavior. Success also played a big part in giving me confidence, perhaps too much for my own good. Resigning from the Marian Choir allowed me to participate in the lectors' ministry and a second choir that focused more of its service on praise and worship. Yes, I was busy in church, but there was no spiritual training for my heart. These episodes are relevant to show the questions of faith that the Lord was prompting in my heart, even as He permitted my rebellion and prideful ways.

We also say goodbye to Jana because she proved not to be *The One*. The return trip to Europe is also connected with the failed attempt to obtain a copy of *The Return of the Prodigal Son*.

Chapter 11 presents my grand folly: the foolish friendship with a soothsayer and the prideful thinking emerging that I could decide my destiny. This Chapter also introduces Élysée, who became my wife.

In Chapter 12, my romance with Élysée blossoms and grows into love. The theme of *The Return of the Prodigal Son* fits in coincidentally, as I eventually found a print copy of the painting. Shortly after that, a "door of faith" opened into a *room* within the Church, which enabled me, a prodigal son of sorts, to begin a better journey of faith.

Having my way

Given the all-clear, I returned home in my triumphal procession. I paraded my bachelor's degree as though it was a victory wreath awarded to an athlete in ancient races. I was full of pride, for I became the first lawyer in my family. Despite the somewhat impossible odds, I'd won a great victory and fulfilled my aspiration. It seemed there was nothing I couldn't do. To prove the point, within a year of my return, I was adding the Singapore qualification of Advocate and Solicitor under my belt. During this time, I was quite hopeful about my prospects with Jana.

The proposed return trip to Europe was carefully planned. I wanted to spend two months traveling leisurely around Europe with Jana to persuade her to consider life in Singapore with me. With this goal in mind, I took up part-time lecturing at a commercial school for law to fund the extended trip. Always one for the challenge, I did this while juggling my Singapore professional examinations.

I was appointed to lecture the Law of Evidence. As a student in London, I relished debating this subject's many rules and exceptions. In the early days of the academic year, I realized a problem as between studying and teaching. As a student, I enjoyed learning interesting topics. It's another thing altogether to teach the breadth of the subject with authority.

I was responsible for two groups of students. The first group comprised young hopefuls who didn't qualify for, or couldn't afford, the regular universities. The second was made up of mature students from all walks of life looking to broaden their minds or considering a mid-career switch.

My own high standards became a rod for my own back. To my consternation, I found the school's materials inadequate for teaching. Fear of being blamed for this content and pride in my own ability challenged me to work hard. So I strove to produce a set of teaching aids capable of delivering the right standard. This effort proved worthwhile.

Just before my inaugural lecture, I learned that my class had enrolled about fifty students. There was an even mix of young and mature students, with the older student group comprising teachers, police officers, doctors and a stewardess. It was relatively easy to satisfy the expectations of the young. Though it's a different ballgame to meet the intimidating, expert gazes of experienced teachers and the professionally qualified in a lecture hall. I cleared my throat and focused my gaze on the students showing interest. As was the custom after the lecture, students gathered round to quiz me. I survived the cross-examination and was given the warm backing of my students, especially the teacher group.

I worked hard for my students and spoiled them rotten by supplying case materials and numerous model essays. My intention was to fast-track the training of their minds with the limited tutorial time, as many were also juggling work and other heavy commitments during the day.

I was still writing romance-filled letters to, and receiving the same from, Jana. Except, that is, for a conspicuous break of two months when I was tied up with work. She was frantic, querying my silence and possible change of heart. My quick replies were, however, messed up by the courier service. I concluded that this ripple in the cosmos was something I couldn't avoid or overcome.

When the year was up, I'd built up a folder of teaching resources and a real sense of fellowship with many of my students. I know of at least one mature student who went on to practice law. I bumped into him in the law courts years later. I enjoyed the teaching so much that, despite the measly emoluments, I continued for another year. I hoped the students benefited from my teaching.

I know I did.

This teaching experience was precious to me, in a way more valuable than the experience of competitive debating denied to me in those years dominated by the Amorites. In the lecture hall, I wrestled with old demons residing inside me, won the warm support of my students and helped shape their minds. I also regained my self-confidence. I wasn't dim, after all.

Search for the Prodigal Son

My path crossed with Fr. Alfred's in the parish one fine Sunday. From our small talk, he learned of my plans to return to Europe for romance and adventure. With an anticipatory spring in his steps, he called me into his office to show me his thumbprint-size picture of Rembrandt's *The Return of the Prodigal Son.*

He shared with me the significance of this extraordinary artwork. The faceless young son kneeling in unreserved repentance represents all sinners. His unkempt clothes, shorn hair, and a single shoe symbolize his spiritual poverty. Represented by the elderly man in this painting, our loving God completely embraces the sinner. Gently overcoming the son's despair, He clasps the young man with a feminine right hand symbolizing comforting compassion, and a masculine left hand showing mercy that welcomes the long-lost sinner back into the family. The stern-looking elder brother on the right of this artwork represents anyone in the family who judges and won't show mercy to the sinner. Fr. Alfred seemed in awe of the painting's solemn, intimate, and timeless message of mercy and forgiveness and expressed his wish for me to find him a larger copy for his use in teaching.

I promised I would.

This was, however, a promise I could only fulfill eight-years later.

Not *The One*

After securing my Singapore professional qualification and completing my first year of teaching, I got on the first flight to Bratislava. I took with me a brand-new camera, *vegetarian* treats from Singapore, and funds for extended traveling in Europe.

Why did I bring along a good camera? I was upset with the loss of the only photographs we had hurriedly taken in a photo booth in the *Bratislava Hlavná Stanica.* With a distance between us, I treasured the snapshots, gazing on her beauty like a lovelorn swain. Not exactly being security conscious, they were clasped between the pages of my *Let's Go* book. The thought of the photographs slipping out was constantly on my mind, but the longing in my heart was too strong to master. The result was their total loss. To celebrate my graduation, I'd led my family on a whirlwind tour of Europe. Running from one train station to another while shepherding them, I carelessly left the book behind on a seat in a *Paris Métro* car.

I stayed in the apartment that Jana's grandmother had bequeathed to her. As soon as I arrived, I felt a distance between us. The following morning, after a few conversations sharing her graduation plans, Jana broke the news about someone new in her life. I was upset at learning this because she could have told me in a letter and spared me this fruitless trip. That being said, the meeting with Jana was important to her, but I just couldn't bring myself to acknowledge the shattered plans at the time. Some of my students thought I was full of passion in the forceful lectures I gave. I can imagine how much aggression I must have projected on poor Jana as if loud speaking could make her change her mind. The melodrama that erupted was tragicomical because I started cooking some of the treats I carried from Singapore while venting uselessly. Masquerading the animated outburst was a sadness steadily creeping to smother this love story—the final curtain was falling on our time together—I was going to leave for good and not look back. With the *vegetarian* treats safely prepared for Jana's enjoyment, I stumbled out with a heavy heart, my luggage, and the purposeless camera.

All is vanity!

She might have found someone else during the two months of my unfortunate silence. My prospect with Jana was dashed by the strange arithmetic of a flitting butterfly. Alas, she wasn't *The One* to make my life complete.

I was deeply devastated and spent the two months wandering all over Europe, nursing a broken heart, thinking about her but unable to pen even a sad song. This wasn't good for my health in another way. In my final year in London, I'd picked up smoking from a young English friend who taught me how to inhale. With my heart spurned, I found solace in days filled with excessive smoking, strong coffee, and reading in quiet cafés.

When I felt less sorry for myself, I remembered Fr. Alfred's request for a copy of *The Return of the Prodigal Son*. This was the distraction I needed. I was familiar with the major art museums in Europe from previous trips: *Kunsthistorisches Museum* in Vienna, *Galleria Borghese* in Rome, *Pinacoteca di Brera* in Milan, *Galleria degli Uffizi* in Venice, *Museo Nacional del Prado* and *Museo Thyssen-Bornemisza* in Madrid, and the *Louvre* in Paris. I believed all of them might sell prints and revised my itinerary accordingly. Even if I didn't find what I was looking for in those museums, I wasn't too worried. I thought I could always fall back on Amsterdam. After all, Rembrandt was a Dutch painter and buried in this city. As I struck the museums off my list, I got more frantic as I approached

Amsterdam. I was wrong. The *Rijksmuseum*, the principal museum in Amsterdam, didn't sell a copy of *The Return of the Prodigal Son*!

Down to the last week of my two-month vacation, I was scheduled to return home from London. I visited the National Gallery and the Tate Gallery in a final try; however, neither sold a copy I needed. In one of the art bookstores on the Strand, I learned that *The Return of the Prodigal Son* hung in and belonged to the Hermitage Museum in St. Petersburg. By then, I'd run out of time to make a dash to Russia. I didn't want to risk missing my scheduled flight home.

Returning home empty-handed, I expressed my regrets to Fr. Alfred.

A fight

I was warmly welcomed back into the Marian Choir. Most of the faces were the same and the routines remained familiar. Saul was still the anchor in the Bass section, and it was convenient for me to lean on his talents and follow his lead. However, in the year I returned, he was diagnosed with lymphoma cancer. Equally sad, Sue and the other girls had by then flown the coop—I was the only one who returned from my studies abroad. Fortunately, there were new faces who became fast friends: Maverick (also a lawyer), Rex, and Puru. I was the best man for Rex and Maverick's respective weddings; I also attended Puru's wedding in Tokyo. They were the three musketeers with whom I still keep in touch. Together with Saul, the five of us spent our days gallivanting, enjoying each other's company, and savoring the distractions life had to offer. The choir had, however, gained experience and ratcheted up its repertoire. In my absence, it'd performed in commercial settings and for private audiences. The pieces were getting harder, and more was expected from the members. I was with this choir for another three years before the fight erupted.

There was no love in my rebellion or my decision to leave the choir. When I joined as a young man, all I could see were angels disguised as choir singers. This choir taught me how to sing not just simple hymns, but also challenging, classical, choral arrangements in four-part harmonies. My four years as a member also sustained my toehold in a church ministry.

In spite of my service, the more I sang, the more the music stimulated a spiritual hunger. My service produced an ache that cried out for knowledge of my Creator, His purposes, and His plans for me. Of course, I didn't understand then why I was dissatisfied. How was I to know? My heart needed regular, full spiritual meals and not miserly morsels here and there. All I sensed at that time was a growing, inarticulate desire for something spiritually more fulfilling. I began asking:

Was my singing helping me become a better Christian?

When I first learned to sing *I Love You, Lord*, I found it beautiful and sublime. As with other pieces or arrangements I practiced and sang, it seemed relevant to my service in the church choir. As time went by, I began to judge the hallmark of performance in the choir's singing, which I felt was discordant with the sacred verses. The congregation usually enjoyed the choir's rendition of choral arrangements, sometimes in Latin or too sophisticated for them to join in. The parishioners often responded with appreciative applause. However, there were moments when I sensed the applause was somewhat disturbing and, on other occasions, the unappreciative silence left me feeling empty and denied. Though I was serving in my parish, guilt and confusion found its way into my heart.

I was yearning for a deeper spiritual experience, and the occasion for the fight arrived before Christmas. The leader proposed charitable visits to homes for the disadvantaged. I was given the task of organizing the visits. Unfortunately, a clash of commitments subsequently emerged for the appointed conductor. Despite confirming the appointments with the leader and the homes in question, I was then instructed to cancel all visits. I remembered my joyful experience with the autistic children in a London orphanage, so my conscience dictated the choir should keep the promises it'd made. That meant adding an uncharitable rebellion to the charitable visits.

I called the members (but not the leader) and persuaded them to attend a meeting. I did so knowing the standing instruction to cancel the visits, and that the leader wouldn't countenance this disobedience. With no love in my heart, I asked the members leading questions about love for the disadvantaged and breaking promises. My friends could only give the reply I was expecting. I found a replacement conductor and musician. My plan to outflank the leader was simple. There was no need for performances with challenging arrangements. Instead, we would sing simple Christmas hymns and offer the gifts of our time and presence. I asked myself rhetorically, "How complicated need charity be?" My heart was convinced that I was simply organizing an informal caroling outing among friends. By the time the leader discovered my mutiny, I'd already secured the high ground, rallied the troops, and executed my strategy for bringing joy to the hearts of the children that Christmas.

The leader eventually acquiesced and participated in the visits to the homes, but it was clear there was no love in my heart. I'd sacrificed friendship, trust, and everything held dear for a pyrrhic victory. Thus, 1 Corinthians 13:3 is correct: ". . . have not love, I gain nothing." There would be no further visits to these homes from this choir. This was my rebellion at Meribah. When the choir's duties for the Christmas season were fulfilled, I attended one more meeting. After the prayers of dismissal had been said, I thanked everyone and said my goodbyes. With love lost, I could no longer remain in a choir that was divided in the direction it should go and distrustful of my intentions.

Wandering in the desert

Having left the Marian Choir, I was on my own again in the anonymous pews, looking for the Lord as I did before. I'd complained. I'd rebelled. There was no love in my heart: only self-justification to defend and protect my ego. I was asking more questions:

With all the good deeds I'd done, how could I be wrong?

How does one learn to be a Christian?

Who could have taught my heart?

I'd heard it being said many times that, "Love is patient, gentle, and kind." If it were so easy to practice this spiritual truth, I could have learned love from the Bible on my own, in the privacy of my room. Yet there was no opportunity to practice and experience love in the quiet bunker of my home. In military terms, my home became a fortress where I could be safe from those who didn't agree with me or couldn't love me according to my expectations.

My heart was in revolt. On many occasions when I was wrong, I found myself excusing my heart for its transgressions, trying vainly to balance my *good works* against my wicked deeds. With a stone for my heart, how could I understand the things that should have been plain to see and hear? When my heart was keeping a strict accounting of the moral high ground I'd secured, how could I recognize my own errors?

At this point, I was practicing law and winning battles in the legal arena. My mind was sharp with careful analysis whenever I needed it. Little did I know my mind was no match for my wayward heart—a heart so incapable of Christian love, it was quite insistent on its own impulses toward self-love, self-preservation, and self-everything! With no one training my heart, my mind struggled to understand the meaning of true love.

Being unable to love others proved my greatest failing—I hadn't grasped what the Bible was saying—to love with the agape taught by Christ. For me, love remains the toughest subject to learn. Even now, notwithstanding the spiritual insights accumulated in recent years, it remains difficult (but not impossible) to love another person.

There was also a gap in my spiritual life. I continued to meet the Lord in the Eucharist at each celebration of Mass and see His love in the kindness of friends and strangers. Though I felt the absence of my Shepherd—far from where I was—truthfully, it was my heart that was far from Him. I didn't even know I was clueless about the Faith. Thanks must be given to God that my uneducated heart didn't cause me to give up the necessary Christian struggle in those days. I plodded on with God's grace.

Staying on the sidelines for a while comforted my ego until the lectors announced their recruitment drive. I decided to try this ministry. I reasoned with myself that reading the Word was similar to my work as a lawyer and should be a walk in the park. It should be just like the submissions that I made in cases for the causes I represented. I wasn't quite right. The training was somewhat lengthy. Each aspiring lector was required to undertake the spiritual preparation needed to support a good reading by studying the relevant passage. The lector needed to read with proper pronunciation and be mindful of enunciation, volume, pace, context, and meaning. I was also pleasantly surprised to learn that a lector proclaimed the Word of God. He or she didn't simply read animatedly or avoid a dull, droll, or drowsy delivery. We were taught that God Himself speaks to the assembly through the lector acting as an instrument of proclamation. This was why a proclamation wasn't so much about performance, but all about the serious training to be an instrument of God.

I remember my first proclamation quite vividly. I proclaimed the second reading serenely, purposefully, and competently. Then, I stepped aside for the psalmist to sing the Gospel Acclamation and began experiencing an involuntary twitching in my right leg, in plain view. My attempts to suppress further spasms by pressing my leg against the low bench only made it more obvious when the bench started wobbling as well! Though I may not have felt nervous, my leg had perhaps something to say.

I stayed with the lectors for about five years until I joined the third choir with my wife in her parish. I was happy for a while to serve as a lector.

The lectors met once a month to discuss plans or reflect on matters affecting our ministry. We took time off once a year to spend a full day in retreat with a spiritual director. In the later years of my service, I recognized the solitary nature of this ministry. We practiced on our own, met once a month, and gathered quietly with our randomly assigned second readers at the scheduled Mass. The sense or spirit of community was quite sparse. The same questions arose as they did when I was with the Marian Choir:

- Is this my Christian life?
- Have I learned what it takes to be a Christian?

During the third year of my service, Michael asked radical questions in a monthly meeting that shook some of us but resounded in my heart:

- Has our service become a routine?
- Are we still growing spiritually?
- Have we perhaps hidden too well our life as a Christian in this ministry and were preventing others from serving?

We couldn't or were perhaps reluctant to answer these questions in our heart. A few of us tried invigorating our spiritual life by signing up for talks and lectures at the Pastoral Institute on Highland Road. We were enthusiastic for a time, but without realizing it, our flesh protested and the desire to learn the Word came to a creeping halt.

The Little Rock Bible course was offered to our ministry and I alone attended. With no support from the lectors, my course attendance came to naught, as no one participated in this Bible study program or showed any interest in forming bible study groups. Despite the Word of God being at the heart of our service, no effort was made to study the Word together as a community.

There were lectors coming and going over the years. So I came to the unfortunate conclusion that this ministry was also unable to sustain my desire for a full Christian life. Indeed, I've noted proclamations from the New Testament that spoke about the need to live my life according to the Gospel, but I didn't have a clue what it entailed.

As a small number of lectors were also serving in the choirs, I decided to join a choir serving in a morning Mass. I was drawn to the

Christopher Choir for a number of reasons. The time slot for this service in the parish didn't make my flesh protest too much. Saul left the other choir and became a member of this choir. The leader was a boon to the choir members with his spiritual prayers and zeal, and my mother surprised me by joining this choir to serve!

The Christopher Choir was quite different in its attitude toward singing, as it was more inclined toward service and worship. The songs it selected were intentionally kept ordinary to encourage the assembly to participate in all the hymns sung during Mass. Singing in harmonies was only tolerated for the sake of occasional color and variety, which Saul was happy to provide with his ample talents. His cancer was in remission, but a grave bout with his illness took away much of the pizzazz and power in his voice. Nevertheless, he was grateful to help. In some ways copying the late Pope John Paul II, Saul never let go of his cross. He soldiered on to serve in an increasingly strangulated voice that seemed no longer beautiful and strong to the world.

In this choir, we were gifted a prodigious opportunity to combine with other choirs in Singapore and from elsewhere in the region to serve at the ordination of Archbishop Nicholas Chia on October 7, 2001. It drew seven hundred heavenly voices together to sing and praise in unison. With a few hundred bishops, priests, altar boys, and an untold number of assembled believers in attendance, I caught a faint glimpse of heaven here on earth.

A trainer from the diocesan music office also came round to teach us how to fulfill our service as psalmists. She instructed us in the prescribed chant tones for Psalms to be sung at Mass. We were discouraged from using other hymns or songs in substitution. The trainer also taught me two valuable lessons that I still remember. Even though it's sung, a psalm should be proclaimed almost as if spoken—the lyrical manner of delivery is suppressed—it is, after all, a proclamation. The second lesson concerned service and performance: should anyone congratulate me for having sung the psalm well, this would have meant a failed service to the Lord for having drawn attention to my singing performance.

I enjoyed my service in this choir and still keep in touch with the leader and his fair wife. The same questions of Christian life continued to follow me into this choir but, by that time, I was distracted by the appearance of Élysée, who later became my wife.

11. Here Is Your God, Israel

Even the demons submit

I was fortunate to begin my career in a respectable city law firm where the founders were distinguished practitioners. In a profession that requires fresh lawyers to work in the backroom, I was fortunate to be allowed early independence in my professional work. The leaders gave me wide latitude, so much so that I found myself invigorated by the collegial and nurturing work environment. In particular, I owe a debt of gratitude to my quietly supportive head of department. There was also a kind senior who generously taught me everything I needed to learn as an aspiring lawyer, to whom I should give a vernal nod. Given the weightier matters of the Faith, I don't wish to go too much into my professional story.

There's, however, one piece of work relevant to my spiritual account. Legal precedents, court cases that establish the law for similar situations in the future, guide the practice of law. My hard work in one case ended in a favorable judgment, with the court decision being written up in the Singapore Law Reports. This case began in my second year as a practitioner. My client encountered a legal issue without any precedent whether in Singapore or in a similar jurisdiction such as England, Malaysia, or Australia. My research carried me far and wide, then landing in the law reports of the Ontario Courts. With the support of the client, I prepared this legal battle on my own. I won in the first instance, lost at the first intermediate appellate court, and succeeded finally at the High Court sitting in its appellate jurisdiction. The precedent was eventually established a few years later and now stands head-to-head with my father's heroic encounter with David Marshall, except that I'm one-up with written proof of my ability. You can imagine how my pride swelled, and I've been babbling on about this achievement ever since.

This groundbreaking precedent and other victories went to my head, and I began fashioning my own towering *Baal.*

Success told in my palm

While I was in Thailand with a British law firm chalking up another tally, I let some non-Christian friends persuade me to meet a soothsayer. He had a reputation for telling the future, supposedly practicing the *science* of palm-reading using details of one's birth particulars. I knew I had no common ground with this man, but my heart convinced me there was nothing to lose. To my rational mind, this was a person with no real power, and my intended consultation was simply a chance to prove him wrong. Truth be told, none of the predictions he made materialized.

Even though I went to this consultation not believing in his power, he did confirm something I'd been thinking about. This is yet another example of my heart set on leading the head astray. Out of interest, I'd been reading about palmistry and its discussion of the Simian Line because my palm lines show an unusual pattern. The soothsayer confirmed what I'd learned about the strength in my Line. Alas, there was no strength to turn away—my hands held the promise of great things to come! Naturally, it was comforting to hear about my future prosperity and happiness; it was what my heart insisted on hearing. So it wasn't the soothsayer who led me astray. My heart had already resolved to see *My God* in my hands —hands that seemingly produced the opportunities in my life. I wanted to believe I could determine my own destiny.

My heart was so far away from the Lord when I was demanding assurances of a promising future or was reveling in vain flattery over my successes or victories. I now know it was gravely wrong to have had any association with this soothsayer. There was no need to please my unbelieving friends or to think the way I did.

Despite this, I was still attending Mass regularly. Yet, even though a common friend gave me a friendly introduction, the local choir leader didn't encourage my participation. So I found myself again in the anonymous assembly, with no one needing my service—I was physically present in the celebrations, but my heart was absent.

I can change my destiny

After two years in Thailand, I was offered a position in a New York law firm with an office in Singapore and returned home. I'd been living the wandering expatriate life and was eager to settle down.

I was introduced to Élysée, a beautiful, soft-spoken, intelligent Singaporean girl who shared the faith. She had long flowing tresses, and an exquisitely melodious voice that never failed to delight me in speech and song. It was always a joy to nestle her slender hand in mine.

Despite her youth, she possessed wisdom that was uncommon for her age. Her observations often bade me ponder the depth in her thinking—she should have penned her axioms and an obelisk could have crossed her! Élysée was also a communicator in her own right, for there was no end to the subjects for our conversation. She was indeed a muse for ideas needing expression, a kindler of my mind's hidden crannies, and an easy soul for ping-pong parley.

Adding to her list of virtues, she was an amazing cook and bakester. Curiously, she picked up these culinary talents after we met. Perhaps this suggests her keen insight to the pathways to my heart.

I knew Élysée for four years before we got married.

During the earliest days of my courtship, another woman put me in a bind. On a European rail vacation in 1993 with my mother, brother, and cousin in tow, we bumped into *Masa* in the carriage that was headed from Rome to Barcelona. This Japanese lady hails from the city of Osaka, Japan. She was traveling on her own and we became warm friends. When *Masa* made subsequent visits to Singapore, she brought along *Nori*, a young neighbor originally from the city of Nagoya. I liked *Nori*, but she didn't speak much English then. Following her visits, I received a few letters from *Nori* though I'd wondered if *Masa* had been behind those letters.

When *Nori* visited again in 2002 with *Masa*, she told me that she liked me romantically. I was honest with her and admitted that I was already in a relationship. I was getting to know Élysée and felt she was *The One*. *Nori* and I, therefore, set up a coded signal. *Nori* enjoyed World Cup soccer as much as I did, so if I were to say Argentina might win the World Cup, it meant I was ready to reciprocate. If, on the other hand, I mentioned Germany, it would supply her with a euphemism indicating my regrets and say she should move on.

After having spent more time with Élysée, I knew in my heart that she was *The One*.

Learning that the soothsayer was in town, I felt a need to make an appointment. My heart insisted again on hearing what the soothsayer had to say. I was an utter, pagan fool for making this consultation: why did I need the confirmation of a choice in favor of Élysée? My consultation could be compared to a legal cross-examination, in which the lawyer asks a leading question crafted to extract a precise answer from the witness. What was I thinking? There was no need for a consultation. It wasn't necessary to prove the accuracy of his prediction. The soothsayer said exactly what I'd expected him to say.

Like the effigy of a golden calf in the Bible, I seemed to be casting one here as well. Why was I making my own idol?

I wanted things reasoned or done my way, that's why. In those prideful days, I'd dropped into worthless, ungrateful, and foolish thinking that I could undo and redo my destiny at will. I even *preached* to Maverick the false sermon that it was within our power to create and open doors in life—man could decide his own fate—that the *low hanging fruit* was within our grasp to pick—take it or someone else will. This erroneous *preaching* was wickedly at odds with my service in the parish and praising the Lord's goodness in my life.

A kindly priest could have advised me: *Get up, the day is at hand.*

With the risen sun behind me, I sent a letter to Nori regarding my thoughts about Germany.

Section IV

THE THIRD ENCOUNTER

12. The Return of the Prodigal Son

12. The Return of the Prodigal Son

Prodigal Son Found

In 2001, I visited the New York office of my American employers. I hadn't forgotten Fr. Alfred's request from eight years earlier, that is, to get him a copy of the inspirational artwork he needed. So I checked out the Metropolitan Museum of Art and other nearby museums during the weekends. Even though I was determined to find a print, this proved to be wishing pigs could fly. I was getting frustrated and was quite resigned to the option of making the long trip to St. Petersburg to fulfill the promise I'd made.

Then I thought about the Internet, which was taking shape at the time. Happily, when I carried out an AlltheWeb search, I found a business in St. Paul, Minnesota selling prints, and promptly ordered two large-sized copies: one for Fr. Alfred and one for me.

When I got home, I arranged for these prints to be mounted in dignified, beautiful frames.

As soon as I was ready to make good on my promise, I asked the whereabouts of Fr. Alfred. I learned he wasn't in a parish, as he was then serving a stint as a lecturer at the St. Francis Xavier Major Seminary in Punggol. After making an appointment, with the help of Rex I delivered the framed copies of *The Return of the Prodigal Son* to Fr.

Alfred. He blessed the prints without any ado. I took my copy home, and two seminarians helped him carry his copy into the seminary.

A great romance blossoms

For our first date, I met Élysée for lunch at a Japanese café in Liang Court. I bantered with her, finding her very easy to talk to and enjoying her company.

After lunch, I felt there was enough time to squeeze in a coffee and asked her, "Can I persuade you to a cup of coffee?" She replied, "You may." I didn't do a double take to catch that captivating, canny comeback. Reader, if you haven't realized by now, I'm foolishly proud of my intellect. It gave me the false confidence to presume many things. Everyday assumptions didn't, however, work so well with Élysée. She was helping me clarify the meaning of the words I'd taken for granted. I was delighted when she agreed to spend more time with me.

She was a young woman of rich, but hidden, depths. On the surface, she exuded gentleness. Just beneath her quiet exterior was brimming, briny intelligence that one could easily miss. As I came to know her better, I found her shrewd, insightful and, yet, full of fun.

We went out for casual dates. Then, there were months of hectic work that prevented me from spending time with her. This time round, the butterfly fluttered without misfortune. I decided to take our casual relationship to the next level. As Élysée loved Italian pasta, I shared with her my experience of delicious pasta in Rome and offered to cook her Roman-style Spaghetti Carbonara. When we were shopping for ingredients at the Marketplace, I confessed to being alarmed at her wanting double cream to go with this creamless dish. There was no need for my fussing. Whether it was a less Roman Carbonara or the fact of my romantic gesture, we became inseparable after this date.

Our offices were inside the business district. This proximity allowed us to meet regularly for lunch at the eateries that dished up the spicy food we both enjoyed eating and the robust coffee we relished imbibing.

We then tried every activity together, only to rediscover the joy of these pastimes in each other's company and to explore each other. There were days of dining, baking, cooking, cycling, running, reading, hiking, swimming, singing, shopping, movies, addictive television series and online games, theater, road trips, short overland holidays, and lounging. We desired any adventure we could plan, conceive, and jump headlong into for the fun and excitement the world had to offer to us.

Life was heady in those days, indeed.

Graduating from our local adventures, we began an exploration of our wondrous world. I was a heavy smoker when I met Élysée, but she was very gentle with this vice. To celebrate my decision to quit in 2003 after twelve years of this offensive habit, she suggested a healthier lifestyle together featuring nature. We were to begin with a visit to Mount Kinabalu in Sabah. Now I've visited a number of mountains in Europe. These alpine attractions offered a cog tram, a funicular railway, or a cable car as a gentle option up to the top for magnificent views and coffee in a superb setting. That was my idea of a trip to the top of Mount Kinabalu. However, when she planned our training in the Bukit Timah Nature Reserve, I was mortified, yet smitten, by the authentic, healthy lifestyle she was advocating. Ever obliging, I struggled with the training but encouraged myself with the simple motto of just climbing the hill or mountain, one step at a time. When we finally scaled Mount Kinabalu in the following year, I realized Élysée had saved my life: for I'd recovered my fitness, strength, and health.

I realized too that all my tough journeys in life, including the journey of faith, should adopt the strategy I'd applied toward climbing Mount Kinabalu—eyes on each slow, steady step I needed to take and eyes off the distant, daunting finish point.

Another mountain of sorts we traversed was the Great Wall of China. A section of the wall we hiked covered over ten kilometers or the length of thirty watchtowers. This part of the wall stretched from the town of Jinshanling to the adjoining town of Simatai, both of which were far from the city of Beijing. We were only able to fully appreciate this wonder of the world, when we hiked along, up, and down this section of the Great Wall, as it wound its way along the contours of a mountain ridge. This visit to the Great Wall was one of two wonders of the world we visited on our adventures together.

Whenever we traveled to places where I'd been, Élysée often quizzed my familiarity with foreign directions. This contrasted with my appalling sense of direction within Singapore. I knew the way to and inside Chatuchak, a perennial favorite for impulsive shopping in Bangkok. I could find my way to San Low Restaurant in Johor for affordable seafood and awesome vermicelli, fried in sinful lard. From the *Stazione di Santa Maria Novella* to the Cathedral on foot, I knew my way in Florence. I seemed the *bon vivant*, who could navigate around the world.

Alas, in Venice on the edge of St. Mark's Square, she confirmed the truth about my sense of direction. I wanted Élysée to savor the sublime, shrimp *tramezzini* at a local *bacari* and remembered the sequence to turn left-right-left from a particular spot. On our way back, I failed to turn right-left-right. We were instantly lost, but she caught the slip! She then gently helped me realize that I'd been memorizing the routes to my favorite places, no matter where I'd been wandering about in the world.

When we traveled together, I'd spoil Élysée by carrying nearly all the luggage. I often reminded Élysée that she was the lightest traveler, ever.

I also enjoyed indulging Élysée with my cooking. The dish she most enjoyed was my Kahlua Salmon creation, with accompanying lasagna-style rice noodles. She loved its sweet, salty, and smoky flavors. Élysée would in turn surprise me with numerous baking treats. One lazy afternoon, she served me a slice of Nutella cake for tea and asked my opinion of it, without telling me where it came from. I thought the cake was moist, chocolaty, and yummy, and innocently asked the name of the shop she'd bought it from. It was her suppressed smile that told me of her original creation.

When we weren't out and about in an ambling adventure, tobogganing down a Swiss hill, or horseback riding in the Giza Plateau, we spent quiet time enjoying each other's company. Such were the days of self-discovery, discovery of each other, and love experienced by two believers desiring to spend our life together.

There were also a number of startling signs in our relationship, which made a case for us to be together as soul mates. One might suppose our common love for animals, singing, shopping, spicy food, full-flavored coffee, cooking, mountains, movies, or traveling might make happy coincidences that any couple could have discovered together in a relationship, in the fullness of time. I'd think the case for mere coincidences was somewhat weakened by the strikingly similar facts: both of us are the middle of three siblings in our respective families; both our mothers have the same Christian name; our phone numbers began with the same four digits! These, too, could still be dismissed as happy coincidences. Then I saw the Lord's helping hand in shifting her office a few times. Each time closer until her workplace was inexplicably right across the road from mine. Our office buildings were so close that we were practically separated by a traffic light on Cecil Street.

With all that was happening, I knew in my heart she was *The One* and made plans for marriage.

Crossing the threshold of faith

In the middle of 2003, the Lord intervened in my history again by inserting me into a permanent community, so I could begin a serious journey of faith.

In the early part of that year, my brother was experiencing a marital crisis. He needed help and I stepped in to provide support, one aspect of which was spiritual. I called the parish and the priest on duty advised me to send my brother to a *community*. A *talk* was being given in another parish. A while later, I asked my brother whether the *talks* were helping him. He told me they were. Without bothering to find out more, I wrongly presumed these *talks* to be comparable to Alcoholics Anonymous, where people aired their marital struggles and received the spiritual equivalent of peer support, guidance, and consolation. I did attend one of the *talks* and bumped into my uncle. He encouraged my brother and me to attend the final weekend retreat, piquing my foodie interest when he said, "Go experience the heavenly banquet."

My brother felt he was alright and didn't wish to continue. I went on my own anyway. Despite my life being happy, I felt obliged to show some gratitude to the Lord by listening to what He had to say to me. I didn't really grasp everything the catechists said at the weekend retreat, given the talks sounded like the many on faith I'd attended before, but the Lord didn't let me go so easily.

He opened my ears to listen to the essential message. On Sunday, before everyone was dismissed, the catechists announced to all the attendees that they were forming a community of faith to last a lifetime. On such a faith journey, we'd learn all about Jesus Christ and how to love each other in the language of the cross that's rejected by the world. I said yes, even though I should have been shouting, "Alleluia!" The world had dulled my spiritual hearing and sight but, thankfully, not enough to say no to journeying with the Lord.

I was open to try this faith journey the catechists were proposing because I'd been searching for a permanent and committed community of faith (not one where people could come and go as they pleased). Moreover, I'd been seeking to increase my knowledge of the Faith. I wanted mainly to learn what the catechists could teach me on this faith journey, i.e. why I needed to love in the way of the cross.

When I said yes, I didn't fully appreciate what I was signing up for. Indeed, my heart was ambivalent about this door swinging open for me. Shame on me also: I was being given the chance to enter the "door of faith," but I murmured in my heart that I could always leave if the catechists were unable to form my faith as promised. Quite unfaithfully, I might add, my heart asked the Lord for a sign, without realizing that I'd found the one gem in the many rooms of the Church. I neither knew nor cared which church group was responsible for the education of my heart because it was clear to me that the Church was offering to increase my faith.

My community of faith was formed on the feast day of Corpus Christi in 2003.

In more ways than I can count the times that Jesus has helped me, He intervened in my history once again. This was my third encounter with the Lord. He intended for me to walk with Him because He was thinking of my marital crisis. My Savior thirsted to teach me His ways and so began preparing me for the calamitous storm that was soon coming for me.

QUESTIONS FOR REFLECTION ON CHAPTERS 10–12

1. Do you see any idols (greed, money, career, success, achievements, patrons, etc.) in your life?
2. Have you seen a fortuneteller?
3. Do you have a victory in your life that makes you feel invincible?
4. Do you think you can control your own destiny?
5. Have you fought with brothers in the church or witnessed fighting that troubled you? Have you drifted away from the Church because of this?
6. Did you wander from one church group to another trying to find meaning and purpose in your spiritual life?
7. In your journey of life, do you find yourself losing the meaning of your faith or drifting away from Jesus?
8. Are you serving in the church? Do you seek acknowledgment for the service you provide? Have you seen signs of performance in your service?
9. Does your service in the church help you increase the knowledge of the Faith, regularly pray, do the will of God, and produce spiritual fruit?
10. Despite being busy with activities in the church, do you have little or no time for daily prayer or evangelizing?

Section V

THE TURNING POINT

13. Life or Death

In this Chapter, I recount the joy celebrating my wedding, grief in the subsequent separation, and consolation in the Lord's help. In my great distress, the Lord responded again to my cry for help. This is a turning point for my conversion: I finally decided to follow Jesus. The events recollected in this Chapter are genuine, even though motifs abound aplenty.

In spite of my faith being formed, I should have been alert to the spiritual danger appearing in my life. These events help me understand that, as a follower of Christ, I can still fall and will need the Lord's grace to recover, pick myself up, and continue following Him. I'll also need His grace to transform, step by step, throughout my lifetime. Even exceptional individuals in the Faith have disobeyed the Lord, did not trust Him, or made mistakes. Why should I be any different? Thus, I'm glad to acknowledge my foolishness and faults.

Without any doubt, the Lord's help in this dark Chapter proves to me His untiring love and redeeming grace. I believe the Lord continues to be faithful, despite my frequent failings. This is the hope in me that I share with you. Having tasted God's mercy so many times, it's my wish that the moral in this Chapter, filled with joy, suffering, and consolation, can benefit you in your own faith journey.

Joining a choir with Élysée

Élysée has the voice of an angel. One day in 2003, while we were lounging in my living room, Élysée stood up and launched spontaneously into song. She sang *My Heart Will Go On*, the challenging theme song from the movie *Titanic* (1997). Her singing cast an enduring spell on me. I gave her a big bear hug and told her I was proud to be in love with a talent yet to be discovered by the world.

Over time, I practiced the art of persuasion on Élysée. I was convinced she should put her gift to use and sing praises to the Lord. Many months later, we decided to join one of the choirs in her parish.

I then said goodbye to my friends in the Christopher Choir and the lectors in my parish.

On a new path together, we went looking for a suitable choir. We took our time, checking out the different choirs serving Masses scheduled on Saturday and Sunday. We finally settled on the *Quintus Canticum Chorus* in April 2004 and remained members for three years.

The choir was easy with its expectations. Everyone was welcome, and no one was pressured to do anything he or she didn't want to. This was both good and not so good. It was good because all members were encouraged to participate freely in the way they felt most comfortable. The lack of discipline, however, gave rise to difficulties because there was no telling who would attend the meetings. Even the psalmists scheduled for duty might, at the last minute, decide not to turn up.

On one memorable occasion, we were warming up for Mass, and everyone was wondering if the psalmist would show up. Just before Mass was due to begin, our organist asked if anyone could step forward. It was crazy to volunteer. Generally, I needed a whole week to be well prepared to stand at the lectern! With the Lord beckoning, I stepped forward fearfully to offer my sacrifice and positively proclaimed the psalm.

Passing on the lessons I'd learned from the Diocesan trainer, I persuaded Élysée to consider serving as a psalmist as well. The lessons advised that seeking applause is the hallmark of a self-serving performance. Indeed, the psalmist serves as a humble instrument of the Lord. With gentle encouragement and guidance, Élysée practiced many hours before she stood at the lectern months later for her inaugural proclamation of the psalm. After that Mass, she shared with me how she'd felt the Holy Spirit guiding and encouraging her.

Like the other choirs, this choir also offered a yearly retreat.

We attended, but I was no longer looking at the choir as an avenue of spiritual growth. By that time, I was walking earnestly with my other community of faith. That community of brothers and sisters regularly breaks the Word, with catechists shepherding and monitoring our spiritual growth.

This left me free to enjoy the choir's social side with its frequent gatherings over food and drink. These presented many opportunities for me to hone my skill of cooking spaghetti *ragù* for a large party of twenty.

The highlight of our time in this choir came in the Christmas of 2006. A few members were discussing how to bring Christmas cheer to people outside the church. Someone suggested a visit to a home for the disadvantaged. Given my prior experience, I contacted a local home for the aged and offered our caroling services, which was gratefully accepted. On the way to the home, the group of twenty-two volunteers warmed up by singing carols on the bus. We arrived in high spirits, and I led the opening prayer to help all of us enter this mission of charity. As we moved from section to section, we realized the home was quite large! It housed many who were old, infirm, and bedbound. We sang our hearts out along the corridors, waved, and tried to convey the joy of Christmas to the residents inside the wards. Then the Lord stepped in. We'd already covered numerous spaces and were wondering what to do next. Some of us were strumming our guitars as if jamming privately, and a few were idling and chatting. As if prompted, one or two of us entered the wards to greet each resident and offered the peace of the Lord. This inspired the rest to follow suit in silent Amen, moving from bed to bed, ward to ward.

We were all grateful for this experience of charity because, for that Christmas, we were given the opportunity to visit those who were out of sight, forgotten, and prisoners of sorts.

Preparation for marriage

We'd had many conversations about spending our life together, so I knew in my heart Élysée and I were meant to be married. I went on my knees to propose on New Year's Eve of 2004.

It wasn't as though Élysée was a poor listener. Rather, I was acutely aware of the inconstant heart I'd experienced in my relationship with others. My whole being knew she'd accepted when her tears flowed freely. I saw it in the same way when my heart first opened to the Lord, and my tears flowed. My beloved even communicated her understanding in a rejoinder, "Yes, until death do we part." We also agreed that her delicate hand was most at home snuggled in my protective clasp if only to define our bond.

We didn't feel any need to hurry, so began leisurely planning for a marriage early in 2006.

We agreed our marriage would be centered on Christ, with the Lord in our life. It followed that we needed spiritual guidance, so willingly participated in the mandatory marriage preparation course organized by the Archdiocese. Fr. Anthony Hutjes was the spiritual director. There were two options: a short weekend or a longer course. The latter involved six sessions spread out over two months, taking place variously in the lecture theater of St. Joseph's and in the homes of presenting couples. We chose the extended course because we were serious about acquiring a deeper understanding of Christian marriage. I shouldn't have been surprised by the strong themes of Christian love that were catechized to all participants. We learned how our spiritual life would grow in tandem with the love we offered each other. God would be the center of our marriage, as the Holy Spirit entered our life.

The marriage preparation course is, without a doubt, a valuable aid for educating and preparing couples who yearn to have Christ in their life. I was, however, surprised by two blunt warnings given by the Church. The first was a simple statistic: that half of us attending the course might experience some form of failure in our marriages. The second warned of the Devil, not the Hollywood version, but one bent on instigating disobedience and interference with God's plan for love, family, and children. I thought it was quite quaint to talk about the Devil in a modern marriage and nonchalantly disregarded this advice.

Élysée chose Fr. Joe as the presiding priest.

Months before the wedding day, there's a formal step. As the representative of the Church, Fr. Joe needed to interview us to ascertain our intentions for the marriage and to ensure we were free from all impediments: a know-your-couple due diligence (if I may give it a simpler tag). A strange thing happened on the day of this appointment: Hipo, Élysée's cat, disappeared! She was frantic about finding him, so I met Fr. Joe without her. He was quite annoyed. The rules for this formal interview required both of us to be present. I offered our apologies, given the unusual emergency, and requested another meeting at his convenience.

It was such a curious incident that Fr. Joe mentioned the cat in his homily on the wedding day.

We turned the wedding celebrations into a massive undertaking by deciding to plan every detail by ourselves. This got us into discussions on the rainbow colors of the tapas desserts, the decorations on the fifty-pound, multi-tiered Black Forest wedding cake, the flavors and accompaniments for the chocolate fountain, and other delectable dishes.

Élysée didn't want the traditional Chinese wedding, so we opted for a European-style wedding at midday: white linen cloths on the tables and wrapping for the chairs, beautiful floral arrangements, with table settings for over five-hundred guests.

To make room for everyone and provide for overflow from the urbane function hall on the mezzanine floor, we erected a spacious canopy tent on the church square. We planned for everyone to mingle, be happy, and enjoy as in a carnival. I had to obtain special permission from Fr. Joe to use the square, and he gave the church's consent on the understanding the celebrations were to conclude by 4 pm. This would make way for the evening novena service scheduled at 5 pm on that Saturday.

For our wedding mass program, we had some difficulties over the choice of the Word of God. We read all forty scriptural passages recommended by the Archdiocese. We were of the same mind on the first reading from the Prophet Jeremiah (31:31-32a, 33-34a). This symbolized our covenant with God and with each other, and our agreement to know God. We also concurred on the Gospel reading from Matthew (7:21, 24-29). This was my choice. I thought this gospel reading reflected our desire to do the will of God, and our desire to build our house on the rock that's God. I didn't see us as the foolish man, who failed to act on the words of Jesus and built his house on sand. We couldn't initially see eye to eye on the second reading. I'd wanted the familiar *love is gentle and kind* reading from 1 Corinthians 13, but Élysée preferred the reading from Romans (8:31b-35, 37-39). She asked me how I perceived our intended union: was it represented by the desire for the full attributes of Christian love described in Corinthians or by the unbreakable bond with the Lord, which also symbolized the inseparability of the marriage? I eventually found Élysée's proposition convincing and came around to her choice for the second reading.

God attended our wedding

On the day of the wedding, I waited for Élysée at the altar, together with three of the brothers masquerading as my best men. We did away with many of the local customs, sticking instead to the tradition of the groom not seeing the bride before the wedding celebrations.

On that beautiful morning, after the blessings by Fr. Joe in the courtyard, Élysée processed down the aisle with her father. She was preceded by a handsome ring-bearer, and her two sisters as bridesmaids. That was the first moment I laid eyes on Élysée in the gown she'd picked out for this special day. She was radiantly resplendent indeed! Her elegant procession has become a magical memory, with achingly beautiful violins still echoing Pachabel's Canon.

Fr. Joe was designated the principal presbyter though I'd invited Fr. Alfred and Fr. Tim as guests. The priests must have discussed presiding arrangements among themselves because I next saw Fr. Tim standing beside Fr. Joe at the altar table.

The Wedding Mass began beautifully with the combined choirs of the *Quintus Canticum Chorus* and the Christopher Choir singing *Lover of Us All* (by Dan Shutte). This had also been the grand opening hymn for the ordination of Nicholas Chia (now Archbishop Emeritus).

The first sign of God's presence was displayed in Fr. Alfred. He'd suffered a stroke sometime in the later part of 2001. Miraculously, he survived three days alone in his room in the seminary until he was discovered after the weekend. Sadly by then, the right side of his body became permanently paralyzed. During the initial part of the celebrations, I noticed Fr. Alfred seated all by himself in the corner of the front row. Then, at the Liturgy of the Eucharist, after the combined choir had completed singing the offertory hymn, *Center of My Life* (by Paul Inwood), he stood up. Steadying himself with his walking cane, my heart leaped for joy to see Fr. Alfred struggle his way toward the altar to offer his sacrifice.

In his homily, Fr. Joe recognized our love for God from the readings we selected and how we desired God to be the center of our life together. Pointing out the warning in the Gospel about the rains, floods, and winds that would batter our marriage, he gave advice concerning the challenges of living together. He reminded us that our marriage wasn't exempt from any of the trials and tribulations. To be truly rooted in God, Fr. Joe felt we needed to move beyond our commitment and share our life completely in God. He also reminded all of us present that no one should divide the marriage that God unites and, of course, he mentioned the curious cat.

The second sign of God's presence appeared at the lighting of the matrimonial candle, portending a warning for me to take note. Now this parish church has a large, spacious, and contemporary design. It's so large that celebrity singers performing in this beautiful church hall have struggled with the acoustics. The doors were shut, and there was hardly a draft in the church hall. Moments after we lit the matrimonial candle, there was a sudden gust of wind that came out of nowhere. It was blowing furiously at the faint, flickering flame. My heart pounded in those brief moments, helpless at the thought of the flame, a symbol of our union, going out before it had a chance to shine brightly. I whispered an urgent plea. As if hearing, the photographer moved forward to cup the candle. The flame then gained strength. With the wedding celebrations concluded, Élysée and I stepped out of the church building, happy to be married.

The third sign of God's presence displayed itself at the lunch following the wedding mass. Trouble had been brewing for weeks before the wedding day. The number of guests had swelled beyond our first, second, and third counts. On our first estimates, the canopy tent on the church square was going to be a spacious extension of the main celebrations in the function hall. When the guest list was finally settled, the tent was almost bursting at the seams. The weather then jostled to threaten havoc. In the weeks leading up to the celebrations, there were heavy, daily downpours. Two days before the wedding, the planner anxiously suggested positioning the tables inward. This would prepare for wet weather but cramp the seating severely. Not wanting to prepare for this contingency, I declined any change to the arrangements. On the day, God showed His mighty hand in the bright sun He brought to shine on the wedding party. The heat was so intense that many said their goodbyes after just two hours of merrymaking. Surprisingly, the planner even asked my permission to pack up the canopy tent at 3 pm, with the food, drink, and guests retreating into the function hall. Without a best man running operations, the wedding program came apart with some happy chaos. I gave up the idea of formal speeches either in the function hall or at the canopy tent and mingled with the remaining guests. The Lord displayed the final act of his presence at the close of the celebrations. By then, only family and a few friends remained, and we decided to call it a day. My uncle needed the restroom, so my mother got me to show him the way. As we exited the function hall, a majestic, deafening downpour arrived. I looked at the clock, noting it was 4 pm, and gasped, "Alleluia!" God generously held off the rain's arrival until the time allocated by Fr. Joe for our celebrations to conclude.

Sinking of the RMS Titanic

In 1912, the RMS Titanic entered service on her maiden voyage. She was then the largest passenger ship, capable of carrying well over three-thousand passengers. When an iceberg struck her a glancing blow, she couldn't stay afloat with more than four of her compartments flooded. The sinking of a maritime behemoth doesn't bear out the only tragedy. It's always sad when a ship sinks. That this ship boasted unparalleled luxury and safety—designed to be *unsinkable*—added nothing. The inadequate safety regulations were at the heart of this tragedy. With too few lifeboats for everyone on-board, more than a thousand lives were senselessly lost.

Élysée and I were nurtured for a Christian life together, expecting only death would separate our union after marriage at the altar. We pledged to be inseparable and gave ourselves to each other. We vowed a solemn covenant before God to remain faithful to the Lover of us all and to each other.

Yet when my marriage struck an uncharted obstacle, it sank just as swiftly and senselessly as the Titanic. Neither tragedy could be avoided. A *postmortem* would offer no consolation, it being all too easy to blame this or pour scorn on that. This is life with its many mistakes, human hubris, and diverse disasters. It would have been quite easy to liken Fr. Joe's warnings about the rains, floods, and winds to the many iceberg warnings the Titanic received.

Was the captain overconfident about the Titanic being unsinkable?

Had I been conceited about the unbreakable marriage bond?

I've been to Rome many times and was well aware of the perennial problem of pickpockets. On my first visit, my waist pouch was packed tightly with my camera, travelers' checks, and passport. Despite this precaution and supposedly being very alert, a pickpocket struck somewhere between the *Termini* and *Ottaviano* stations. The pickpocket managed to lift my passport from the pouch, despite my eyes being fixed frontward on my bags! On subsequent visits, I observed and took note of the many techniques employed by pickpockets: the distractions of the opened-newspaper, the swaddled-baby-mannequin, the false complaint, and other misdirections.

Yet twelve years later, I was still unprepared for the encounter with a pack of ten at *Spagna* Metro station. When Élysée and I got onto the platform, I noticed the all-female gang and moved past them with caution. However, in the agonizing minutes before the train's arrival, two of the girls moved quickly to our left, two positioned themselves swiftly behind us, and the rest of the pack inched toward us. I realized too late that we were encircled like prey! Help must have been given because I did quite the unthinkable. I motioned Élysée to move toward the main pack, creating confusion to the four then on our left. Somehow this unraveled the pack's strategy to disturb, distract, and divest. When the train doors opened, their moment was lost. I nudged Élysée into the carriage and heard the spine-tingling cry of a banshee in my ears as the doors shut. This brush with a pack of ten caught me off-guard, as did other encounters in Cairo and Istanbul.

We all do our best to prepare for life's adversities, but glancing blows still get the better of us: Julius Caesar was brought down in a safe place on the Ides of March; the Titanic failed to sail further; my marriage rent asunder. How does one escape the snare of the fowler?

Within a year of our marriage, the Devil blinded us to each other and to our God. Concerned with suffering, Élysée questioned my praying for faith and love. I acceded and stopped praying for these. Then, she felt I didn't put her first ahead of my other commitments. I compromised again and did my best to adjust my obligations. Finally, she felt the Lord crowding our space as if watching our every move. In exasperation, I cried out, "Let's take God out of our equation!"

Yes, I should be damned for asking God to leave. It was I who let the darkness enter our marriage. I let the Devil take a hold of her hand, and her hand slipped away from mine. Then I stood by when Élysée left our home in the summer of 2007, then our marriage, and finally the Faith.

It would be too convenient to shift the entire blame to the Devil for the colossal failure in my marriage. I didn't even want to acknowledge the Devil. Yes, it was I who allowed the Devil to snag a toehold in our marriage. Foolishness ensued and reduced the foundations of the marriage to sand. I promised to build the house on the rock, but didn't act on the words of Jesus. I promised to love and cherish Élysée, but let the bitter root take hold. Like Adam before me, I accepted the fruit and death became inevitable. Thus, I'm fully responsible for the collapse and ruin of my marriage.

Our Redeemer was no longer the center of our life.

I attended Mass on my own and dined by myself. Then, I was utterly on my own. Somewhere along the stone path, I forgot how to cherish the other who represents Jesus Christ.

Speaking only for myself, I said and did things that were hurtful, awful, and quite the opposite of the love a believer should give his beloved. She's the one whom I professed to have and to hold, for better, for worse, for richer, for poorer, in sickness, and in health. Through the unloving way I gave myself to my better half, I lost everything.

Warm conversations, once filled with lively laughter, turned into short, sharp spats spewing so sour soliloquies.

Psalm 22

The best way to give an insight into my feelings at this time is to use metaphors, symbols, and imagery. This may seem dramatic, but grief is never easy to recount. When all seemed hopeless again, the Lord gave me hope through His Word in Psalm 22.

Not able to look at snapshots of us, I was inconsolable, given the sentimental chasm threatening to engulf me. I became edgily agitated, unable to speak about the prospect of civil divorce and unwilling to listen to anyone. Sadly, my actions or inaction weren't those of a man with integrity.

In my heartache, family and friends were no longer welcome. People had been offering advice even though I didn't request it. There were pointless conversations in which kind souls offered platitudes or asked questions for which there were no obvious answers.

Some were unsentimental, urging me to change my history: "Find another wife. You're still young." or "You need someone to keep yourself company in your old age." They seemed to think marriage so disposable, like tech gadgets requiring replacement by the latest models. Anyone trying to smear the good name of my wife suffered my vociferous, vitriolic rebuke, and my door clanging shut and tight, croaking, "No more cruelty, please."

All social contact intensified my distress. I was vainly struggling to suppress the sadness welling up like a gray geyser gathering to groan. Longing for solitude, I hid myself away. It was as if a sword had struck me, and much of my body was cut off. What remained entered a fiery ordeal. The seven nations then attacked me all at once: anger, greed, sloth, pride, lust, envy, and gluttony.

- I was angry at the wrecking of the marriage.
- Then I thought of ways to amass even greater wealth as if this could turn the tide.
- I hid in the shadows, still, alone, sleeping but finding no rest.

- My pride swelled to imagine nothing amiss in the fast-sinking marriage.
- I glanced at women passing by and wondered who would take her place.
- Envy entered the fray, which instigated my resentment of couples in budding romances and young families living happily together. The signs of marriage were everywhere, with couples holding hands and many children making noises full of family life. At the other end, old couples tenderly held each other, even as their candles were dimming. All these happy signs intensified the bitterness taking root in my heart.
- I sought solace in richly flavored, cloyingly sweet and well-marbled sustenance, albeit I found no satisfaction, except for the garbage truck repeatedly reproaching, rigorously raging and rapaciously repressing that which remained resolute.

No one could understand my anguish, console the sadness, or soothe the turmoil in my heart. As in the courtyard, many mistrusted me—didn't you—why couldn't you—it was you. I felt the silent accusations like sixty brutal daggers. Like a soldier returning from the battlefield, having lost everyone in his platoon: how and why did I alone survive? Avoiding friends and family, I sought the help of counselors, but one turned on me, another accused, the third passed away, and the fourth went missing. I was alone once again, as I'd been for a long time, unable to escape the eviscerating desolation.

I was expelled far from the garden but, unlike Adam, was without my Eve. Soon after, the Accuser pronounced my sign, "Broken," and married life, "Dead." Thus, I swallowed the lie that I would never find happiness again. I shamefully hid in the safe shadows, with only the garbage truck and a charcoal-colored cat for company.

Hipo was a stray but most handsome Ragdoll, with a white patch on his chest. Even though I wasn't crazy about cats before Élysée, I grew to love hers. In some ways, he was like a dog: calling me, rolling in front of me. With his forepaws on my knee and standing on his hind legs, he would stretch his neck skyward to show how much he enjoyed the many scratches and strokes I offered him. He loved to crunch, crackle and chew whole chicken bones; better than all the dogs I had as pets. The food that made him lose all proper manners was fresh mackerel, lightly cooked in its own juice. If I didn't pay attention, he would be up on the stove in a furious flash, frantically licking away at the mackerel juice as if the sweetest milk. His best attribute was an ability to croon tunes in his mewling, unlike any cat I'd ever come across. He was quite a singer if he wanted to be. When the days weren't so dark, lonely, and uncertain, Hipo was my companion, never tiring of singing, scratching the shelf or receiving rubs. To encourage his good nature, I gave him a new name, "Hip-Boy" because that was what he was.

Questions and dreams

I suppose those who believe themselves victims in the breakdown of a marriage, ask the same questions:

- What happened to life together, a life filled with joy, laughter, and many quivers of arrows?
- Why did the Lord halve my life?
- How do I talk with my idols? Could they speak, see, hear, smell, touch, walk, or make a sound?

This life, without my wedded equal, seemed like a barren tree that failed to produce its fruit. My state of being had become a vineyard overgrown with wild weed, wantonly wasting the harvest of laughter, the pitter-patter of padded feet, and might-have-been cries for comfort and sustenance. The prospects for forgiveness and reconciliation became judged as a valley scattered with vast quantities of bones, quite dried up, without breath, or life—dead as my marriage was.

I tried to find comfort in idleness, darkness, and emptiness as if I needed to return to the womb. I'd failed in my life's chief purpose and hoped to reset. My mind then turned to *that* exit door, thinking of the many ways to depart from a life so filled with woe, sorrow, and grief. In spite of my growing negative desire, I was denied any passage out, not without pain or shameful stain. With each passing day, I was filled with baffling bleakness. The sleep that came was neither restful nor comforting. Entering a deep depression, the visits by the garbage truck became insidiously insistent for a few years.

One night, alone in the deep depths of my despair, I had a terrifying, crushing dream. If I had to describe the nightmare that troubled me, it'd read like this:

Whyfor was I standing still in Love's trench,
Wedded LC's dressed in white camouflage?
Cramped her hand in my hand, dismissed the stench.
Whither thou goest . . . cool cat's still still at large?

Then her faint fingers slipped my careless last clasp.
Smelling bread, how, why was Death in her stead?
Dashing 'twixt catacombs, I wailed—aghast.
Smiling were the dead, wearing sailor threads:

Wrested here, heaped there, losses everywhere.
We keeled over and slipped into the sea,
Resting so deep where God seems not to care.
Canary sings, alas, indifferently.

Word from God

I woke from my nightmare in the early hours. There was no comfort in waking; how could there be? I was on my own, soaked in a cold sweat, acutely aware of my affliction, yet bewildered. Whether asleep or awake, I couldn't escape my entanglement. The tormenting dream dragged me to the chasm as if to push me down far below the bottomless pit. I'd stared into the deep abyss and found only wasting, woeful wretchedness—so this must be hell on earth.

I wailed as only one could in this deathly despair, as upon finding his cherished partner torn into pieces, or a favorite child gurgling blood and breathing her last, or a dearly-loved parent, choking, succumbing to the summons by Death.

I knelt down before the Lord and pitifully asked for consolation, a Word, and His help. I randomly turned the pages of the gospels, and my finger came to rest on Mark 16:33-39: "The Death Of Jesus." As I read it, my heart grew weary. Its meaning, though beautiful, was too heavy for me; I was already bent double with grief, sorrow, and feelings of hopelessness. I asked the Lord, "How am I to die on my cross?"

Prompted, I noticed the parallel reference to the side and turned to Psalm 22. From young, I'd neither understood nor accepted this cry of Jesus, "My God, my God, why have you deserted me?" Ever unschooled and foolish, I continued to resist the way of my Lord even in those moments. I didn't stop wondering why Jesus—the Savior of the World—was feeble in His last moments on the cross. Yet, there I was very much enfeebled, suffering life's many troubles, but only bewailing the death of my marriage. For the first time in my life that night, I read all of Psalm 22:

> My God, my God, why hast thou forsaken me?
> Why art thou so far from helping me, from the words of my groaning?
> O my God, I cry by day, but thou dost not answer;
> and by night, but find no rest.
>
> Yet thou art holy,
> enthroned on the praises of Israel.
> In thee our fathers trusted;
> they trusted, and thou didst deliver them.
> To thee they cried, and were saved;
> in thee they trusted, and weren't disappointed.
>
> But I am a worm, and no man;
> scorned by men, and despised by the people.

All who see me mock at me,
they make mouths at me, they wag their heads;
"He committed his cause to the Lord; let him deliver him,
let him rescue him, for he delights in him!"
Yet thou art he who took me from the womb;
thou didst keep me safe upon my mother's breasts.
Upon thee was I cast from my birth,
and since my mother bore me thou hast been my God.
Be not far from me,
for trouble is near
and there is none to help.

Many bulls encompass me,
strong bulls of Bashan surround me;
they open wide their mouths at me,
like a ravening and roaring lion.

I am poured out like water,
and all my bones are out of joint;
my heart is like wax,
it is melted within my breast;
my strength is dried up like a potsherd,
and my tongue cleaves to my jaws;
thou dost lay me in the dust of death.

Yea, dogs are round about me;
a company of evildoers encircle me;
they have pierced my hands and feet–
I can count all my bones–
they stare and gloat over me;
they divide my garments among them,
and for my raiment they cast lots.

But thou, O Lord, be not far off!
O thou my help, hasten to my aid!

Deliver my soul from the sword,
my life from the power of the dog!
Save me from the mouth of the lion,
my afflicted soul from the horns of the wild oxen!
I will tell of thy name to my brethren;
in the midst of the congregation I will praise thee:
You who fear the Lord, praise him!
all you sons of Jacob, glorify him,
and stand in awe of him, all you sons of Israel!
For he hasn't despised or abhorred
the affliction of the afflicted;
and he hasn't hid his face from him,
but has heard, when he cried to him.

From thee comes my praise in the great congregation;
my vows I will pay before those who fear him.
The afflicted shall eat and be satisfied;
those who seek him shall praise the Lord!
May your hearts live for ever!

All the ends of the earth shall remember
and turn to the Lord;
and all the families of the nations
shall worship before him.
For dominion belongs to the Lord,
and he rules over the nations.

Yea, to him shall all the proud of the earth bow down;
before him shall bow all who go down to the dust,
and he who can't keep himself alive.
Posterity shall serve him;
men shall tell of the Lord to the coming generation,
and proclaim his deliverance to a people yet unborn,
that he has wrought it.

Comforted by my full reading and heartfelt grasp of Psalm 22, I was finally able to rest.

It took me some time to better understand that Jesus had been praying to the Father, imploring the Father and praising the Father in his final, agonizing moments on the cross. The Lord made me grasp the fulfillment of this Psalm in Him—God had acted as He said He would—Christ had come into this world, suffered in my place, then died on the cross to bear my sins. Eminently amazing was God's next act: my Savior rose and triumphed over suffering and death. In and through this Psalm, He promised to rescue my soul; then, I too will give Him praise. Through the cross, Jesus showed me the victory of His love over Death. He offers the same fulfillment for me as His follower: I can have a share in His victory, if only I *would* carry my cross and accept my suffering for the sake of the agape, the Christian love. I can't continue to think of myself a victim or believer without hope.

At this crossroad of my faith journey, I finally made a decision to seriously follow my Lord. I desired my Lord to teach me His ways that I may learn how to love and carry my cross.

QUESTIONS FOR REFLECTION ON CHAPTER 13

1. Have you suffered a tragic loss, or experienced the grief of losing a loved one?
2. Did you love this person (i.e. put the needs of your beloved ahead of your own)?
3. Do you blame God, yourself or anyone else for a terrible suffering you experienced?
4. Have you "removed God or His Church from the equation?"
5. Do you hope to learn the Christian agape from our Savior?
6. In the depths of your despair, have you turned to the Lord?

Part Two

Submissions for a Transformative Journey

If any man would come after me, let him deny himself and take up his cross and follow me. For whoever would save his life will lose it, and whoever loses his life for my sake will find it.

—Matthew 16:24–25

Section VI

THE NARROW GATE

14. Rebuilding My House on the Rock

A serious journey continues in earnest

Jesus is the narrow gate. (John 10:9) The Lord has been urging me to enter the gate of the sheepfold by listening to all He says. Indeed, His Good News is necessary and urgent for the salvation of not just my soul, but every soul.

I thought I was left on my own to find the King of Kings. Yet, I'm an adopted son by faith and should have recognized His thirst to teach, guide, and save me. How could I forget my Lord's promise that nothing could separate me from His love?

All this happened while I was looking for *The One*. Why did it take my heart so long to recognize the only One? The only One, who is my Lord, remains true, faithful forever, and merciful beyond comprehension.

Thankfully, I entered the "door of faith" opened by my Savior and began my spiritual journey.

Twelve years wrestling with the Word

As I write these words, I've been walking with my community of faith for twelve years. Even though I've been wandering in a spiritual desert, there's no doubt that the Lord has been by my side. Yes, my life's been turned upside down. What was the *benevolent* cause? I supposed a woman searching for her lost *drachma* brought happy turmoil to my life.

As my faith has matured a little, I see the earlier spiritual confusion arose from the inadequate formation of my faith. To catch up, I've been walking as faithfully as I can. I've been studying the Word of God with my community, allowing the Lord to cut and slip through the place where the soul's divided from the spirit.

Structured faith formation

The Church has taught me the Divine History of Salvation—Abraham, the Exodus, the Covenant at Sinai, the Way in the Desert, the Conquest of the Promised Land, David and the Kingdoms, the Exiles, and the Prophets. I also learned the Patriarchs, the Leaders, the Judges, the Kings, the Figures, the Restorers, and the many themes from A to Z found in the *Dictionary of Biblical Theology* by Xavier Léon-Dufour.

Yes, I *have* finally grasped the Good News. Our God came down from the heavens to meet you and me. He has revealed His wonderful plan of salvation for everyone. To prove His incredible love for all mankind, God allowed men to kill His Son, Jesus Christ. This understanding of God's plan of salvation is now sustaining my faith as I continue on my spiritual journey, and I'm confident the Church will continue to help me by providing the faith formation, which was lacking in my earlier years.

I'm also grateful for the serious examination of my faith by my catechists at each liturgical stage. My catechists have followed me on my journey as responsible shepherds, regularly scrutinizing and encouraging me as the Lord forms my faith. These examinations are, without any doubt, slowly and gradually contributing to my spiritual growth as a follower of Jesus Christ.

I've come to realize thus far my great need of grace from God because, on my own, I can't fulfill the Lord's commandment to love.

Without the scrutiny of my faith, I'm convinced my heart would have continued to say, "I'm already converted. Speak to someone else who doesn't know Christ." If this had happened, no man (including I) would have been any the wiser about my poor faith.

Brothers and sisters in God's community

During the many years I journeyed with my brothers and sisters, the Lord held me tight, even though I wanted to turn my back on my community of faith. He gave me brothers and sisters who have so little in common with me, and it hasn't been easy to love them as they are. There are always temptations and distractions offering alternatives outside the community of God, but I've learned that none can fulfill their promises of a balm or relief from suffering.

The Lord has opened my eyes to the reality of my community and the parish to which it belongs. All of us make up the Body of Christ, and all belong to Him. This reminds me not to be so proud of my intellect, life experiences, or aspirations.

Loving the other who is a brother and sister of Jesus Christ

The Lord obliges me to relate to each individual as he or she is. If I reject my brothers and sisters, I'm most certainly rejecting my Savior. Though I haven't met my Lord face-to-face, I regularly meet those who make up His Body on earth. If I can't love my brothers and sisters as they are, how can I say I love my God? If I don't love them, I won't love my neighbor either.

Through the brothers and sisters He has put in front of me, I appreciate the Lord's program to teach me how to love. My own heart had been turning to stone. It's been easy to make demands of others, to expect them to conform to or satisfy my expectations. Through the Word, it's His Spirit speaking to my spirit that urges me to be at one with my brothers and sisters so we may be united together in Him. Then, the world may learn from this love of the Father. (John 17:21-23)

Carrying my cross

I accept my heart has been illiterate, and there's more of the Faith I must learn. Jesus has promised His help to battle the seven nations, which constantly assail my heart and tempt me to insist on having my way. I've responded to His help by listening to the Word as best I can, as I continue in the desert with the Lord as my guide and Teacher, learning all I can about the cross.

I'm also thankful now for being able to appreciate the timeless love He showed all mankind by taking and sharing our pitiful path of "being born, toiling and dying." (St. Augustine, Discourse 130,2) This is the harsh life of a slave, full of suffering and seemingly meaningless, which Jesus experienced when He dwelt among men. When He entered His passion, Jesus completely accepted the will of His Father and obeyed it. He acted on the Father's plan to redeem every sinner, accuser, and scorner—by allowing men to nail the Christ to the cross.

Sadly, my many sins still grieve my Savior. This will continue as long as I show little love, and my words and deeds oppose His will. It's the language of the cross that saves—the *prodigal* love of God for all mankind—that He has put in front of me to contemplate, cherish, and copy. Hence, I must welcome the cross in my life. If I remain open to His teaching, I'll be able to carry my cross of love.

Little by little

With Jesus as my spiritual trainer, I *have* to carry my cross to grow my love of the other. Why must I do this? Because His Spirit lives within all the brothers and sisters. My cross isn't heavy because it's supported by His great love. Tiny step by tiny step, I'm reducing my own needs and interests. With every confession of my failings, my

Lord helps me to *die* and *resurrect*. Each little *resurrection* aids the gradual transformation of my heart, helping me to love a little more. Walking this path, I have to reject the false happiness prescribed by the world and start embracing the true happiness offered by the Lord.

As I'm rediscovering the love of the one, true God, I accept the direction of my onward journey and must learn obedience to all His teachings about life. I also recognize the effectiveness of the teaching I've received so far. Hence, I'm obliged to share this experience with those of you who wish to see and hear.

What's this experience?

It's the training of the heart that can't love, like my selfish heart that always desires what I want and not what God wants.

I'm moved by my gratitude for the Lord's saving help to write this earnest appeal to you, my brothers and sisters in Christ. How do you benefit from my experience?

I've been a worshipper of idols, soothsayer's friend, and a prideful believer who still can't love as well as I should. Despite my many sins, my Lord has shown no desire to give up on me. I've no doubt my Lord will not stop wiping my slate clean and teaching me His ways, provided I turn to Him, listen to all that He says and try my best to follow in His steps.

Given that the Lord has worked so hard for me to learn His love, it goes without saying that Jesus—the Savior of the World—also wishes you to experience the full measure of His love.

Who should embrace faith formation?

I've written Part 2 with Christian archetypes in mind. I appeal to Andy who has strayed, Andre the regular churchgoer, and Andreas the lukewarm. We should all do what Jesus tells us to do. With the will of God in mind, I hope you'll take this opportunity to reflect on the state of your life as a Christian. If I had to sum up this book in a single sentence, it would be that—the crisis of faith begins in our heart.

Why *is* that so?

I believe the majority of Christians have *not* received an adequate, continuing education of the Faith. Left on our own, we've neither formed intimate communities of faith nor learned to love our brothers and sisters. If we'd been diligently studying the Word of God every day, this would have allowed the Lord to teach us to love. After you've digested and processed Part 2, I hope you'll ask yourself:

Have I loved?

Have I kept the Word of God?

Am I *being* and *doing* as a Christian?

If you haven't, don't feel discouraged. Do *not* be afraid because God wants to help you. The first step for a sincere believer is recognizing that he or she needs God's help. This is conversion. Turning to God in humility saves us. This is still needed after our baptism; we need to keep turning to God for everything in our life. Please, I also beg you not to take my writing out of context. Measure what I say against the words of Scripture and the Church teachings I've included. Take some time for reflection.

What am I trying to achieve in the second part of this book? I'm hoping that you'll read through to the end and keep your heart open to the exchange of ideas.

I'm also hoping you'll knock on your church door, and give your heart a chance to receive the necessary spiritual education. We should all be very concerned for our eternal life with God. Faith formation is a means to that end, and it begins with discovering the will of God in our life here and doing it now.

What's God's will for our life?

It is to love others as completely as He loves you and me! And if we haven't, we really should get ourselves ready to love by learning this all-important duty.

I should remind you of the caveat I mentioned in the Preface: that I shouldn't write too much about various aspects of the Faith.

Why not?

The most obvious answer is that it's for God's Church to transmit the Faith to you. The second obvious answer is that my own faith formation is incomplete, so I'm humbled by how little I know. I did briefly study sin and suffering, topics academic theologians have written volumes about, so I know I can't do full justice to such themes in this book. All Christians inspired by this book should seek faith formation and learn the complete Jesus Christ on their own journey of faith.

Even though it's not my job to teach you the Faith, I'm hoping to continue the conversation on the reasons that get in the way of faith formation and the new life belonging to every Christian. I hope the exchange of ideas will prompt you to consider both whether you're living according to the Gospel, and whether it's been fruitful or barren. These are truly serious questions touching on the faith, piety, and love of every Christian.

I've also mentioned that you should consult your pastor. This book prompts many serious questions, and I'm counting on the help of your pastor to help you reflect. Please use this book and benefit yourself by consulting your pastor.

In scrutinizing the archetypal Andy, Andre, and Andreas, I've been prompted to turn to Jesus for His advice. Please heed what the Lord says in the Parable of the Sower:

> Listen! A sower went out to sow. And as he sowed, some seed fell along the path, and the birds came and devoured it. Other seed fell on rocky ground, where it had not much soil, and immediately it sprang up, since it had no depth of soil; and when the sun rose it was scorched, and since it had no root it withered away. Other seed fell among thorns and the thorns grew up and choked it, and it yielded no grain. And other seeds fell into good soil and brought forth grain, growing up and increasing and yielding thirtyfold and six-

tyfold and a hundredfold. And he said, "*He who has ears to hear, let him hear.*"

And when he was alone, those who were about him with the twelve asked him concerning the parables. And he said to them, "To you has been given the secret of the kingdom of God, but for those outside everything is in parables; so that *they may indeed see but not perceive, and may indeed hear but not understand; lest they should turn again, and be forgiven.*"

And he said to them, "Do you not understand this parable? How then will you understand all the parables? The sower sows the word. And these are the ones along the path, where the word is sown; when they hear, *Satan immediately comes and takes away the word which is sown in them.* And these in like manner are the ones sown upon rocky ground, who, when they hear the word, immediately receive it with joy; and *they have no root in themselves, but endure for a while; then, when tribulation or persecution arises on account of the word, immediately they fall away.* And others are the ones sown among thorns; they are those who hear the word, but *the cares of the world, and the delight in riches, and the desire for other things, enter in and choke the word, and it proves unfruitful.* But those that were sown upon the good soil are *the ones who hear the word and accept it and bear fruit, thirtyfold and sixtyfold and a hundredfold.*" (Emphasis added) (Mark 4:3-20)

Contrast with the Christians who are bearing fruit

This appeal isn't addressed to those of the faithful who already possess the Word of God in their life, family, and community. They're earnestly laboring toward a fruitful yield pleasing to the Lord. There are two ways to identify these faithful Christians.

1. They *listen* to the Word, accepting that the Lord instructs them through His Word. They don't take

anything for granted, not even their baptism or the promise of heaven. Psalm 95:8 urges us: *If you would listen to Him today*, and these faithful listen intently, revere solemnly, and hope humbly in the Word because faith comes from listening.

2. They may already be producing fruit described in Galatians 5:22-24: ". . . the fruit of the Spirit is love, joy, peace, patience, kindness, goodness, faithfulness, gentleness, self-control; against such there's no law. And those who belong to Christ Jesus have crucified the flesh with its passions and desires."

In the new life of a Christian, the fruit is identified as obedience to the commandments of Jesus Christ. We should especially obey the greatest command, ". . . You shall love the Lord your God with all your heart, and with all your soul, and with all your mind," (Matthew 22:37) and the accompanying command, ". . . you love one another as I have loved you." (John 15:12)

Without a doubt, these brothers and sisters are actively serving their families and communities with the love of God in mind. The Apostle James advises that, "But be doers of the word, and not hearers only, deceiving yourselves," (1:22) and these brothers and sisters do just that. When these faithful Christians allow the Word to penetrate their heart, it:

- helps them discover or uncover their failings;
- aids the struggle to overcome their faults; and
- encourages them to keep and apply the Word in every part of their life.

Depending humbly on the Lord for everything, they live their new lives according to His plans. At least two or three times a week, this group meets in a community of faith to scrutinize and celebrate the Word. Every time they pray, they're spending quiet time in the presence of our Redeemer—listening, learning, longing for the Lord. I'd include in this group of the faithful those who are walking in fits and starts given that many adults, including me, need time and the patience of the Lord. We have to change a lifetime of habits and behavior contrary to His teaching. These brothers and sisters are thereby collaborating in a structured program of faith formation, seeking help from the Church to bear spiritual fruit.

They should be praying the Liturgy of the Hours throughout any given day.

What's the Liturgy of the Hours? These are the daily prayers prescribed by the Church, and they're contained in a book known as the Divine Office or Breviary. The Apostolic Constitution says that all the People of God need to pray, with the most important "Hours" being the Morning Prayer and Evening Prayer. There's a little more on Prayer in Chapter 20.

In a way, the two-stage miracle mentioned in Mark's Gospel (8:22-26) is relevant to help us understand that, despite possessing the Word in our life, many of us are like the blind man. We need time and the help of the Lord to see *plainly*. I firmly believe all, or as many of us as possible, should sign up for a program of faith formation that the Lord provides, as Teacher, through His Church.

Why do all of us need faith formation?

Because Jesus Christ is waiting patiently to ask us, "What do you ask of God's Church?"

And the answer is, "Faith."

"What does faith offer you?"

"Eternal life." (Catechism of the Catholic Church, 168)

QUESTIONS FOR REFLECTION ON CHAPTER 14

1. Reading this Parable of the Sower, how do you see yourself receiving the Word in your life (e.g. by the edge of the path, on patches of rock, in thorns, or in rich soil)?
2. Do you spend solitary time every day with your heart turned toward heaven in prayer?
3. Have you committed yourself to grasp and grow your faith? Do you remain steadfast in the face of any difficulty?
4. Do you share your faith with your family and loved ones, growing together in the love of the Lord?

Section VII

"Feed my lambs"

15. Appeal to Andy Who Has Strayed

In this Chapter, I'm going to reach out to the group of Andys. If you aren't Andy, this Section doesn't apply to you, although you're welcome to continue reading out of interest. The first question before us is how does one identify the believer who has strayed. Andy might be:

- disenchanted because the Faith couldn't give him or her the freedom he or she wanted;
- any member of the faith who felt aggrieved by injustice inside, or outside, the church;
- someone who is disappointed or embittered by the suffering in his or her life; or
- a believer who has lost hope: this Andy might even think him or herself a hopeless sinner.

I've shown a lot of pride in my life, but I no longer presume to have all the answers. Only One has the right answers: He is the Wonder-Counselor. All I'm doing is reminding you that the Eternal-Father loves you. Even though your loved ones may have abandoned you, the Lord won't desert you. He cares for you still.

God's will to search for the stray

Many Andys have lost faith. If you're one of them, you may think there are good reasons for your disappointment. You may think the Lord doesn't care for you because He didn't give what you reasonably expected.

I write to help you remember the tireless, saving love of the Savior of the World. If you feel lost, remember the Lord's consolation and promise in the Parable of the Lost Sheep in Matthew's Gospel. (18:12-14) This parable teaches us about God's amazing love, mercy, and compassion. Our Lord is more concerned with the recovery of the one lost sheep than with the other ninety-nine that aren't. Jesus said clearly and compassionately that, ". . . it is not the will of my Father who is in heaven that one of these little ones should perish." God shows a similar concern for the sinner as if He cared less for the healthy.

Remember, our God takes no pleasure in any of His sheep losing the way or anyone's death. If you are lost, God is very concerned about you.

God keeps His promises

Andy could be a Prodigal Son, (Luke 15:11-32) perhaps rejecting God or turning away from the Lord. If so, take courage. Know that the Lord is inviting you to return to the fold today. Remember that God never forgets you or stops loving, no matter what happens. In St. Paul's Letter to the Hebrews, we *are* reminded that Abraham obeyed the call of God to set out for the Promised Land. He lived in tents, in unknown places, while he waited a very long time for God to act. (11:8-12) Abraham never lost faith. Similarly, despite Sarah being past childbearing age, the old couple were blessed with an uncountable number of descendants.

What's the connection between Abraham's faith and the Christian who strayed from the path?

It's that God keeps His promises!

God fulfilled the promise He made to Abraham.

How do we know this to be true?

Consider how many descendants of Abraham are living today. More than a billion share the same faith and many more call Abraham the ". . . father of many nations . . .". (Romans 4:18) Likewise, God has promised to forgive all the wrongs we've committed. (1 John 1:9) He will make us children of God (John 1:12) if only we'd turn back to Him, and keep faith in God as Abraham did.

We should do our best not to forget. God has told us so many times and in so many ways that He loves each and every one of us.

Aggrieved Andy

No judgment or revenge

You may have left the Church because you were put off by the politics, infighting, or signs of weak faith shown by some believers in the parish. If so, the Word in the Letter of James (4:11-12) tells us not to slander or judge each other. Only One is entitled to both define the laws and judge others for breaking them, and He is the Lord! We've no right whatsoever to judge our neighbor.

Similarly, the Word reminds us not to seek revenge. If there's to be any payback, it's for the Lord to give. So while we wait for the Lord's justice, we should give our enemy food if he's hungry or a drink if she's thirsty. (Romans 12:19-21) In other words, believers should copy the way of Christ by responding to evil with love.

Don't trust in Man

Someone (in or outside a church) might have failed Andy. Here's the dilemma. Wherever we look, there are individuals claiming authority. They have plans. They expect us to follow. Yet we know we should be following the Lord. The Word confirms that true happiness only comes from placing our hope in God. (Psalm 146:2-6)

Why then do we put our trust in Man?

We may be looking for someone to give us happiness or security. This can be a leader or, closer to home, anyone who assumes responsibility for our safety, happiness, or livelihood (as in a parent, spouse, or employer). Never forget this is a two-way process. We give others hope because we may be the ones providing vision, leadership, or security. However, illness or death can prevent people from keeping their promises: ". . . a son of man, in whom there is no help. When his breath departs he returns to the earth; on that very day his plans perish." Similarly, when promises become socially or financially inconvenient, dependents are disregarded. The fact the agreements are written down makes no difference. Many don't think twice about breaking promises, vows, and relationships. The resulting disappointment can be hard to swallow. We know it happens. We just hope it won't happen to us or vainly hope not to be the promise breakers.

I'm not saying we can't rely on others or allow others to put their trust in us. What I'm really saying is that there's only One in whom we can truly trust—He is the Lord. Throughout time, His promises of help and salvation haven't changed.

Look only at the Lord

In the Letter to the Hebrews, St. Paul tells us never to lose sight of Jesus. If we keep steadily on His path, Jesus will lead our faith to perfection. (12:1-2)

God showed His love to mankind through the ministry of Jesus. He died for our sins and was resurrected to give us life. St. Paul helps us understand that someone might die for a worthy person, but Christ died for all of us while we were still sinners. (Romans 5:7) It's the will of God that all sinners be reconciled with Him. The Lord wishes everyone to be filled with joyful trust in the Good

News that He has been offering throughout time: God loves you and me so much.

If any believer needs a good role model, follow the perfect example of the Lord.

Show mercy

At the heart of our Christian faith is the radical love for the other believer, who possesses the spirit of Jesus Christ (Romans 8:9):

> For if you forgive men their trespasses, your heavenly Father also will forgive you; but if you do not forgive men their trespasses, neither will your Father forgive your trespasses. **(Matthew 6:14-15)**

The Lord is calling you and me to show mercy just as He did for every believer. In baptism, the Lord cancels all our debts, and showers love and mercy on everyone who believes in the Good News. We can never measure God's mercy because He forgives all our sins, time and again, even when we repeat them. In the spirit of this limitless mercy, He obliges us to show the same mercy to those who fail us.

How do we show God's mercy to the offensive people He places in front of us?

No matter the many kinds of wrong done to us, we should forgive our brothers and sisters seventy-seven times. I recall a homily by Fr. Anthony Hutjes about a Christian friend of his. This friend had a standing three-strikes policy, i.e. he obeyed the command to forgive, but stopped short at three chances of mercy and refused to go any further. This is what we need to fight against—*comatose* Christianity! Jesus teaches us that Christians are different from non-Christians because we were all called to *love our enemies and pray for those who persecute us.* (Matthew 5:44-45)

Now this might strike you as crazy. You might ask, "How can

one ever love an enemy?" You might also be thinking, "No one is this perfect."

Well, why do we (or the other believers who make us angry) go to church? Are we not sinners—enemies of God—who need to be forgiven and helped by the Lord? Everyone has done some wrong in his or her life, and may continue doing so until the last breath. In the end, He is the only judge. Yet while we live, He consistently shows Himself willing to forgive all our wrongdoings. All we have to do is ask. Just as we ask for forgiveness when we've trespassed against God and/or our neighbor, we should ask for grace from God to forgive those who trespass against us. This is how a Christian should love. He loved us when we were His enemies, so we need to obey His command and love our baneful brothers and slanderous sisters.

Can we presume that Andy is unwilling to show mercy?

If Andy is unable to love his or her enemy, does that mean Andy does *not* want to copy Jesus Christ? In many cases, this would be the wrong question. We should really be asking if Andy has had the opportunity to live the way of Christ.

Can you see the difference? No?

Let's try the analogy of skydiving. We know we have to jump out of the plane with a parachute. Suppose we practice this successfully many times while the plane is on the ground but, when it comes to jumping out of the plane in the air, fear overcomes us. Now picture a believer who confronts an enemy and is told to copy Jesus Christ, i.e. love this enemy. Without an active Christian life, this would be the first time Andy actually goes *skydiving.*

This is the difference between theory and practice.

Without leading a steady Christian life, it's hard for Andy to love his or her enemy. To succeed, Andy must be accepting guidance from the Word or have had the opportunity to practice giving and accepting forgiveness in a community where the Bible's lessons are welcome. We all need the communion of brothers and sisters. This community will enable us to practice and sustain the life in Christ. It'll also help us to keep the Word and love in the way of the cross (or using the analogy: jump out of the plane and skydive with Jesus).

How does one learn to show mercy?

We take the first step toward practical forgiveness by praying for those who hurt or harm us. By communicating with God through prayer, we receive His help in letting go the ill feelings or sense of injustice.

We also do *not* forgive by repressing the anger and doing our best to forget. We *do* so by moving on. This requires a conscious effort to leave the hurt, anguish, or resentment in the past where it belongs. The anger is done; *let it go.* The present and the future can never be happy when we carry forward anger or the desire for revenge.

When we celebrate the Eucharist, we recall the Lord's sacrifice—He died so we can all be saved. Now, when we show mercy (James 2:13) to the brother and sister needing our forgiveness, understanding, or compassion, we honor the Lord!

What about the injustice we suffered?

Are we not entitled to compensation? Can Andy return an eye for an eye?

Well, there's no room for accounting in Christian love. Remember, our Lord has taken pity on us and canceled our debts. (Matthew 18:27-28) There's no *accounting* for us. Given the good prospect of our redemption, shouldn't we be prepared to do the same for those indebted to us?

The act of forgiveness isn't just a loving choice to free a brother or sister from the long shadow of sin. We also benefit! By forgiving, we pull out the roots of bitterness that grow and make trouble in our heart.

If we don't forgive, the pain remains and might eventually kill our love for God and neighbor. Death becomes inevitable at the hand of unforgiveness: a death of understanding, of kindness, and of love. This spiritual death is how the hearts of believers begin to turn to stone.

Forgiveness is one of the hardest things to do because our heart may not have learned how to love.

Don't worry if you still lack the strength to forgive. With the help of the Lord, agape, the Christian love, will eventually grow in our heart. This is why we need the Word to teach the stubborn heart. We need to pray, begging the Lord to shape our heart to learn mercy, forgiveness, and love in the language of the cross. We'll also need our brothers and sisters in a permanent community of faith to make all these happen.

Andy's suffering

Andy could be a Christian who suffered and cried unceasingly for help. Perhaps you've also experienced unbearable suffering, overwhelming difficulties, or a crippling disease that wracked you with pain and misery. You may have lost everything precious in your life or wanted to redress an injustice, but when you prayed for help, neither the Lord nor your brothers and sisters appeared to answer.

As a result of this silence, did you lose faith?

Ask and it will be given?

The words in the Gospel according to Matthew seem to be offering a blank check of sorts. (7:7) Many believers feel expectations when they read, "Ask, and it will be given you . . . For every one who asks receives." They suppose God is promising to answer their petitions and will give them what they pray for.

In this quote from Matthew's Gospel, what does God wish to give every Christian?

For guidance, I turn to the Word again and I'll share with you three of the keys that I've learned.

- The first key: the Lord gives to those who keep His commandments and live the life He commands. (1 John 3:22) How does a Christian do this? Please read the rest of the book.
- The second key: the Lord will hear our prayer and give us whatever we ask, as long as it's in accordance with His will. (1 John 5:14) How do we discover the Lord's will? The answers can also be found in the rest of the book.
- The third key depends on the context for these words from St. Matthew. Taken as a whole, the passage means we should be asking for the *Holy Spirit.* (Luke 11:13) We should be asking the Lord for everything that will help us to grow in faith, hope, and love. (1 Corinthians 13:13)

Is the Lord mean for not giving us what we use prayer to ask for? How can it be? The Lord knows we're fighting battles against idolatry, infidelity, abuse, oppression, violence, and rebellion; not forgetting the judgments we make of our brothers and sisters. I also hope none have forgotten our common fight against all the different types of destructive behavior that lead to poverty, injustice, and terrible crimes—by crimes, I'm not just talking about the terrible things done by nonbelievers. Knowing this, why isn't every believer grateful for the breath to live this day? Why aren't we happy with the different talents and strength He gives to each of us, and the freedom to live according to His will by entering the fight against the previously stated? What more do we really need?

Some people might say, "Give me what I want first, then I'll do the will of God." This is not a *good* offer. God has already given everyone the means to love in our life—aren't the gifts He has given us sufficient?

Sadly, God's generous gifts may never be enough. Let's consider a few lessons offered by the Bible. Having witnessed Jesus perform the miracle of the loaves, why did the people want to take the Lord by force and make Him king? (John 6:1-15, 27) Why didn't the nine lepers, who were believers, return to give praise to God? (Luke 17:11-19) Isn't it also true of Chorazin, Bethsaida, and Capernaum? Jesus performed many miracles in these towns, yet the miraculous help of God had little or no effect on the people's desire to convert. (Matthew 11:20) Is it any wonder that man is *not* ready to live with God?

If the people in those days killed Jesus despite the great works He did, what makes us believers think we won't kill Jesus a second time around?

Seek the Lord in prayer

The Spirit consoles us when we align ourselves with Him through prayer. Psalm 42 teaches us how to struggle against despondency and the troubles in our life, as Israel did through prayer and quiet time with the Lord:

> As a hart longs
> for flowing streams,
> so longs my soul
> for thee, O God.
> My soul thirsts for God,
> for the living God.
> When shall I come and behold
> the face of God?
> My tears have been my food
> day and night,
> while men say to me continually,
> "Where is your God?"
>
> These things I remember,
> as I pour out my soul:

how I went with the throng,
and led them in procession to the house of God,
with glad shouts and songs of thanksgiving,
a multitude keeping festival.
Why are you cast down, O my soul,
and why are you disquieted within me?
Hope in God; for I shall again praise him,
my help and my God.

My soul is cast down within me,
therefore I remember thee
from the land of Jordan and of Hermon,
from Mount Mizar.
Deep calls to deep
at the thunder of thy cataracts;
all thy waves and thy billows
have gone over me.
By day the LORD commands his steadfast love;
and at night his song is with me,
a prayer to the God of my life.
I say to God, my rock:
"Why hast thou forgotten me?

Why go I mourning
because of the oppression of the enemy?"
As with a deadly wound in my body,
my adversaries taunt me,
while they say to me continually,
"Where is your God?"

Why are you cast down, O my soul,
and why are you disquieted within me?
Hope in God; for I shall again praise him,
my help and my God.

How does the Prince-of-Peace help us?

The Lord helps us by generously giving the Spirit to us. The Spirit aids us in the struggle to give up selfishness (the character of sin) that prevents us from giving all of ourselves. Little by little, the Lord helps us acquire the courage to love in the long, arduous journey of life.

In the next Chapter, I write more about suffering. For now, take a moment to contemplate a truth professed in St. Paul's Letter to the Hebrews: Jesus prayed humbly during His life on earth. What was the result of His many prayers?

It was that Jesus Himself learned to obey the will of the Father through suffering. (Hebrews 5:7-8) In this light, why should we be excused from suffering or obeying God's will?

No, we can't escape suffering by expecting God to take it away! Instead, copying Jesus as best we can, we learn to offer up humble prayers to God because with His help, we can continue to love despite our difficulties.

Yes, we receive the help of His Spirit through daily prayers.

Can we persevere in faith?

Like you, I've cried in the darkness, where no one listens except God.

Does He hear?

If He does hear, how does He act?

The Lord gives us His promise that justice will be done, but the Word tells us we can't demand an instant response. No matter how long and hard we pray, justice comes to the Christian whose faith remains steadfast. (Luke 18:6-8)

Don't lose faith. Take courage, pray, and spend quiet time with God.

Now ask yourself, "Do you trust in the Lord? Can you stand firm till your last, dying breath?" You have to because this is faith. All Christians need to be unwavering in hope. If any believer decides, however, to place a time limit on God, he or she should study what a very beautiful widow had to say about putting the Almighty to the test.

The hopeless sinner?

Despite your strong commitment and brute determination, you could be feeling that you just can't overcome your sins. It's easy to lose motivation when we see how many sins there are, all the forms they take, and the poor spiritual results thus far. I won't add to your burden. I'm also a sinner and know how unendurable the burdens can be.

Why are some believers troubled by the idea of sin?

The answer lies in our view of original sin. Some believers see this as God putting handcuffs on every newborn. Some think it unfair and impossible to escape. Why? They claim God ought not to have created a flawed creature i.e. one born with the capacity to sin.

Yet these imaginary restraints are the opposite of God's incredible plan of salvation for all humanity. The Church helps us understand the loving design of God. According to the Catechism of the Catholic Church (CCC), God created man as a rational being with free will. (1730) We're in control of our actions. That's why we're free to decide whether to accept His love and follow Him. It's God's will that we love.

Suppose we make mistakes. Does God's love disappear?

Absolutely not! He loves us all, saint and sinner alike!

Of course, exercising this free will can result in catastrophic mistakes. On the other hand, this freedom can also produce the most beautiful expressions of human love. Our head may know the difference between good and evil, but does our heart choose well? Even if we can't choose well, we should take courage because all our heart really needs is love-training and practice.

What *is* sin?

It's easy to be selfish because of our free will. Some of us may be saying in our heart: "Me first!" "I want!" "Make the other person do the right thing!" In our faith, the many types of sin are simply the different ways in which we show disobedience to God; I know this because I'm such a sinner. There are believers who choose to ignore the rules they think are outdated. They suppose the morality represented by the idea of sin is too conservative. Some suppose the Church is unreasonable to restrict their freedom to do whatever they like.

What does the Church say about sin? The CCC defines sin as any offense against God; i.e. it's doing something we know God has said is wrong. (1850)

Let's examine a major sin—pride—and see how it manifests itself. With pride, some think they're entitled to redefine good and evil, to say what's acceptable and so suit their purposes. When we think like that, we become self-righteous and reject God's love. The arguments we sometimes make reveal our false expectations or disobedient thinking:

- God is full of love.
- He won't allow bad things to happen to good people!
- I'm a good person, so He will always protect me.

Does the wrong thinking stop here? No, it seldom does. Such thinking might produce other threads:

- I'm a believer. Therefore, God will do the right thing.
- Not only will God protect me, but He must also punish the wrongdoer.
- I also expect God to compensate me for all the injustice I've suffered!

Some of us presume to know all the correct things for God to do.

When God *neglects* to give us what we want or *reasonably* expect, a few might even get angry with God, turn their heart away, or lose faith in Him or His Church. Those who do so fail to realize that this type of thinking is a not-so-subtle rebellion against our God, as subtle as the rebellion in the Garden of Eden.

Our love of self is disobedience rooted at the heart of sin.

Free from sin?

Some of us choose or try to obey the commandments of God.

What does the Word say about obeying the laws? It's simple. St. Paul tells us in the Letter to the Romans that God has laid down a framework of laws to tell us what's sinful. (3:19-20) God isn't just judging whether we follow the letter of these laws, but He is looking at the spirit in which we obey.

We should ask ourselves, "How many of us keep the laws faithfully?" These apply not just to the headline commandment, ". . . You shall love the Lord your God with all your heart . . .", (Matthew 22:35-40) but it includes the sometimes less convenient laws like, ". . . you love one another as I have loved you." (John 15:12) If we're unable to love our neighbor, is it pointless to keep all the commandments? Does this mean that we should give up our faith?

Definitely not! This is just proof that we all need help in growing our faith.

God knows we're weak and that our heart fails to choose well. This is why God sent us His son to teach us everything about love.

Turn to and trust in God

Many people also misunderstand the word *repentance*. They think it's up to us believers to change our behavior and turn away from our sins. The Catechism of the Catholic Church teaches us that repentance is changing our attitudes toward Jesus.

When we repent, we're accepting that Christ is the only Redeemer, who can save us from death (the product of our sins or failure to love). We repent by admitting our weakness before God and choosing to depend totally on His mercy. As Christians, baptism has a pivotal role. Baptism is the most important sacrament because it unites us with Christ. At that moment, we accepted His promise of salvation and took our first steps in a new life.

Naturally, we entered His Church full of sin; baptism then cleanses us of our sins. (CCC 977)

It would be perfect if our new life stayed free of sin!

Sin after baptism

Baptism marks the beginning of our new life in Christ, but the Church steadies us with the sad truth. (CCC 978) Baptism itself doesn't make us strong. Unfortunately, our capacity to sin remains. We remain weak and prone to be led astray by temptation. Even if we give up most sins in our new life, other sins remain, or new ones rear their self-loving heads.

Just think how proud some believers are of the many sins that they have given up, or that they commit fewer serious sins than their brothers and sisters! We should take care not to exalt our righteousness before God. Everyone's a sinner before God. All Christians remain in need of His mercy, regardless how many sins we succeed in giving up. Baptism is just the first of many steps in our transformative journey.

What's the long-term goal?

The goal is for all believers to be transformed into followers of Christ, who can love as Jesus loves us. This requires a lifetime of struggling with selfishness, falling down, and getting up—never taking our eyes off the Lord. There's much joy, however, in the transformative journey because the Redeemer is always with us. Also, we *have* the brothers and sisters in our community of faith. We aren't alone in the race to the heavenly finishing line, and we're certainly not fighting our demons on our own.

You might be wondering why so much trouble remains after our baptism. The topic of suffering is discussed in greater detail in the next Chapter.

Which Christian has conquered sin?

"If we say we have no sin, we deceive ourselves, and the truth is not in us." (1 John 1:8) This is the kind advice given by St. John to all Christians; he couldn't have been addressing nonbelievers or casual readers desiring to learn wisdom from the Bible!

It seems the tendency to sin—the desire to reach for the forbidden fruit (or do whatever we like) continues after baptism. Is there no hope for believers? Asking this question would be the ultimate betrayal of faith! If it weren't for the mercy of the Lord, can any Christian survive His call to account for every sin committed? (Psalm 130:3-4) We should never stop seeking the Lord's forgiveness, (1 John 1:9) and let Him teach us all that's good—for breaking with sin is a lifelong struggle.

Yes, there's always hope in the Lord's mercy: this is the hope in me that I communicate and share in this book.

Did the first Christians have no struggle with sin? St. Paul in his Letter to the Romans shares with us his inner struggle: ". . . but we ourselves, who have the first fruits of the Spirit, groan inwardly as we wait for adoption as sons, the redemption of our bodies." (Romans 8:23) That's why we praise and revere the one, true God, who is always prepared to forgive and help us in the fight against sin throughout our life.

If it were possible to stop sinning on our own, we might be tempted to think we've no need for God or His mercy!

If it's hard to break with sin, are we free to continue sinning? Of course not! St. Paul made it clear that we belong to Jesus Christ. Having been freed by our Redeemer, we can't remain enslaved to sin. (Romans 6:15-19)

Can we ever stop sinning then? Yes! The day we stop sinning is that day when we're completely united with God and can love like Him. We can take joy in this seemingly unattainable goal because it's patently clear that Jesus Christ will do the work of transformation in every believer. All we need to do is believe this truth in our heart, cooperate with the Lord, and trust Him to help us.

How do we cooperate with the Lord and receive His help? Continue reading Sections VIII and IX of this book. To do our part, we need to act beyond an idea, a wish, or good intentions.

How do we trust in our Savior to help us? We need to do everything Jesus tells us to do. Only when our faith is properly formed and we're able to love like Jesus, can we hope to conquer sin in ourselves.

Christian action, not platitudes

In his book *A Grief Observed*, C.S. Lewis wrote about the grief he suffered when his dearly beloved wife died. He described how a few well-intentioned Christians offered him words of scripture they hoped would console him. At page 25, C.S. Lewis said he rejected the consolation of religion.

It seemed a horrible thing for him to say! How can a Christian reject the Word?

Well, it depends on the spirit in which scripture is offered. Some people quote the Bible because it's a natural and easy thing to do. No matter how relevant the passages selected, the gesture may not be sincere in the circumstances and even come across as thoughtless.

I think C.S. Lewis was saying he needed the quiet company of a Christian. Yes, love is often better expressed with the hard labor of one's company, time, and listening ear!

When we look around, we see brothers and sisters who need consolation or just our fellowship. Approaching them directly without waiting to be asked may be resented. Offering unsolicited counsel or quoting slogans from the Bible isn't helping them. These are the people who need us, not our platitudes or judgment.

In another book, *The Secret Thoughts of an Unlikely Convert, An English Professor's Journey Into Christian Faith*, a kind pastor offers Christian hospitality and a listening ear. He and his wife tirelessly help a lost sheep rediscover the love of Jesus Christ. *Vulgar* Christians had previously put off the author with scriptural catch phrases—perhaps looking for an instant conversion without offering love's labor. (14; 24; 17)

These are real examples which reinforce the ultimate lesson, i.e. to love a sinner as Jesus has. We can benefit fellow sinners and ourselves by allowing the Lord to teach us on the subject of love.

How do I know so much about vulgar Christians? I'm one of them. I also need to learn how to love, as Christ loves me.

Sin and sin again—how do sinners repent?

According to the CCC, repentance begins with the admission of our faults. We need to be honest. After all, we can't deceive God. He knows we're sinful, but because He is merciful, He will forgive us. (1847)

Remember that repentance is turning to and accepting the mercy of the Lord.

Once we've spoken the words of repentance and shown contrition as best we can, does this mean we can continue to indulge freely in our sinful behavior of the past?

No, we shouldn't continue to sin!

After our baptism, even though our many sins have been washed away, we're still free to sin or disobey God. Each new sin separates us from the grace of God. This is why we have the Sacrament of Penance and Reconciliation, through which we seek reconciliation with our ever patient God whenever we have a chance. Yes, Christians burdened with any serious sin need to turn back to the Lord.

You might be thinking: the hopeless sinner is back where he started. He's proven he can't love, be unselfish, or change his sinful behavior. Surely it's a waste of effort to make further attempts to improve? I have five good reasons why our fight against sin is never hopeless.

1. Conversion begins with the acceptance that sin is a (continuing) rebellion against love. When we cheat, lie, get angry, steal, and so on, we miss opportunities for love by hurting ourselves and those around us. We could have done the right thing, not lied about being sick for work, not cheated on our ex-

pense claims, not squeezed the third-world hawker over chump change, etc. When we repent, we're choosing to recognize the opportunities we've missed for love. An honest admission of failure will help us begin addressing the cause of our inability to love.

2. There's no time limit for the transformation of our heart. Most of us may need the whole, or a better part, of our lifetime to reverse the many years of accumulated, ingrained selfishness or rebellious behavior. This, of course, runs the risk of dying in a state without grace. To avoid this tragedy, we ought to start the fight against sin today! Having said that, there's a possible obstacle against this fight. Well-meaning Christians in the parish may bully the Andys by expecting them to improve pronto! The wise course is to give every sinner the time to study and meditate on God's teaching together with his or her brothers and sisters. After all, the Lord has given all believers this time of waiting as our opportunity to be saved. (2 Peter 3:15) People move at their own pace or not at all. If the believers are to accept the complete Word of God and allow His love to completely govern their heart, it must be a free choice. Christians should just be happy that a sinner has returned to the fold and is willing to begin his or her lessons on love.

3. Let God help us. If our lifestyle is presently disordered, we might not even see our sins plainly or know how to begin doing the right thing. This is why I've been advocating faith formation in this book: to expose you and me to Jesus Christ, the true Teacher. We need to depend on the Lord for

spiritual help, growth, and transformation. Put in a different way, where are you in your journey as a Christian? Are you at the end of your faith journey, with your heart completely transformed to love God and your neighbor? No? Perhaps you're at the beginning of your faith journey, having just experienced initial conversion, and you *are* presently following Jesus Christ and learning His ways? No? Rejoice, because no matter where you are on your journey, God loves you and wants to help you!

4. We shouldn't fight our sins on our own. The Lord has said He will fight our battles for us against our enemies (the seven nations or capital sins)—read Chapter 18.

5. In communion with our sinful brothers and sisters, the lessons in love can begin. When our brothers and sisters eventually relate to us, they accept us as we are, warts and all. Why should we love a brother or a sister with all their faults and shortcomings? Because God loves each and every one of us as we are. This is the Lord's teaching. It follows that we should love our broken, unhelpful, or ungrateful brothers and sisters as they are. To be clear, all Christians who are sinners are to love the sinner, not the sin. It's also not right to mock a sinner who prays, but apparently can't or doesn't display the righteousness, which we expect from one who *prays* a lot. Too many Christians obsess about correcting the faults of others, when the Lord has been clear about the planks in our own eyes. When brothers and sisters show patience, understanding, and acceptance, the sinner is freed from the stress

> of *Christian* expectation—victory from sin will come with the help of the Lord and in His time.

Instead of striving to be sinless, the Lord urges us to love and thus begin the journey to cultivate a humbled, contrite heart.

Courage—admit our sins

Every believer needs to turn to the Lord for His mercy. How then do we turn to God? To encourage us all, read the following extract from Psalm 51 describing King David's unreserved response to God concerning his grave sin:

> Have mercy on me, O God, according to thy steadfast love;
> according to thy abundant mercy blot out my transgressions.
> Wash me thoroughly from my iniquity,
> and cleanse me from my sin!
> For I know my transgressions,
> and my sin is ever before me.
> Against thee, thee only, have I sinned,
> and done that which is evil in thy sight,
> so that thou art justified in thy sentence
> and blameless in thy judgment.
> Behold, I was brought forth in iniquity,
> and in sin did my mother conceive me.
> *Behold, thou desirest truth in the inward being;*
> *therefore teach me wisdom in my secret heart.*
> Purge me with hyssop, and I shall be clean;
> wash me, and I shall be whiter than snow.
> Fill me with joy and gladness;
> let the bones which thou hast broken rejoice.
> Hide thy face from my sins,
> and blot out all my iniquities.
> *Create in me a clean heart, O God,*
> *and put a new and right spirit within me.*

> *Cast me not away from thy presence,*
> *and take not thy holy Spirit from me.*
> Restore to me the joy of thy salvation,
> and uphold me with a willing spirit.
> Then I will teach transgressors thy ways,
> and sinners will return to thee.
> Deliver me from bloodguiltiness, O God,
> thou God of my salvation,
> and my tongue will sing aloud of thy deliverance.
> O Lord, open thou my lips,
> and my mouth shall show forth thy praise.
> *For thou hast no delight in sacrifice;*
> were I to give a burnt offering, *thou wouldst not be pleased.*
> *The sacrifice acceptable to God is a broken spirit;*
> *a broken and contrite heart, O God, thou wilt not despise ...* (Emphasis added)

As you can see from this Psalm composed by David, the first step is to admit our trespass or failing. Yes, even though David was to God, ". . . a man for himself after his own heart . . .", (1 S 13:14) he committed grave sins, as all men do. This Psalm also shows us that an unreserved confession is like a sacrifice—the sacrifice of our broken spirits—for we believers can't seem to do what's right and good. Even St. Paul admits the inward struggle when he finds himself doing the very things he hates. (Romans 7:15) Take courage, our loving God is very much interested in the Christian with a humbled and contrite spirit, who trembles at His Word. (Isaiah 66:2)

Why does God love weak sinners?

Some churchgoers watch those around them and see people like Andy who appear unable to change. What do these churchgoers do next? They say to these Andys, "You can be saved," then heap burdens on them. They expect them to give up their sins before entering the doors of the Church. Do tell me, which believer:

- enters a church without sin;
- does good work without sin in his or her heart; or
- returns from a pilgrimage free of disobedience?

It's very difficult to give up sin before becoming a Christian ready and willing to love. So we should move away from the thinking that a sinner should fight sin on his or her own. Such a sinner fights a losing battle. When Andy grows demoralized and gives up the fight against sin, he or she thinks there's no choice but to turn away from the Lord and give up the spiritual fight. This is utterly wrong!

Let's assume that Andy has gone astray. I hope Andy will see through the lie that God doesn't love a weak sinner. I hope he or she'll turn back toward the Lord. Why should the sinner turn back? What benefit will he or she receive?

God loves every sinner. He is waiting for all sinners to turn to Him for help! Remember the Lord left behind the ninety-nine that weren't lost or sick to look for the sinner. Think also of the Father's joyful response when the Prodigal Son was seen making his way home. Jesus gave us this parable to help us understand the true meaning and benefit of repentance. Yes, the benefit that Andy receives is the salvation of his or her soul through the forgiveness of sins. (Luke 1:77) All this is made possible by the most tender mercy of our God. (78) Andy should take his or her courage in both hands. The Lord is calling Andy to join the saints in the journey of faith. Fight the good fight, finish the race, and keep the faith. (2 Timothy 4:7-8)

As for me and my house, I choose my God and His plan of salvation for us.

For the New Evangelization to fulfill its mission, the pastors must commit themselves unreservedly to help every Andy: those who have strayed, have a weak grasp of or are struggling with the Faith. I make my appeal to all pastors of souls in Section X.

QUESTIONS FOR REFLECTION ON CHAPTER 15

1. Do you think the sheep that Jesus was searching for (Matthew 18:12) is spotless, blameless, or a sinner who has lost his or her way?
2. Have you turned away from the Lord (even for a moment)?
3. All Christians are sinners who need the mercy of God. Yet, are there prostitutes and tax collectors you disdain in your Church?
4. Are you able to show mercy to the sinners who hurt you?
5. Do you allow God's will to be done (that you are prepared to lose everything in your life)?

16. Why Must Christians Suffer?

Sharing what I know

I'm going to share what I've learned about suffering from my study of the Word of God. This requires me to refer to what the Bible says. I'll also share how the Word has helped me in my experience of suffering. All I hope is that you'll keep an open mind and continue reading to the end. If you have any questions, write them down and discuss them with your pastor.

The Bible gives us the truth. Suffering began with our first parents, Adam and Eve. As their descendants, we copy their disobedience in various ways. Every now and then, a handful of the faithful breaks away and shows great love. For most people, however, suffering continues.

Why does suffering continue? As long as we remain unable to love, i.e. the Christian agape is missing from our words and actions, suffering is the price we pay for remaining selfish and persisting in doing whatever pleases us rather than what pleases God.

There are two basic aspects to the experience of suffering:

1. Some suffering is experienced when we interact with the disobedient hearts of men and women.

Keep in mind that we might be the ones causing suffering to others.

2. Some suffering is caused by natural forces in the physical world we inherited as the descendants of Adam and Eve. Some people are bold and seek to control this world, but we need to speak the truth. God bestowed the sun and the rain on this world and its inhabitants. No matter whether we're good or bad, the sun shines and the rain falls. We're warmed, there's something to drink, and the combination enables farmers to grow our food. But in stormy seas, we're like fish caught in a treacherous net. We're also told that natural disasters and pool accidents do not prove the guilt of those who suffer and die. A hurricane may arrive our shores, but we don't have the science to weaken its power. A tsunami destroys everyone and everything in its path. We could do nothing to redirect or destroy an asteroid headed toward earth. Of course, we try to prepare for emergencies, put safety measures in place, or evacuate as many people as possible, but we can't stop nature in her tracks. This is physical, emotional, or economic suffering produced by natural forces beyond our control.

We need to face facts. Everywhere we turn, suffering is present in its many forms. It's an unavoidable part of the world we live in. We should always use the best of our abilities to reduce the harm and loss, but the Word tells us there's suffering and we can't escape from it. What's more, we've been told that Jesus didn't come to take all the suffering away, (Mark 1:32-38; Luke 4:40-44) and before He returns, there will be great suffering to come. (Matthew 24:6-14)

In the first part of the book, I shared my own experience of suffering. What insight did I offer? According to current standards,

I'm intelligent with the qualifications to prove it. I calculated the odds and executed my plans, trying to direct and control the outcome I desired. Yet I couldn't save myself from pain and grief. Why couldn't I have my own way all the time? The Word told me that *a large army will not keep a king safe nor does the hero escape by his great strength.* (Psalm 33:16) So, not surprisingly, I couldn't avoid suffering.

I hope you'll use these ideas to begin a discussion with your pastor or start your own study with your brothers and sisters. The Word of God offers a rich treasure trove of learning that will help every believer in the difficult journey of life. Your brothers and sisters can also share their own experiences. Together, all can learn what God wishes to teach us about this life and the world we live in.

Original suffering

To understand how humanity got here, we need to start from the account of creation in Genesis. After creating everything, our Father gave loving advice to Adam and Eve. For a full life without death, suffering, or want, our first parents were told: ". . . You may freely eat of every tree of the garden; but of the tree of the knowledge of good and evil you shall not eat, *for in the day that you eat of it you shall die.*" (Emphasis added) (Genesis 2:16-17) Adam and Eve had a free choice, but they chose poorly. They *had* a full life with God, but God's friendship and generous gifts were *not* enough. Was their disobedience willful, negligent, or careless? However it's put, they disobeyed God's kindly advice.

What's the deadly consequence of this original sin? Humans suffer and die.

All humanity inherited this original sin, which has three tentacles:

- not following simple instructions;
- not trusting God's will; and
- believing a lie.

Adam and Eve were deceived into believing that God didn't love them enough. They wanted to be like God with their eyes opened, (Genesis 3:5) and responded to God's love and generosity with unspoken ingratitude: "Not enough." Adam and Eve had to be expelled to a mortal life in the natural world because they could next pick from the tree of life. (Genesis 3:22) Adam and Eve's descendants have copied this disobedience and rebellion by not trusting in God. Because of the original sin, humanity inherited a life of toil, suffering, and death. (Genesis 3:16-19)

Divine plan of salvation

Although Adam and Eve fell from His grace, God put a divine plan of salvation into action. In this plan, He has been teaching our predecessors in the faith that choosing to love leads to life. Everyone who desires to do the will of God is given many chances to be restored to *life* (with Him) and avoid *death* (without God's love). Hopefully, all of us will embrace every choice that leads to *life*.

What can we do to cooperate with God's plan?

Avoid the path chosen by Adam and Eve. Turn to the Lord for help and salvation, and receive the most generous gift from Him!

In his Letter to the Ephesians, (2:7-10) St. Paul teaches that salvation is a gift from God, i.e. we can't earn or buy the right to be saved, say, by doing *good* deeds. We can't claim the credit for our salvation. Only grace, through faith, can save us.

So what's the grace of God?

Even though there's no entitlement to grace, it's every spiritual goodness that the Lord generously gives us e.g. the grace to trust in God despite our suffering and difficulties; the grace to forgive every hurt; the grace to love each difficult person on our life's long journey etc. To participate in God's plan of salvation, we must want to receive this grace of God.

Do we just believe and need do nothing more to receive salvation?

No, there's more to this gift of salvation. We *were* created to live a good life.

What's this? The good life is certainly not the modern misconception of a life of comfortable excess, throwaway luxury, or sensual pleasures. This good life is all about following God, listening to Him, and doing everything He says. That's the way He meant us to live. When we obey God's will, we'll discover the richness of His grace.

It follows that we're the beneficiaries of the Good News. As sinners, we benefit by unconditionally accepting the death and resurrection of Jesus Christ (Mark 1:15) in our heart, which proves God's justice.

What's God's justice?

As a result of Adam and Eve's original sin, humanity forfeited the intimate, face-to-face relationship with God. Mankind's exile from Paradise led to an unending show of disobedience, despite many promises to obey God's commandments. Despite all our sins, He will show justice by exonerating anyone believing in Jesus, the Son of God, not out of onerous duty, but in faith—as in the simple love of children for their father. This flows from the divine plan in which Jesus offered His life for the redemption of all sinners. (Romans 3:23-26)

Yes, when all humankind finally realize how much God loves everyone that He sent our Savior to take every misdeed upon Himself, all should be grateful and thank God for His justice. In this way, we should want to lead the new life according to Christ, which will help us reunite with God. Moreover, we'll be justified or acquitted, and our sins will be forgiven—all are gifts from God through Jesus Christ.

Love and suffering

Is the design of man flawed?

One might ask, "If disobedience led to all our troubles, why didn't God simply make Adam and Eve incapable of mistake, noncompliance, or rebellion?"

If we'd been made a bit robot-like, such docility might answer the vexed question about God's plan and the problem of disobedience. In my imaginary Paradise, we would need some programming to command Adam and Eve not to select the wrong choices. For the encounter with the serpent in the garden, let's consider the following programming:

- Avoid any conversation with the serpent.
- Reject all false statements or suggestions.
- Don't eat from the tree of the knowledge of good and evil.

Except such simple commands leave wriggle room for Adam and Eve to think, act or get around the restrictive programming. When one takes into account the endless scenarios, counter-responses from Adam or Eve, and deceptive scheming by the serpent, the second command opens the door by allowing them to listen to the serpent. Adam and Eve would still misjudge "falsity," and end up failing to comply with the last command by, say, sampling (rather than eating) the forbidden fruit. Providing a thousand lines of prohibitive programming might succeed in policing free will and forcing the desired outcome, but what kind of life would that have been for our first parents with martial law, prohibition, or curfew? For *God* to eliminate all wicked or wrongful possibilities at inception, Adam and Eve would have to become like complete robots. If that were to happen, humanity would be living unfree lives—how can any of us do without the freedom of thought and action?

This tells me that God didn't make Adam and Eve less than human. In His wonderful design of humanity, Adam and Eve were made free to think for themselves, without repressive restrictions on their freedom to choose whether to love and obey. So, God has given all men and women the freedom even to choose *life or death, blessing or curse.*

In this light, original sin wasn't about:

- ambiguity in God's instructions,

- the insufficiency of God's love for Adam and Eve, or
- too much freedom;

Rather it was all about a disobedient choice. Mind you, it wasn't just any disobedience. Our first parents basically disobeyed God's all-important house rule. Adam and Eve utterly disregarded God's warning that the particular disobedience would result in suffering and death.

Cuffing suffering

We could also ask: "Why can't God eliminate all the suffering that happens in everyone's life?" This question acknowledges the possibility of evil being conceived, i.e. men and women are free to think and act. However, given the possibility of evil acts, we'd be expecting God to police and arrest every harmful action before it causes any suffering. However, much of the suffering we experience arises from interaction with our neighbors. Consequently, *God* will have to intervene when another is going to cause us to suffer and vice versa, i.e. there's an immediate curtailment of your freedom and mine. The way I see it—that's the problem with trying to eliminate suffering. If God were to stop one of our actions, we'd have experienced *immediate* suffering because of God finding us guilty right here, right now. In this way, *God's* elimination of suffering wouldn't produce a happy ending for every sinner in the present life.

Well, back to the drawing board. How can suffering ever be eliminated?

Freedom and learning God's will

Let's return to the original advice given by God. He is, after all, our Creator, and has the answer to the problem of suffering. We know that God gave Adam and Eve an instruction. It's easy to focus on the instruction as an unhappy prohibition and forget the Lord had allowed Adam and Eve to eat from every other tree in the Garden of Eden. He also gave Adam mastery over all creatures on earth. We shouldn't forget the joyful gift of companionship in Eve that Adam received from God. Our parents were given purpose in the Lord's Garden. It's clear that God had a plan for Adam and Eve to live well in Paradise, but they chose to disregard God's advice and thereby rejected His wonderful plan.

It follows that the first step toward the elimination of suffering is rediscovering God's advice for our new life in Christ, i.e. we need to learn God's will. All Christians should consider how to respond to God: will we choose the path of *life over death, blessing over curse*? (Deuteronomy 30:15-20) In this, remember God's caution to all believers: "Be not like a horse or a mule, without understanding, which must be curbed with bit and bridle, else it will not keep with you." (Psalm 32:9)

We've been given freedom:

- Are we going to use it responsibly and obey God's will?
- Do we need our freedom shackled (or curbed with bridle and bit) because we just can't handle the consequences of exercising our free will?
- Are we going to behave just like Adam and Eve—ignore God's instructions, in part or in whole, and do what pleases us?

If you need more confirmation of God's caution, read the Parable of the Sower again in Chapter 14. Note the reference to believers who experience difficulties *along the path, on rocky ground, among thorns.* God doesn't take away life's suffering even though we've decided to believe in Him. Instead, the Lord asks whether believers *see but not perceive, and may indeed hear but not understand; lest they should turn again and be forgiven.* God is asking believers if they'll look past their suffering *on rocky ground* or *among thorns*, convert, and have faith in the Lord's plan of salvation. Yes, the Word tells us that the only way for humanity to return to Paradise is to learn to trust in God by doing everything He tells us to do, despite our suffering.

Those questioning the perfection of our maker's design should reconsider. Why? Because our *prodigal* Father showed His abundant love by giving us free will from the beginning and trusting us with it. If you ask me, freedom is one of the top-five fantastic, free gifts we've received from God. Instead of stripping away free will, He left us free to contemplate, choose, and decide throughout our life.

Love in God's plan

What's the significance of free will in the plan of God? Springing from this freedom is our potential for extraordinary love. Because God is love, we cannot fail or forget to love. (1 John 4:8) He made us so we could live in love and in God. (4:16)

We see the truth of God's love beginning with His constant companionship with Adam and his family outside Paradise. He never abandoned them! Our God continued this relationship with Abraham and the other father figures. Where appropriate, He made covenants with them. He accompanied Moses and the people in their incredible journey out of Egypt. Then our God became man in the magnificent ministry of Jesus Christ.

From early history to the present day, the Lord has helped the people of Israel, simple Apostles, defenseless martyrs, persecuted saints, and all other holy men and women who remained steadfast. Each of our predecessors-in-faith met with difficulties, suffering, and helplessness. Yet they kept in their hearts an unbroken, common thread of hope *through the ages*, passing the faith unfailingly from one generation to the next, namely the promise of reconciliation with God through the saving power of Christ Jesus.

Despite suffering, being humiliated, or experiencing confusion, many Christians remained able to love because of this hope. Even those caught up in random destruction caused by earthquakes, extreme weather, and other natural calamities continued to love. They're the best of us, and in the face of competition from those who chose sin, these followers of Christ embraced hard choices of love. They led by example, choosing the path of *life* and *blessing.*

Using their eyes to see and ears to hear, they recognized the love of God in their history. This is the other unbroken thread of faith running through the fabric of time: these faithful men and women have expressed their love for God and one another. Each of their lives, filled with love, is an echoing sign of faith from the beginning.

Without any doubt, these clear-sighted expressions of faith also prove the existence of God in the history of man. There's no need to look for the Lord in the celestial heavens or in the genome He designed. Such Christians radiate the *prodigal* love of God, which they have received in their life. What *is* this Christian love the faithful radiate? It is service, sacrifice and the giving of self. Thus, God has left a unique imprint in each Christian who has carried his or her cross in every age.

When we choose to obey God's commandments, teachings and advice, we'll be exercising our freedom for the love and glory of God. By loving God and one another, we'll have demonstrated the noblest expression of humanity's free will. When I refer to *love*, I'm talking about the standard of loving even one's enemy that Christ set for every Christian committed to following Him. (Matthew 5:44)

As I see it, this is the significance of freedom in God's plan! If God were to police and stop suffering, judging everyone here and now, there's a risk that love would be snuffed out; love had to be given a chance to spring up and flower. That's why He didn't weed out the darnel at the outset. (Matthew 13:28-30) It follows that the second step we should take is to use our free will to love in the way that Christ loves everyone. We *have* to want the path of *life* and *blessing* offered by God.

The third and final step toward the elimination of suffering should be our reconciliation with God at the end of our life's journey.

Those who offer the opposite of love are doomed to fail. We see this truth in the Old Testament in teachings about Cain and others, who opposed the loving plan of God. Look around today and we see murderers, oppressors, cheats, and even religious men and women claiming to love God but doing the loveless opposite. Yes, I was one of them and I'm still capable of all sorts of serious sin.

When we question the need to obey God or trust His plan for us, our free will begins leaning along the lines of Adam's disobedience. How soon can one see the terrible result of free will that's exercised badly? Read what Cain did to his brother, Abel, in chapter 4 of the Book of Genesis.

Sin opposes love; love covers sin

We give ourselves the chance to learn wisdom by looking back with a critical eye at the choices we've made. We should revisit the teaching in Genesis 2 regarding original sin. Adam and Eve believed the falsehood that God didn't love them enough because they were forbidden to eat fruit from one particular tree. If we can grasp this teaching, it becomes easier to see the thread of disobedience that's woven into the history of mankind and into our life. All humanity inherited the same rebellious disposition with most of us having little or no desire to trust God's advice or His plan—we want to do whatever we like.

Put another way: if we truly love God *in our heart*, it should be easy to obey all God's commands. But do we love our enemies? Are we able to forgive seventy-seven times? Have we loved God and our neighbor? Many of us believers say we love God, but how many accept all the Lord's teachings?

What's the result of disobedience? When sinners don't obtain the outcome they expect, they become frustrated or angry, i.e. they begin to make others suffer. Yes, every believer possesses the power to inflict suffering upon his or her neighbor. Every time we ignore love in our choices, we're choosing to sin. This always produces more suffering.

What if you're an innocent victim of suffering? For the answer, you should revisit what St. Paul said about justice in his Letter to the Romans, (12:19-21) which was discussed in the previous Chapter.

Why *is* sin an offense against God? We know God is love. He advises us to love. In love, the giving of self is free, but when sinners put their own needs or agenda first, they're likely to hurt themselves or their neighbors by taking what they want. Such selfishness is contrary to God's plan of love, which is evident in the freedom and other phenomenal gifts He has given to all humankind.

Why do sinners ignore God's advice? Because they feel insecure, they deny (or have lost hope) that God has a plan for them—as did Adam and Eve. They lack the humility to trust in God to help them or to wait for the Lord's help. In their pride, they believe in their own strength or wealth to provide the security or outcome they want. If they fear they may not get what they want by fair means, they may become aggressive and kill. In using the word *kill*, I'm referring to the risk that a sinner may take the life of another. There's also the other risk that he or she may snuff out the love, friendship, or trust in family, friends, and neighbors to reach his or her self-serving goals.

What did God teach us about the fight against sin? Jesus told us to *shoulder His yoke and learn from Him . . . and we will find rest for our souls.* (Matthew 11:29) We rest and relax when not obsessing about keeping laws or behaving in ways we've been told are free of sin. When Jesus washed the feet of the disciples, (John 13:4-5) and taught the parable of the Good Samaritan, (Luke 10:30-37) He was really training us to follow the New Commandments, i.e. His yoke. These have the agape or Christian love as their focus, for our type of love means service and the giving of self. Not only do we need to put God first in our life, but we must also put the needs of others before our own needs. This is the love that Jesus wants us to copy from Him. Others benefit because they experience love and not suffering from us.

Christians reduce the suffering in the world by choosing to love; waiting, not demanding, for God's justice. When more and more Christians begin to love and serve, the world becomes a better place.

The serpent encouraged the false thinking in Adam and Eve that God didn't love them enough. How do we know if God really loves all humanity? God allowed all men and women to kill the

Christ with their sins. In the divine plan of salvation, there can be no doubt about the Father's love for all mankind.

When we truly love God *in our heart*, we *will* copy the love He displayed on the cross. Love requires the opposite of sin, i.e. the death of self. When we think less of our own priorities, the persistent practice of love can cover all our sins. (1 Peter 4:8)

When every believer chooses to love in the way of the cross, we'll be humbly taking steps to reconcile with God, walking toward Him and not away. These are the necessary steps to be taken by each follower in his or her new life in Christ.

But why must we suffer?

God has designed a plan for every believer to be saved through Jesus Christ. During our life on earth, He has set out a path for Christians to follow as we learn how to love. Even though we believers *understand* the Good News, many don't fare spiritually well with the suffering in our life.

What do you suppose we're doing when we mumble in our heart:

"Why did the Lord let the innocent suffer and die?"

or

"Why did God allow bad things to happen to me?"

or

"Why me?"

If such thinking is in our heart, then we *are* showing ourselves unwilling to trust in God!

Think back to the Garden of Eden. God had given Adam and Eve so much, but they didn't think the plan of living an abundant life with God was enough. That was why the serpent could tempt them with the lie that they could surely be like gods; i.e. the rebellion was already in the hearts of Adam and Eve. The serpent cheated Eve, so she ate from the forbidden tree. She then gave the fruit to Adam, who also accepted the lie and showed the same disobedience.

Coming up to date, I used to question why the Lord wasn't more generous in His healing when there were so many deserving candidates. In my heart, I wondered why the Lord had only permitted just sixty over miracles at Lourdes, repeatedly asking why He wouldn't save more worthy candidates. Why couldn't I accept just one miracle as a concrete sign of His supernatural work? Would this not be proof enough that He lives and that He is still here with mankind? How many times must God perform miracles before I was convinced?

My faith had been shallow indeed. I've been making demands of God and disregarding His generosity all around me.

By questioning the sixty-nine signs He has displayed at Lourdes thus far, I'd been shamelessly ignoring His divine revelations in today's world. These signs today, however, are hills in the balance compared to God's revelation in the birth, death, and resurrection of my Lord Jesus Christ. I shouldn't forget the many spectacular signs, which the Lord has given mankind from the beginning of time, including the extraordinary signs of human love everywhere, which are miracles in their own right. I say this to myself, in particular, because I might unfaithfully continue to look for signs in others to bolster my faith.

The Word has thankfully helped me since to look past the evidence of faith. Now, not counting the great bounty I've already received in my life, I'm able to recognize and be grateful for the blessings I receive each new day. From the moment I rise, I'm thankful for all that brightens and warms my senses. I'm also grateful for the fresh air I breathe, the clean water I drink, and the incredible variety of nourishment that sustains my life to do the will of God. Times are hard and my body grows feeble. Even so, I'm grateful to receive the love of my family, brothers and sisters, and friends in a *today* filled with plentiful possibilities of the cross of love.

I've also been given the grace to appreciate the gift of just being alive today. Before I retire each evening, I ask Him for another day—one more day—to learn more of His ways, convert some more, and love a little more.

By questioning God in my earlier journey, "Why?", I'd been falling into the same error as Adam. The Accuser doesn't stop aiming to cheat me with the same falsehood that my God doesn't love me enough to give me what I want. I should be mindful that the Lord doesn't have to give me what I want ASAP, if at all. I acknowledge my heart's a bottomless pit, always wanting more gifts and bailouts from God. There were never enough gifts from God to satisfy my greedy heart. I'd been unable to trust God's plan that didn't include the outcome I was expecting.

In nursing the self-pity about the suffering in my life, it's clear to me now that I've been blinding myself to the goodness of the Lord. I've received undeserved gifts from the maker of heaven and earth, and will no doubt receive other generous gifts in time to come. What happens to help me trust in God? He gives me the help of the Holy Spirit to grow in faith and see plainly His help in the blessings and gifts I've received. He also gives me spiritual sight and hearing to understand a little of His plan.

There had been recent times when I became anxious and ill feelings threatened to engulf me. The Word in my life, however, helped me recall my Lord's love shining brightly on the cross, and I was able to lean on Him to remain steadfast and march on.

Yet there's a paradox about suffering and love. Even though the cross represents so much suffering, the Lord showed His amazing love to all mankind and triumph through the cross. Man can be saved if he truly believes in Jesus, our Savior, and begins carrying his cross. *Life*, in this way, triumphs over *death*. Thus, the man *who loses his life for the sake of Christ will find it*, which is why I have to lose my life i.e. to accept the suffering that goes with Christian love. I have to keep trying to do what the Lord has asked me to do. (1 Corinthians 15:58) Every time I succeed in giving something of myself, serve someone else, or let another benefit at my expense, I'll be experiencing a little resurrection over *death*, *kiasu-ism,* and *kiasi-ism.*

Indeed, the suffering in my life has enabled me to learn God's will little by little. In the Letter to the Hebrews, St. Paul reminds me how parenting is supposed to work. When a father corrects his son, he isn't trying to discourage the boy. If the father didn't love his own, he wouldn't continue to offer advice and teaching. When I relate to God, I need to acknowledge that suffering is a necessary part of my spiritual training. He trains the ones He loves and punishes those He acknowledges as His sons. This method of parenting has always been the way by which every father cared and accepted responsibility for the upbringing of his child. (Hebrews 12:5-8) The Lord has been correcting me and I'm now happy to learn from Him the suffering love that saves.

God suffers with us

If you're still unable to love or troubled by the suffering in your life, consider the advice of Bishop Baldwin of Canterbury in *Treatise 10*:

> That is why he says: "Set me as a seal on your heart." As though to say: Love me, as I love you; have me in your mind, in your memory, in your desire; in your sighing, your groaning, your weeping. Remember, man, in what state I fashioned you, how far I preferred you before the rest of creatures, the dignity with which I ennobled you; how I crowned you with glory and honour, made you a little less than the angels, and subjected all things under your feet. *Remember not only the great things I did for you, but what harsh indignities I bore on your behalf; and see if you are not acting wickedly against me, if you do not love me. For who loves you as I love you?*
>
> Who created you, if not I? Who redeemed you, if not I? Lord, take away from me the heart of stone, a heart shrunken and uncircumcised—take it away and give me a new heart, a heart of flesh, a clean heart. (Emphasis added)

The way memory works is selfish. It tends to remember only the convenient and pleasant things. When we're sighing or our suffering is unbearable, we should remember how much Jesus suffered for us.

The Lord continues to love every sinner, even though we reject His love. This is God, the one who created us. He wants to save every wrongdoer, one by one. He will do so repeatedly. Why *is*

God so faithful, abounding in mercy, with a love that can't be measured or fully understood? I've no doubt that He is waiting patiently for every sinner to seek His help because with His help . . . *the man who stands firm to the end will be saved.* (Matthew 10:22) For this precious reason, we should reject our heart of stone and beg for a clean heart, a heart that can love God as He loves every one of us.

The next time you cry in your suffering, "Where *is* my God?", I bid you to consider this radical proposition of faith: God is by your side in your suffering of today, as He was yesterday, and will be with you tomorrow. Remember that the Lord has always been with us outside the Garden, in the burning fiery furnace and under a furze bush in the wilderness.

The Lord positively understands your suffering because He has already endured so much pain, humiliation, and suffering to tell humanity how much He loves all sinners. In addition to loving you and me and offering to wipe the slate clean, God wishes everyone who is suffering to reconcile with Him.

Milk and solid food, Part I

Looking back on my early journey of faith, I used to see my suffering as a series of opportunities for the Lord to intervene and perform miracles. You might say I was waiting for the Lord to show His mighty arm through external signs! It was spiritually childish to demand proof of His works. The basis of faith is acceptance of spiritual truth, without the need for proof. I had to wait until my faith had grown a bit before I could see suffering for what it really is:

- a training exercise for my heart;
- a spiritual struggle; and
- an opportunity to trust in the Lord.

When I stopped grumbling about the suffering in my life, I began to see Jesus Christ working in me.

Immature faith

When I was a child in the Faith, my belief in God was shallow. It skirted the essential Christian struggle to renounce the world, carry my cross, and follow Jesus Christ. I was satisfied with the *milk* given to me because I wasn't ready for the *solid food* that Paul spoke about in 1 Corinthians 3:2-4. Similarly, I was happy with the *Apollos* I found in priests, parish leaders, choirs, and other ministry groups. It provided spiritual milk that sustained:

- my unformed faith with my self-serving activities in the parish;
- the limited charity I performed; and
- my small joy in the many gifts I received from God (because they were never enough and I was soon asking for more).

Visible signs of faith

When I drank only spiritual milk, I kept looking for visible signs, hoping to witness an occasional miracle or God's intervention in my life or the life of my family and friends. On an everyday level, I also wanted to see an increase in parish numbers, but only with people of the right type. In the church ministries where I served, I expected my brothers and sisters to be pleasant, kind, and considerate to enable the parish to become a place of peace and genuine worship (if only I'd known what true religion meant). This was why I avoided *church politics* and was quick to condemn anything I felt was spiritually insincere or hypocritical.

This made me petty.

The wailing, ringing, or beeping distractions of handphones during solemn celebrations never ceased to annoy me. I didn't want to excuse latecomers for disturbing my experience of the sacred, as though I was paying 100% attention to what was going on at Mass.

I looked the other way, not wanting to borrow trouble when I saw arguments in the car park immediately after Mass.

I wanted everything about my religious experience to be peachy and *just so*. Sadly, this proved the shallowness of my faith. When I returned home from a pilgrimage or after watching a good movie like *The Passion of the Christ*, I was filled with strong religious feelings for the Lord. Such feelings were, however, fragile. Anyone touching a nerve would disrobe my faith that's still without a wedding dress. Sadly, I didn't recognize then how limited my faith was. If the Lord didn't give me victory, His help or a sparkling sign of faith, I allowed my faith to flag and decrease.

It was the same during my travels around Europe. Until I was distracted by the discovery of a new place to eat or drink, the many undeniable signs of faith delighted me:

- Incorrupt remains of St. Bernadette.
- The inexplicable miracles of healing attributed to Mary's shrine in Lourdes.
- Martyred Christians in the Colosseum and elsewhere who became a sign that eventually converted the Roman Empire. It wasn't just the wholesale killing of our Lord, the Apostles, other leaders, and martyrs that impressed me, but also the Faith managing to survive many centuries of persecution, in its early days, as a bizarre, cannibalistic sect.

Back home, when I came across a historical reference in the Bible, such as Nebuchadnezzar, I delved into my books, looking for evidence that the sacred scripture was grounded in history. When searching for the historical basis of the Church and the Bible, I felt the miraculous foundation of the Church was evident in the warning given by Gamaliel to the Sanhedrin. This Elder advised his peers in these terms: ". . . keep away from these men and let them alone; for if this plan or this undertaking is of men, it will fail; but if it is of God, you will not be able to overthrow them. You might even be found opposing God!" (The Acts of the Apostles 5:38-39) The works of men always break up of their own accord, typically in three generations as some sayings attest. But if the inspiration for the Church is God, the enterprise will be unbreakable. Why? To break an enterprise inspired by God, *man* has to fight the Lord, and no *man* can win such a battle. So I bolstered my faith with the enduring two-thousand-year history of the Church, merely noting the incessant persecution and killing of its founder, nearly all the Apostles, and untold numbers of holy men and women.

Such evidence of faith comforted me in those earlier days.

Suffering, strengthening, singing praise

For a time, I was happy to mouth the usual words to praise the Lord for all the good things and blessings He showers in my life. You've read the account of my academic failure transformed into an unimaginable, if not miraculous, vocation of law. I got what I wanted and that made it easy to thank the Lord for the favor He granted me. Then there were the droughts, famines, and tragedies that prompted me to question His silence.

When I despaired the amputation of my married body, I cried in my heart:

"Where *is* my God?"

"What *has* happened to my joy of fatherhood?"

"Where's my bliss of life together?"

The Lord seemed unwilling to intervene in any choice that was empty of love, in the disfigurement of the marriage sign, and in the ensuing crisis of my faith. I hoped in vain for positive help from the Lord and failed to see the Lord slowly, but amazingly, converting my heart.

How did the Lord do this work of conversion? I'm convinced the Lord took pity on the tragedy unfolding in my life and helped in my inadequate spiritual training. My Savior inserted me into an ecclesial community and took my faith formation to a higher ground. Over the years following the failure of my marriage, my inner turmoil slowly lessened. Little by little, He strengthened my faith—accompanying me through the raging seas onto dry land.

I began to hear His voice more clearly through the study and celebration of the Word in my community of faith. I grew conscious of the Spirit whispering to my heart: *Hope in God; praise Him still.* Gently, He helped me believe in the power of prayer. With my faith strengthening, I then accepted the necessary suffering in my life.

Who could have come to the aid of my broken spirit, except the Lord as He has promised? I certainly couldn't have done this on my own strength. I've been journeying twelve years with my community of faith. The shepherds guiding us offer faith formation that's bringing me deeper into the heart of the Faith.

What had I hoped to see on my journey of faith at the outset: a man wearing fine clothes?

The Lord is faithful indeed, and I testify to this. He is gradually remaking me into a likeness that resembles His image. (Colossians 3:10)

Along this narrow path, I'll have to continue rejecting the Accuser. This Adversary keeps telling me that there's no hope from a God who claims to love me. The Beguiler rails that God has done nothing to give me what I want, seemingly giving me unbearable suffering, losses, and failure. I now possess a little more strength to remain constant and reject the falsehood that I have options: to stop wasting my life, to change my history by taking another wife, or forging another fatherhood.

Yes, I've learned from Psalm 42 to *put my hope in God: I shall praise him yet, my Savior, my God.*

Through the hard work of my catechists as faithful servants of Christ, I find my faith maturing. Without flinching now, I can grasp and accept the stark message of deliverance in Habakkuk 3:17-19:

> Though the fig tree does not blossom,
> nor fruit be on the vines,

the produce of the olive fail
and the fields yield no food,
the flock be cut off from the fold
and there be no herd in the stalls,

yet I will rejoice in the LORD,
I will joy in the God of my salvation.
GOD, the Lord, is my strength;
he makes my feet like hinds' feet,
he makes me tread upon my high places.

The suffering in my life has strengthened the seed of faith planted by the Lord. The Lord has been with me all this time, helping me like a gardener tenderly nursing a barren fig tree, which is what I am.

QUESTIONS FOR REFLECTION ON CHAPTER 16

1. Do you reject suffering?
2. Do you ask God to take away the suffering in your life? Did God answer your prayer?
3. Have you questioned why God allows *good* people to suffer and the *bad* to escape suffering?
4. Have you taken for granted His gift of life to you, in a today filled with sunshine, rain, and every possibility for you to bear fruit?
5. How have you responded to the many other gifts received in your life (e.g. love of your family, work, freedom, peace in your country, etc.)?

Section VIII

"Look After My Sheep"

17. Appeal to Andre the Churchgoer

In this Chapter, I'm reaching out to members of the second group of archetypes. They *are* regular churchgoers. Some also help run the ministries that serve the parish.

To make this discussion easier, I'll refer to each believer in this group as Andre, reminding you that I was an Andre in the early years of my journey of faith. Andre, I've no doubt you're sincerely faithful. Yet, as you'll note from my account in Part 1, I didn't know what Christian life resembled or required, even though I was active in church.

If you're living your life according to the Gospel, this Section isn't relevant to you. If, however, you're not sure about the Christian life you ought to have, I urge you to read on.

In writing this appeal to Andre to consider faith formation, I need to pose two questions:

- Are you aware of your vocation as a priest, prophet, and king?
- Do you know what Jesus requires you to be and to do as His follower?

For the sake of Andre's eternal happiness, I'm going to set out what I've learned about the vocation, mission, and service required of every Christian. I write this hoping you'll realize your position in the spiritual race St. Paul spoke about. If you're still on the starting blocks (or nowhere near the spiritual track and field), please take action today to avoid being left behind—like the bridesmaid without any oil.

Knowingly, actively celebrating the Eucharist

Let's start by stating the obvious. The Eucharist holds a central place in Christian life. Given the fundamental significance of this sacrament, I worry whether Andre understands enough to celebrate in the right spirit.

Many believers think all that's needed to be a good Christian is attending the Eucharist. By doing this one important thing, they feel they're leading a Christian life. Put the other way round, Andre might have little or no Christian life outside Mass on Sunday.

Please don't misunderstand me. This discussion doesn't downplay the importance of the Eucharist. Instead, it recognizes the importance of the call to all Christians to live "a life worthy of the gospel of Christ." (CCC 1692; Phil 1:27) By itself, Christian life isn't about a competition in which only the highest achievers earn a place in heaven.

So I invite you to explore this topic with me to get a better understanding of the Christian life that's so important to the faith we profess.

Source and Summit

Why is the Eucharist so important to Christians? The Catechism of the Catholic Church tells us the celebration of the Eucharist, usually called the Mass, is the source and summit of the Christian life. (CCC 1324) It's important to Christians because we give thanks to God, remembering the perfect sacrifice of the Lamb of God, Jesus Christ, and draw life from the Lord. (John 6:51-58) At the Eucharist, the People of God come together to praise and worship, and are united with heaven.

Sunday Mass

In the Church, Sunday is the foremost day of obligation with churchgoers regularly attending the Eucharist or Mass. Beginning with the preceding evening, Sunday is also prescribed as the day on which we celebrate the paschal mystery. (CCC 2177) Given it's the Lord's day of rest, we're obliged to rest, together with the Lord and His Body, the Church.

Fully aware

Even though Andre may attend Mass faithfully every Sunday and on days of obligation, does he or she understand what happens during the Mass? For example, does Andre grasp the importance of the Liturgy of the Word and the Liturgy of the Eucharist?

Sacrosanctum Concilium is an important conciliar document produced by the Second Vatican Council on the Sacred Liturgy. At paragraph 11, it confirms that the liturgy only produces its full effects when the minds of the faithful match their voices. Mere attendance and participation aren't enough. That's the letter, not the spirit of the law. The congregation must be actively involved in the rite. Failure at this stage may prevent the worshippers from deriving any benefit from the divine grace. This places a heavy duty on the pastors to ensure that those assembled are fully aware of what they should be doing during Mass.

It's an alarming thought that Andre may be attending Mass, but gets no benefit because he or she doesn't understand what's going on. To avoid this, Andre should consult his or her pastor for guidance.

Active participation

At paragraph 14, *Sacrosanctum Concilium* continues talking about the Church's desire for the faithful to be active participants. Everyone should be fully aware of their role as a redeemed people in a holy nation. (1 Peter 2:9) So the Church requires all pastors to strive zealously to produce active congregations in their churches. This is not limited to the Eucharist, but applies to all activities in and around the parishes. Necessarily, pastors must consider how much more formation to offer all Christians.

Ask yourself: "Do you neglect to participate in the Eucharistic celebrations?"

If the answer to this question is, "Yes," do you suppose your faith needs learning and training?

Not anonymous

When we gather, the Church is clear we aren't an assembly of anonymous strangers, merely present as silent spectators. (*Sacrosanctum Concilium* 48) We assemble to celebrate the central mystery of our faith. We need to be active collaborators in this sacred activity.

If we are to be active, we need a good understanding of the rites and prayers. We also need to know what we're doing so that our celebration joins us together as God's chosen people.

Sacred Liturgy not entire activity of the Church

Andre may be tempted to think that the Sacred Liturgy is all that the People of God do. In fact, there are six other sacraments essential to our Christian life:

- Baptism;
- reconciliation;
- confirmation;

- marriage;
- Holy Orders; and
- Anointing of the Sick.

So how does Andre live a full Christian life? If you've been trying to figure out what you need to be and to do as a Christian, please read on.

Beyond Baptism, for those who already believe, the Church teaches all Christians, ". . . to observe all that Christ has commanded." Such teaching reinforces the need for obedience, faith, and penance. It also encourages all to remain pious, be charitable and, as apostles, become the light of the world. (*Sacrosanctum Concilium* 9) When Christians follow these commands, they glorify the Father before men.

Let's accept that Andre may be sincerely devout. Even so, this doesn't mean he or she understands the complete tenets of the Faith—what it means to be a Christian. We start with the clear reference to charity. I hope Andre is actively charitable: not just with material contributions, but also with time and self for the benefit of family, community, and society. Then there's piety: how does Andre show piety? Andre should be actively revering God, be in communion with the Lord and, because he loves God, be fulfilling his spiritual duties toward the Lord. How does Andre discover his duties? If he actively studies the Word of God, the Lord will give Andre the instructions needed to live a full Christian life. In other words, Andre needs an active Christian life beyond devotion.

There's more: what *is* the work of a disciple? It's assuming the duty entrusted by Christ to His disciples to communicate the love of God to an unbelieving world. Remember, Baptism makes us today's disciples. As lay apostles, we're the ones tasked by the Lord to do the work of communication. This challenges those who prefer remaining passive. If asked, they justify their failure to act by claiming the responsibility of proclaiming the good tidings falls on the Church. I hope you aren't one of them. The clergy and the religious have never been solely responsible for announcing the Good News.

Do you remember, in the Preface, I asked who the *Church* is to you? The Church is you and I! If we ignore our duty as lay apostles, who will be sent to share the Good News that God wishes reconciliation with all peoples?

How can we not share the amazing agape we've received from God?

How can we not struggle in the face of persecutions, rejections, and doors clanged shut, all in union with our crucified and risen Savior, who showed us the Way on *Via Dolorosa*?

More importantly, how do we account to God in heaven for the many people with whom we could have shared the Good News, but didn't?

How does Andre develop his or her Christian life?

We don't belong to this world. (John 15:19) We're merely passing through, with many opportunities to exercise our freedom according to the will of God. At the end of our life, we surrender ourselves to the Lord's judgment and mercy. While living out the precious time we've left, the Word and the Catechism can:

- help us understand our belief;
- prompt us to do the will of God; and
- develop our spiritual life so that we're filled with love and obedience.

How does the Church help Andre develop his or her Christian life? Let's examine what needs to happen:

> While not being formally identified with them, catechesis is built on a certain number of elements of the Church's pastoral mission which have a catechetical aspect, that pre-

> pare for catechesis, or spring from it. They are: the *initial proclamation of the Gospel or missionary preaching* to *arouse faith*; *examination* of the *reasons for belief*; *experience* of *Christian living*; *celebration* of the *sacraments*; *integration* into the *ecclesial community*; and *apostolic and missionary witness*. (Emphasis added) (CCC 6)

The Church makes it clear that all of us need lifelong Christian education or faith formation! With our faith formed well, we can attain a full Christian life. We do this by:

- celebrating the sacraments every day;
- living our Christian life in communion with our brothers and sisters in ecclesial communities; and
- responding to our vocation as witnesses for the Lord.

With the love of God *in our heart*, we're then able to venture out like missionaries, explaining the reasons for our belief and communicating our hope so that others may inquire about our faith. By being open, we'll eventually become role models and share the experience of living as a Christian. This confirms that, by joining the Church through our baptism, we became jointly responsible for delivering God's message of love.

In ancient times, this message was hidden from the world. Then God sent Jesus to reveal the truth to all humanity. At first, only the saints heard the Good News. Now it's our turn to bring the Good News of God's love to those in the world today still without hope. We (and not someone else) have the responsibility for proclaiming the Good News to everyone, making all perfect when they recognize Christ is among us. This reflects St. Paul's promise that, when we live our life rooted in Christ, our understanding can develop to the point where we really know God's secret. (Colossians 1:25-29;2:2-3;6-8)

Obviously, we can't fulfill our mission if our faith isn't formed well, especially if we aren't living a life according to the Good

News. So are you surprised that all Christians need to live a full Christian life or announce the Good News? That just a few hours on Sunday, within the four corners of the church building, doesn't make up our Christian life? If you're surprised, read again paragraph 6 of the Catechism of the Catholic Church quoted above.

In your defense, you might say, "Although I've welcomed Jesus Christ in my life through baptism, I haven't yet received enough training of my heart and so can't live my whole life according to Christ." If this were your response, I'd say, "Praise the Lord," and urge you to take courage. It isn't too late to knock on the doors of your church and gradually learn how to live a full Christian life.

You are an apostolic and missionary witness!

Priest, prophet, and king

The Church helps us recognize that we, the laity, make up the People of God and the Body of Christ. When we entered the faith through baptism, we received a share in the Lord's priestly, prophetic and kingly office. (CCC 783) This means every Christian bears the joint responsibility for mission work and the services flowing from it.

What then are the mission work and the service of a Christian? Before the contents page, I offered the definition in Matthew 16:24. The First Letter of Peter also tells us plainly that Christ left an example for every Christian to follow the way he took. (2:21)

This is, however, just scratching the surface. There's a greater depth to the spiritual job description for all Christians.

Service & Mission

It begins by being and doing more than the Christians who only attend Mass on Sundays and other days of obligations. Remember the label, "Sunday Christians," is a byword for ignorance or indifference. For every day of our life, we *are* to be priests, prophets and kings with a mission to serve our Lord, who is the only true priest. (CCC 1545)

Our priestly office

Lumen Gentium, also known as the Dogmatic Constitution, is the keystone of all the conciliar documents that emerged from the Second Vatican Council. Paragraph 10 sheds more light on our common priesthood, saying that the anointing of the Holy Spirit consecrates each baptized Christian. This gives each Christian the right and duty to offer spiritual sacrifices such as praise, worship, and service. All Christians should proclaim God, who has called us out of the darkness and into the light.

No matter where we go, we *are* disciples. We're obliged to bear witness to Christ. Should anyone ask, we should explain our hope of eternal life.

We don't, of course, have the privileges of ordained priests to dispense the sacraments. Instead, as members of the laity and the common priesthood, we share the all-important mission of bringing the Gospel to the places where we live, work, and play.

Do we understand and possess the Gospel?

During the week, do we study the Word?

Do we also have a relationship with the Lord through daily prayer in quiet time?

There'll also be occasions for our priestly sacrifice by way of our love, charity, and self-denial. We love by giving ourselves entirely for the benefit of the other, without condition or expectation. Jesus puts this person in front of us to love, and he or she could be a neighbor or the least of His brothers or sisters.

How many of us have prepared ourselves to live in this Christian dimension?

Our role as prophets

Lumen Gentium tells us that by becoming a living witness to Him and establishing a regular spiritual life, we're also prophets. (12) Once enrolled as a member of the People of God, we can't waver in our belief. Our obedience to the living Word of God needs to be absolute. From the Bishops down to the ordinary members of the lay faithful, the application of the Faith should be steady, with morals unwavering in our life.

Like the prophets of old, we can't pick and choose what to believe. The Faith comes as a single package! Ask yourself:

"Do you have trouble accepting any teaching of the Lord?"

"Do you have difficulty practicing any of His commandments?"

If you have, take courage. This just means you need faith training or more of it. All of us need the grace of God to understand and do His will.

What if you're already busy serving in a ministry within the church—are you excused from learning? No, you're not exempt. As you'll see when we reach Chapter 22, I refer to St. John Paul II's exhortation at paragraph 47 of the *Catechesi Tradendae,* where he gives strong advice to all church groups not to neglect the study of the Faith.

Our kingly office

Lumen Gentium describes how Jesus communicated a royal power to His disciples so that, by being truly penitent and living a holy life, they might conquer the reign of sin in themselves. (36) In turn, this power is shared with us. If we serve Christ with humility and patience, we can lead our brothers and sisters to the King of Kings. The Lord wants to spread the Faith through the laity to establish a kingdom of truth.

What's the truth?

That Jesus is the Christ, and He is, ". . . the way, the truth, and the life. . .". (John 14:6)

This third office we share with Jesus requires us to show leadership by living a holy life, not according to anyone else's expectations but as best we can. Through the example of our life and our commitment to God, we lead others to Jesus Christ. So the Lord saves every believer who is willing to listen to Him. This tells us we can't stay passively in a room or building. We should go out like our Lord, from one village to the next.

What if you're having difficulty serving your kingly office or offering spiritual leadership? Take courage. You need help first. What help do you need? Read the next Chapter.

More than Sunday Christians

In this Chapter, Scripture and the documents published by the Second Vatican Council remind us that we are to be Christians praising, serving, and loving beyond worship on Sundays and other days of obligation. Each of us needs to live a Christian life outside the church building as well. This is the deeper facet of the Eucharist we need to grasp.

Do you recall the concluding words said by the presiding priest at Mass? You sometimes hear, "Go in peace," but there are other forms, which reveal the true nature of the *dismissal*:

- "Go and announce the Gospel of the Lord."
- "Go in peace, glorifying the Lord by your life."

The forms of dismissal tell us that we've heard the Good News, and Mass doesn't end there. We need to continue after Mass by communicating and sharing what we've received and learned from the Lord—as I'm sharing the *hope* with you in this book.

The Second Vatican Council has advised the breadth of Christian life and vocation beyond Mass and outside the parish on Sunday. We shouldn't continue imagining that the responsibilities of the apostolic mission, witness, and service belong solely to the priests and the religious (as I did in my earlier journey of faith). If we're still neglecting our lay apostolate, we ought to reassess our Christian life and commitment to our Redeemer.

We should struggle to do more for the sake of piety and love of

God because He has given us the Good News at great cost to His Beloved. All sinners are truly precious in the eyes of God because Jesus suffered and died for His great mission to give everyone a priceless opportunity to be saved. We share the important offices of priest, prophet, and king graciously with Christ himself; as such, full Christian lives are needed for every believer. If any of us lacks the time or energy for the Lord, we should perhaps read Chapter 19 about the lukewarm Christian.

If, however, we recognize our poor Christian life or the ignorance of our vocation as priests, prophets, and kings, it's never too late to ask the Church for catechesis and formation. I'm convinced that the New Evangelization must begin with the faith renewal of all within the Church. Why? Because a fervent and full mission awaits every believer as a sweet offering of thanksgiving to our Redeemer. We belong to Jesus, are the Body of Christ, and serve together with our Lord in His loving plan for those in the world still searching for meaning, hope, and love.

All believers should consider the fruit of their faith. If there's none, everyone should gather their courage and take immediate steps to rediscover their baptism.

QUESTIONS FOR REFLECTION ON CHAPTER 17

1. Do you attend Mass (or Eucharistic celebration or worship service) with your community?
2. Do you have a sense of community in the church you attend?
3. Do you understand what goes on at Mass?
4. Do you serve inside and outside your church?
5. Do you have an active Christian life outside the church, beyond Sundays? What is your Christian life?
6. Is the homily given at Mass the primary source of your faith education?
7. If the homily isn't the primary source of your faith education, how do you broaden and deepen the education of your heart on a continuing basis?
8. Do you have a pastor (or priest) monitoring the flowering of your faith?
9. Are you actively fulfilling your lay apostolate for the love of Jesus Christ?

18. Is a Faith Journey a New Idea?

We now come to exchange ideas on a faith journey that seems old but is actually timeless in our faith. When the Lord called our Jewish brethren to leave Egypt, they followed Him on a journey. It lasted forty years, during which He taught them His ways. Taking the same spiritual path less traveled, today's believers are invited to leave our Egypt and follow our Lord because He will teach us His ways and transform our heart. I'm on such a path, and it's my hope that the Lord will change my heart. So this journey doesn't belong to the past. It's relevant today, i.e. the Word of God has life and our God isn't just of the dead, but also of the living. (Matthew 22:32) A fresh journey is still being offered to every believer, today.

Of course, rather than a reference to a country in Northeast Africa, Egypt is a metaphor for all that enslaves us spiritually. The slavery usually shows itself as a disordered life in which attractions or distractions lead to a more general failure to follow Jesus Christ.

Is the period of forty years relevant in today's world? Yes, of course! Our heart needs to be prepared for the trials of our faith. (1 Peter 1:7; Zechariah 13:9) We'll prove our faith over time, in the crucible of life's many tribulations, through steadfast struggling.

Indeed, a lifetime may be needed to transform believers into Christians ready and willing to love.

If we accept the Lord's invitation and begin this journey, He will do the main work of fighting the seven nations or seven deadly sins in our life. (Deuteronomy 7:1-6; Amos 1:3-15) These seven nations are larger and stronger than us, so we shouldn't be fighting them on our own. We can, however, survive everything that happens during this journey if we trust in the Lord completely.

When Jesus invites us to follow Him, where do you suppose the Lord will lead us? He wishes to free every believer from all types of slavery and speak to our heart in the spiritual desert, a place where only His voice can be heard.

As a topic, slavery is complex, so I'm only going to touch on it generally where it concerns the Christian life and the need for faith formation. I hope this Chapter will prompt you to think about whether there's slavery in your life and, if so, encourage you to begin the spiritual journey.

The Lord calls us out of Egypt

There's no need to "look" for the Lord

For a long time, I thought I should search for my Lord among the poor and the disadvantaged. I've since learned there's no need to search for Him. St. Paul confirms that God is with us here and now. (Romans 10:5-13) It's pointless to beg Him to come down from heaven—He is already here. We waste our time searching for Jesus in the underworld—He is already risen. If we don't feel His presence in our life, it might be that we lack faith.

If our heart believes, He is near us.

When we confess the Faith in our heart, He will save us.

The Lord comes to meet us!

God didn't limit His activities to the past. The Bible records the many occasions on which our predecessors-in-faith encountered the Lord. What's the celebration of Christmas, if not joy at the first coming of our Savior—the Word "made flesh"? (John 1:14)

He didn't stop visiting the faithful when the Bible had been written. The Lord continues to meet us today. He is with us every day of our life, everywhere, when at least two or three are gathered in His name to praise, worship, and pray. (Matthew 18:20) Think also of the Lord coming to invite each of us and all mankind to enter his kingdom, "early in the morning," at the "third hour," the "sixth hour," the "ninth hour," and the "eleventh hour." (Matthew 20:1-16)

If there's still doubt whether the Lord is with us, remember what Jesus said: ". . . and lo, I am with you always, to the close of the age." (Matthew 28:20)

Modern slavery

Some Christians don't feel like slaves. They're leading seemingly happy and contented lives with no obvious pharaoh tormenting or overseers literally whipping them, so they doubt the need for God's help. It would be different if the metaphor of Egypt was real for them, but they have grown so used to their enslavement, they misunderstand the idea of slavery.

What's the misunderstanding? It usually flows from underestimating or dismissing the power of the capital sins or *nations*. We should list them again: pride, greed, envy, anger, lust, gluttony, and sloth. Is it too medieval or just inappropriate to talk about sin in today's secular world? I think not. These seven sins continue to enslave and oppress many of us, every day. You don't think so?

For this exchange of ideas, I'll address two themes, e.g. the worker and hunger. This is the age of science and enlightenment:

- humanity has made incredible leaps in scientific achievement;

- the internet has made information widely available and opened up myriad kinds of access to so many that the world is said to be a smaller place; and
- more nations are cooperating and assisting each other than in the past.

We'd like to think slavery has been vanquished because so many societies boast of their progressive thinking. Some of us suppose food is plentiful because we find it available everywhere in our successful *modern* economies. So how can slavery and hunger be relevant to Christians in today's world?

Let's begin with a look at workers in the bustling and prosperous cities. How many of us have personally groaned in our encounters with injustice or heard weeping cries in our workplace for being forced to work excessive hours or meet oppressive deadlines? Do we quickly forget the warring factions in the office? Do we turn our eyes and ears away from the backstabbing, petty gossip, or unjust whispers that seem *utterly* necessary to ensure survival and promotion, or advance career prospects at the expense of others?

Now think about some business owners and major stockholders in corporations. Could they be the New Pharaohs in today's world? I hope I won't be misunderstood. I'm sure many business leaders, owners and investors are socially responsible. They reward their employees, invest in local communities, and limit the environmental impact of their activities. Instead, I'm asking:

- Do you have any personal experience with an employer that has lost its moral compass or deceived the public?
- Does short-term thinking and profit-maximization cause the enslavement you've experienced because management thinks it's acceptable to squeeze profits out of you and your co-workers?

If the answer to these questions is, "Yes," you might be a metaphorical slave in New Egypt with the New Pharaohs acting in the same way as the slave masters of old. Yes, their appearances have certainly changed, but they *are* slave masters if they maximize profits by cutting human costs to the bone without counting the moral price.

Looking around the world, do we not hear the cries of 168 million children, who are without textbooks or a decent meal? Many of these children find themselves forced to work in sweatshops by business owners who callously cut corners every which way they can. Children are the ideal slaves because they have little or no say about their rights or entitlements. These New Pharaohs take advantage of conditions of abject poverty by exploiting the cheap, mute labor to maximize profits.

Do we also forget the millions of other workers without rights or entitlements, who grind the hours daily in a nondescript factory for a dollar—a slave's wage?

Why are the laborers oppressed? Should the suffering of the workers be none of our concern?

Moving on to hunger: why are a billion souls not eating well, when so many of us exchange pictures of our food and have portions so large, we can't eat it all?

A new version of Egypt is all around us, i.e. not so far away that we can avert our gaze. It's also in our homes, schools, and cities. Yet too many of the faithful have become blind or desensitized to the oppression they're experiencing, or to the silent cries of their neighbors near home and those abroad. They celebrate their presumed freedom by filling their bellies with fish, cucumbers, melons, leeks, onions, and garlic. These material benefits should not seduce us. We should open our eyes. But the reasons for not leaving New Egypt or not following the Lord are the same today as they were thousands of years ago.

The slaves have adapted to their enslavement—they're unable or reluctant to change. This makes "New Pharaoh" a metaphor for greed, oppression, and fear in a place where slavery for many is the norm. I should remind you that these metaphors don't just apply to owners and their workers. An individual can be a slave (or victim) to any of the capital sins.

Before going further, I should make clear that it isn't my intention to oversimplify the moral discussion about slave wages, oppressed labor, or unjust hunger. While it's clear that actual and spiritual slaveries do exist in their many forms, a worker might be genuinely happy to work for a dollar-a-day because there's no other work in his or her town, and a dollar might fetch far more in that economy than it would in ours. Competition in a capitalist system is often healthy because it helps corporations innovate and encourages the workers to give their best work. As for the problem of hunger, it may be that businesses, agencies, or charitable organizations haven't yet found viable pathways or processes to distribute food to every corner of the world.

That said, I'm using the themes of slavery and hunger to discuss our spiritual life, asking what difficulties a Christian faces in New Egypt.

- That we're unwilling to begin considering or examining the slavery in our life. Listen to the complaint some Israelites made to Moses while he was working hard to arrange for Israel's exodus from Egypt: ". . . you have made us offensive in the sight of Pharaoh and his servants, and have put a sword into their hand to kill us." (Exodus 5:21) Instead of being grateful for the chance to escape the obvious slavery, they preferred to put up with it. Are we slaves of sorts? If so, are we all for not rocking the boat?
- Inertia holds some believers as slaves. Over time, they have grown used to the devil they know and accept the disorder, torment, and oppression, i.e. some slavery can be bearable with attractions or distractions to take their mind off the actual or subtle slavery in their life. The problem with this attitude is that these believers forget life on earth is temporary. In the struggle to find earthly happiness, they forget eternal happiness until it's too

late. They then lose the opportunity to prepare themselves for the life with Christ here and beyond.

- Having grown used to our own enslavement, we're probably desensitized to the reality of our neighbor's slavery. So we fail to see the countless weak and defenseless who can barely keep alive or get by. Are the marginalized and downtrodden in our neighborhood as well? If we have our eyes wide open, we'd see them, these slaves trapped in New Egypt, but we might be spiritually numb to the enslavement of our neighbors.
- That we're not willing to trust in the Lord. When Moses finally persuaded the people to leave, this was their unkind response to the first sign of trouble: ". . . Is it because there are no graves in Egypt that you have taken us away to die in the wilderness? . . . Is not this what we said to you in Egypt, 'Let us alone and let us serve the Egyptians'? For it would have been better for us to serve the Egyptians than to die in the wilderness." (Exodus 14:11-13) Fear is a strong emotion. It's so strong that it may blind some of us to the awesome help offered by the Lord, as seen in the exodus from Egypt. How many of us continue to serve the New Egyptians? Only those who are able to trust in the Lord for everything that happens in our life cast out fear.

Why should we leave New Egypt and follow the Lord? Because He is the Savior of the World, of course. When we enter the spiritual desert, He will affirm our identity as sons and daughters of God, as He did for Himself during His forty days in the desert. He has triumphed over death and suffering, and He wants to help us triumph as well. These are sound reasons for following the Lord and learning His ways in the spiritual desert; assuming, of course, that our heart believes in the Lord and everything the Bible says.

New Egypt in technology

In the last few decades, humanity has made incredible strides to make the benefits of the world accessible to more people. In this, the uses of technology are too many to count, but include the power of the internet to magnify creativity, increasing productivity by leaps and bounds, and empowering even the disadvantaged through social networking. We'd like to think that technology has improved our lives, and it has.

On a personal level, my mother in Singapore could Skype me in New York, and we're delighted to talk from opposite sides of the Pacific Ocean.

Having said that, many users are at fault in our use of technology. New Egypt lurks in the stream of consciousness that technology makes possible. Instead of spending time nurturing face-to-face relationships, we feel obliged to make instant links and connections. As addicts, many of us distract ourselves from what should be important in the here and now. We've become slaves to the siren song of our laptops, the demanding ringtones of our smartphones, and the insistent beeps from our other communication devices.

On the darker side of the internet, there's torment, confidence schemes, and harm perpetrated by bullies, tricksters, and predators. We shouldn't forget the modern mongers of bigotry and false facts that sow their wicked agenda among the innocent and gullible; especially as the young haven't been properly trained to use technology.

We think of zombies and mind-robbing aliens as subjects for horror films, but the truth is that the New Pharaoh is anything or anyone who's already enslaved the minds of inexperienced, vulnerable or gullible online visitors and users of technology. We also see his slaves mindlessly killing time on game Apps; walking and texting on the streets, but not looking where they're going; and driving, but dangerously not keeping their eyes on the roads. The pretense of life in social communications has similarly stolen our attention in the conjugal bedroom, at our family dining tables, in the pews, and when we meet real people. Even when our family and friends are by our side, we give our attention to cyberspace at their expense. The joy of warm conversation and togetherness *is* becoming a faint memory for some.

Why did God come to give Himself to Man?

The following passages from the Catechism of the Catholic Church teach us why our God comes to give Himself to us:

> 50 By natural reason man can know God with certainty, on the basis of his works. But there is another order of knowledge, which man cannot possibly arrive at by his own powers: the order of divine Revelation. Through an utterly free decision, God has revealed himself and given himself to man. This he does by revealing the mystery, his plan of loving goodness, formed from all eternity in Christ, for the benefit of all men. God has fully revealed this plan by sending us his beloved Son, our Lord Jesus Christ, and the Holy Spirit.
>
> 68 By love, God has revealed himself and given himself to man. He has thus provided the definitive, superabundant answer to the questions that man asks himself about the meaning and purpose of his life.
>
> 69 God has revealed himself to man by gradually communicating his own mystery in deeds and in words.
>
> 70 Beyond the witness to himself that God gives in created things, he manifested himself to our first parents, spoke to them and, after the fall, promised them salvation (cf Genesis 3:15) and offered them his covenant.
>
> 71 God made an everlasting covenant with Noah and with all living beings (cf Genesis 9:16). It will remain in force as long as the world lasts.
>
> 72 God chose Abraham and made a covenant with him and his descendants. By the covenant God formed his people and revealed his law to them through Moses. Through the prophets, he prepared them to accept the salvation destined for all humanity.

> 73 God has revealed himself fully by sending his own Son, in whom he has established his covenant for ever. (T)he Son is his Father's definitive Word; so there will be no further Revelation after him.

Many of us are searching for the meaning and purpose in our life. Look no further—the Word of God contains all we need to know about the most important truth! Through the Word, God wishes to teach us His ways, which will give us *life*—through an authentic and active relationship with the Lord.

What will the Lord do in the journey of faith?

The Word in the Book of Deuteronomy reminds us that the Lord led the people into the wilderness and kept them there for forty years. (8:2-6) This was a humbling experience. It also gave the people an opportunity to know their inmost heart: "Know then in your heart that, as a man disciplines his son, the LORD your God disciplines you. So you shall keep the commandments of the LORD your God, by walking in his ways and by fearing him."

In today's journey, Jesus offers knowledge of salvation. (Matthew 11:28-30) If we walk with the Lord and put our trust in Him, we'll learn the path to life. We'll also *discover* our *inmost heart*: whether we truly love God and our neighbor.

How do we learn from God? By allowing the Lord to teach us through the Word.

How can we begin this learning? By following Him on a journey of faith!

The Lord fights our battles

The Lord reassures us that He will lead us in all our struggles and difficulties.

In practical terms, what does *fleeing* from our New Egypt involve? Rather than requiring a major reorganization of our life, it begins with a symbol. No physical journey is required—not just yet—the first change to be made is the spiritual decision to turn to the Lord and hope for His help. This is how we believe in Jesus Christ—not with lip service, but with a firm commitment to follow Him. Similarly, a struggle with a nation doesn't mean an actual fight with a sovereign state. We *are* to make preparations and spend real face-time with the Lord in the spiritual desert, where no communication device can distract us from listening to our Teacher or learning from Him. In this spiritual journey of faith, the Lord uses His Church and His Word to teach us.

How do we know the Mighty One of Jacob will come help us fight our battles? Moses told the people that God will be with Israel every step of the way. Just as the Lord fulfilled His promise to the Jewish people, He promises to help us too; God won't fail us or desert us in our spiritual battles. If we become disheartened, He will comfort us. (Deuteronomy 31:8)

The Lord will do the work of transformation

The Bible contains many accounts of the Lord fighting battles with and for His followers in faith. My favorite is drawn from Chapter 7 of the Book of Judges. Gideon, the judge, was to lead an army of thirty-two thousand to confront the army of Midian. In ancient battles, the largest army generally won. When more people enlist, it's easier for soldiers to believe they can win the fight and return home safely. Yet before battle was joined, the Lord instructed Gideon to allow everyone who was frightened to go home. This reduced the ranks to ten-thousand. There's something odd with the Lord's military strategy! The Lord, however, decided that ten-thousand was still too many to confront the Midians. In the end, Gideon led three-hundred onto the battlefield. They didn't even carry weapons. All they had were horns, empty jars, and torches, but trusting the Lord had their backs. That, so few faced the massed ranks of Midian allowed the world to see the power of the Lord. It also highlights the faith of Gideon and the men who obeyed the Lord's commands!

With God on our side, we win our battles, no matter how fearsome the enemy may seem.

When we read the Bible and see how many battles were fought, it's tempting to think God loved war and wanted to spill the blood of His enemies. Yet that's to misunderstand why so many accounts of battles were included.

The Word teaches us that the Lord will fight our battles (including the war against sin), if only we would put our trust in Him! A mere three-hundred unarmed men seem terribly weak against an army of enemy warriors, but with His strength, we can fight the seven nations in our life.

Why will the Lord fight our battles? He knows these nations or sins are larger and stronger than us. We need His help because every heart has the potential to be rebellious, unfaithful, or frightened. Doubts in our heart make it difficult to trust in the Lord, learn from Him, and convert.

Now come the essence of the biblical message in the battle against Midian. As the three-hundred walking out onto the battlefield with Gideon were forced to admit, they couldn't claim credit for the victory! The Lord will fight for us in a way that makes it impossible for us to claim the win for ourselves. There's no room for pride. Humility's the only requirement. We'll always have to acknowledge His help, particularly when it comes to the major battles to convert or transform our heart.

The Lord will fight our battles if only we let Him.

At this point, we should look back at the Letter to the Ephesians. (2:7-10) The Word proclaimed by St. Paul reiterates the same message: we can neither earn the free gift of salvation nor *claim the credit* for our own salvation.

Do we do nothing?

Even though the Lord will fight our battles, this doesn't mean we can passively accept the benefit of His help. Remember Gideon and the three-hundred had to step onto the battlefield against the army of Midian. They didn't remain in the safety of a building or room. They demonstrated their faith and trusted in the Lord by obeying His command to march out.

Naturally, it seemed scary to confront a great army, but they knew the Lord was on their side. He had fulfilled His promises to the people of Israel many times before, and there was no reason then to doubt the Lord's promises.

We live in a world surrounded by troubles and difficulties. Doing nothing is definitely discouraged. We need to remain vigilant against attacks by the Accuser. This Enemy tempts the weaker members of our Church and mocks our Creator for allowing the suffering, tragedy, and calamity to continue in this world.

Yes, our Lord promises to fight for us. If only we would believe this truth in our *inmost heart*, but how difficult this is for many of us who waver and doubt! To win the battles against sin, which gives us troubles and difficulties, we should want to be one of the three-hundred and be seen to step out onto the battlefield of our life!

How do we become one of the three-hundred? The first of three steps to take is to believe in the Lord and follow Him.

Following our Lord and trusting in Him, we take the second step to remove ourselves from the things or places that enslave us. When the Lord came to the aid of our Jewish brothers and fought the battles against Pharaoh, He needed His people to move out of Egypt. Moses said to the people, "Remember this day, in which you came out from Egypt, out of the house of bondage, for by strength of hand the Lord brought you out from this place . . . This day you are to go forth, in the month of Abib." (Exodus 13:3-4) The Lord could have fought Pharaoh and allowed our Jewish brothers to remain in Egypt, but it was the Lord's plan that His people leave for the Promised Land.

Let's examine another Word and understand if God really wants us to do absolutely nothing. When King Jehoshaphat heard an enormous army was advancing from Edom, he issued an order that everyone in Judah should fast. A meeting was announced and every town in Judah sent representatives to seek help from the Lord. After all had assembled, the King confirmed the power of the Lord to help them. No matter what the threat, God would prevail. Then God spoke through Jahaziel and told them not to be afraid. This wasn't their battle. All they had to do was demonstrate their faith by marching out against the invaders on the following day. There would be no need to fight. They were to be present to keep faith, pay attention to the salvation God would deliver, and give witness of the Lord's mighty works!

In this battle with the army of Edom, God was with our Jewish brothers and won the battle for them. (2 Chronicles 20:2-7,14-16,17) The Lord did what He said He would do.

We need to march on with the Lord

The Lord performed a miracle by parting the sea, but he also told Moses not to lose heart. The Lord instructed Moses to tell the sons of Israel to *march on*. (Exodus 14:15-16) In the journey of faith, we should leave our New Egypt, walk with the Lord, and listen to His teaching. Do you remember the caution discussed in Chapter 14 under the Parable of the Sower, ". . . see but not perceive, and may indeed hear but not understand; lest they should turn again and be forgiven?" Jesus is also addressing Christians, telling us that we need to struggle with the Word: struggle to see, listen, and understand; and struggle to do the Lord's will. This is the third step we take when we follow the Lord on the lifelong, spiritual journey.

When times get tougher, we continue the essential spiritual struggle—we march on, without worry or doubt.

Trust in the Lord always

There's no doubt in my mind that the Lord will fight our battles. To which battles am I referring? These are the battles against the seven nations, the sins that enslave our spiritual liberty as children of God. We need to march on the journey of faith, and never lose sight of our Lord as we follow Him. Yes, all of us should turn to our Lord and trust in Him; only He can win these spiritual battles for us.

If our neighbor is still trapped in New Egypt, we could serve the Lord by passing on our hope of salvation. By doing so, our neighbor has a chance to embrace the same hope, seek the Lord's help and begin the same journey. If we're finding it difficult to follow the Lord or serve our neighbor, isn't it time to examine whether the hope of the Good News is truly in our heart?

What if we lack the strength to leave our New Egypt? Even in this struggle, we can depend on the Lord's help. Whether it's leaving New Egypt or persevering in the long march, the unchanging requirement is to have faith in our Lord.

We can never have doubts or reservations. We should never lose faith in the trials we face.

As long as we seek the Lord in daily prayer and ask for His help in our heart, He promises to help us.

Remember, don't ever doubt the Lord!

The Lord may not respond so soon. If so, we need to be relentless in our prayers and remain steadfast. Only then can we see what the Lord will do for us.

We should also be patient and humble. We ought not to think our Lord will or must fight our battle today, sooner, or in the manner of our choosing. The Mighty One chooses our journey, paths, battles, and encounters—all in His time. We should allow the Word in our daily life to form us, teaching us when to keep still, and when to move forward. This confidence should give us peace to hope in the Lord's help against the seven nations at war within us.

Let us be instructed by the Lord, learning from the same paternal caution that He gave to the children of Israel:

> Then I said to you, "Don't be in dread or afraid of them. *The LORD your God who goes before you will himself fight for you, just as he did for you in Egypt before your eyes*, and in the wilderness, where you have seen how the LORD your God bore you, as a man bears his son, in all the way that you went until you came to this place." Yet in spite of this word *you didn't believe the LORD your God*, who went before you in the way to

> seek you out a place to pitch your tents, in fire by night, to show you by what way you should go, and in the cloud by day. (Emphasis added) (Deuteronomy 1:29-33)

As a father goes in front of his children and, if necessary, fights alongside them, so God goes in front of us just as He led the faithful out of Egypt. He led them in the wilderness along the road that He chose. So, on our journey, He will go ahead, find a spiritual camping ground, and make a light so we can see our way in the darkness of our life. God will choose the path we should take.

All we need for the journey to be a success is faith in God—in our inmost heart.

Milk and solid food, Part 2

I continue my reflection on the solid food of faith from Chapter 16. My own faith has been growing slowly but steadily, because the Church is giving me faith formation on my spiritual journey.

Life isn't fair to everyone. In this, it makes no difference whether we're one of the faithful. I don't know where the notion came from that God doesn't or shouldn't allow bad things to happen to good people! Anyone can experience and need help with tragedy, injustice, and loss. Faith formation isn't an opiate with which to numb us to the pain and suffering in life. Instead, it represents the Lord's help given to those who wish to learn His love and get ready for what He has told every Christian to do.

When we have the love of the Lord in our inmost heart, it gives us courage and helps us understand our purpose in His wonderful plan.

Gradually maturing faith

As I've described in some detail in Chapter 14, my catechists have been guiding my study of the Word. Together with my brothers and sisters, I'm scrutinizing and learning the Word week in, week out. Using the parallels and footnotes found in the Jerusalem Bible,

I find, ". . . the New Testament lies hidden in the Old and the Old Testament is unveiled in the New." (CCC 129) Through the Word and the Church teachings taught gradually by my catechists, I'm reacquiring the first love for my God.

I'm thankful to appreciate His magnificent plan to save all mankind: including every sinner that was ever born and those yet to be born.

Yes, I've no doubt that our God loved the world so much that He gave us Jesus for the salvation of every soul.

When great men of faith slipped

Am I rediscovering the Faith using rose-tinted glasses?

No, I'm not.

I've learned at least four bittersweet themes showing the need for unwavering obedience and trust in God:

1. *Moses* was described as the greatest prophet of his generation. (Deuteronomy 34:10) He spoke with God face-to-face, and the Lord caused him to perform great signs and wonders in the land of Egypt. Despite his many years of faithfulness in the desert, he didn't believe the Lord could proclaim His holiness to the sons of Israel at Meribah. As a result, he wasn't allowed to enter the Promised Land. (Numbers 20:12)

2. *Samson* was Israel's strongest judge. He brought terror and laid waste to the enemies of Israel. He failed, however, to heed the Lord's command, gave away his secret, and was then shorn of his great strength. (Judges 13:5) He became an object of amusement to his enemies.

3. *David* was a great king of Israel. God called him *a man after My own heart.* He won the favor of the Lord, fearlessly slew Goliath, and acted as God had commanded him in many victorious battles. When

he became a murderous thief who *took the poor man's lamb*, he suffered the Lord's wrath through the death of his first son. (2 Samuel 12:14)

4. *Solomon* has been described as the wisest king ever. He was the builder of the Lord's temple, but he also displeased the Lord by following the idols of his foreign wives, and the Lord allowed his kingdom to be torn apart in the following generation. (1 Kings 11:9-11)

What have I learned from my study of these four predecessors-in-faith? Each of these men slipped because they lost sight of the Lord, even if it's for a short spell. Great individuals of faith were quite capable of making mistakes or experiencing moments of weakness. This realization makes me tremble because I'm a man much weaker than any of them. I'm humbled by my weak faith and this forces me to accept that I can't remain faithful by depending on my own strength and will. I'll need the brothers and sisters that He gives me. Ever striving to let the Word penetrate my heart of stone, I must see, hear, understand, and convert, for I need to acquire a humbled, contrite heart.

I must depend on the Lord for help to learn single-minded, unfaltering obedience, and trust in Him because He is the Almighty—the greatest lover.

The Lord's work of gradual transformation in me

In past Penitentials, I was conscious of the advice, "Go and sin no more." With much determination, I would try not to sin for a while, but there was a problem. I was only using my own strength!

In those days, I didn't have a steady prayer life, nor was I living a Christian life; worse still, the Word of God was completely absent from my daily routine.

Not appreciating the breadth of God's love for all mankind, I didn't realize my pride had hindered many chances for me to reconcile with my Lord of Mercy. That's why I failed to stop sinning and why each failure led to longer entanglements. Then, I stayed away from the Penitentials for a very long time. In hindsight, I realize that I needed more than just self-control. I needed to turn to the Lord and seek His help in all my fights, every day.

Why should I turn to the Lord? For the help of man isn't dependable!

This battle can only succeed when I'm in a community led by shepherds journeying with us. By praying together and scrutinizing the Word regularly with spiritual brothers and sisters, I'm allowing God's Word to penetrate my implacable heart and transform me slowly but surely. The Lord is patiently waiting for my complete cooperation to win the battle against the seven nations within me.

Now with the solid food of faith, I see a few signs in my own person. I've embarked on and will continue my journey of faith. With the Lord helping me, I've resolved not to turn back to New Egypt.

My words may seem to echo Peter's declaration: "You are the Christ . . . the Son of the living God." (Matthew 16:17) Even so, I'm still an *old man*, ever hoping for a wedding dress. According to the moral standards of the world, I should be denied entry to the wedding feast. God, however, doesn't give up on me and continues to call me to attend His Heavenly Banquet.

I know I cannot take for granted the hope that He will save me. Regardless of the hope presently in me, I have to lean on the Lord for everything. By doing so, I've made a sincere decision to follow Jesus. By following the Lord, I'm working hard to keep His word and do His will. That's why I need to renounce this world, which regularly tells me I don't deserve God's love or that my efforts to learn His ways are all a waste of time.

What's the result of this step? I'm on my way to attend the wedding feast that the Lord is preparing. However, I can't attend the wedding without a wedding dress.

What's this wedding garment that I keep referring to? It's the transformation of my heart. This should happen on the day when I'm able to love with a humbled, contrite heart. It's a feat that's only achievable with the help of the Lord.

Moving forward on this spiritual journey, I'm quite capable of willfully, negligently, or carelessly denying the Lord, as Peter once did. I can lose my spiritual footing more easily than the great men of faith I mentioned above. Israel needed forty years in the desert. Should I expect to achieve within a year, or a few years, my *metanoia*, which is the ". . . intimate and total change and renewal of all my opinions, judgments, and decisions?" (*Paenitemini,* Chapter 1, 34) No! I have to trust that the Lord's help may be given in His time, taking into account my lifetime of spiritual blindness, deafness, and rebellion.

New grace every day

Through His Word, the Lord teaches me that His grace is given every day anew.

How do I receive grace from my Lord every day? Through,

- the Eucharist;
- study of the Word;
- daily prayer; and
- communion with my brothers and sisters who are taking the same steps in the journey of faith.

This means I have to keep my eyes on the Lord throughout each new day. When others have fallen so easily, I've no doubts it'll be just as easy for me to stumble and easier still for me to return to my New Egypt.

If I *remain apart from his vine, I can do nothing and will wither.* (John 15:5-6) My ears are ready to listen to the Lord's warning and heed His advice concerning the two paths of life or death, blessing, or curse. (Deuteronomy 30:15-20)

If I don't receive His grace every day, how can I hope to grow in faith and in the love of my God? How else will I possess a closer relationship with Jesus and be transformed? Even though I haven't been receiving His grace, I won't fret. I should simply acknowledge this failing, pick myself up, and turn back to the Lord.

Doing the will of God

I also know a touch more of what St. James meant by good deeds. (James 2:14-26) My belief in the Lord is truly in my heart when I:

- keep the Word;
- carry my cross; and
- bear fruit by doing the will of my God.

The good deeds I shall do will begin the day when I can love as my Lord loves me; when I can copy and reproduce the agape that Jesus is teaching me.

So I'll shout all the louder. Yes, I dare to touch His cloak. I shall be grateful for the fallen crumbs—hoping in the Lord's mercy always—trusting that He will eventually conquer the seven nations within me and give me His peace. I desire my Lord's grace, and the teachings of the Church to renew, strengthen, and deepen my faith—hoping the treasure of Jesus Christ will grow in my earthen vessel. So I can say to my soul, ". . . put your trust in the Lord."

I sense my gradual healing from the depression I suffered. My desire grows to seek reconciliation. I can also accept my broken marriage. In this light, I won't hide but display my blighted sign, wishing to keep all my vows till there's no breath left in me.

On many occasions in the recent past, I'd set out two-by-two to proclaim the Good News to the residents of Tampines and Hougang in Singapore. Initially, I was discouraged by the rejection and shut doors, but I'm learning to be unfazed by the seventy-seven doors that won't welcome my announcement of the Good News. The Lord has slowly helped me to understand that all I do is knock on doors. Some will open. I then announce the Good News to those willing to listen. There's no burden on me to convert anyone. Instead, it's the Lord who will give faith, and He alone does the real work of conversion. When I reflected on my sharing with those listeners, I realized that the words I spoke were for my benefit and gradual transformation—I received faith as I shared it. I needn't have wondered or agonized to know if those who opened their doors understood or were moved by faith—it isn't my battle alone. If I don't announce the Good News, how else do I love my God and share His love for mankind? How else do I fulfill the necessary Christian mission: to communicate the Lord's desire for the world to be reconciled with Him?

This is my understanding of the Lord's will for me at this time.

My desire grows to obey the command of Jesus in Matthew (16:24-26) to carry my cross, follow Him, and risk my life for His sake. Isn't Jesus the Savior of the World and my Lord? It's also very tough, but I'm learning to love and accept my brothers and sisters as they are. I attribute all to the Word acting in my life.

I need *not* look elsewhere for proof of faith. With unwavering hope now in the Lord's promise to lead me, I'll hold up my limp arms and steady my trembling knees.

The Almighty has been faithful to His people Israel. The Lord has fulfilled His promise by raising Jesus, the living and eternal King from the royal line of David. With no more doubt in my heart, I trust that the Lord will continue to be faithful to me (and to you as well).

Questions for Reflection on Chapter 18

1. Are you searching for the Lord?
2. Are you searching for the meaning and purpose of your life?
3. Did the city promise so much and deliver so little to you?
4 Is the Lord calling you out of New Egypt?
5. Will you allow the Lord to lead you and fight the seven nations on your behalf?
6. On your own, are you able to discover the will of God and do it?
7. What's stopping you from trusting the Lord's plan and providence for you?

Section IX

"FEED MY SHEEP"

19. Appeal to Andreas the Lukewarm Christian

In this Chapter, I come to the third group of Christians. For ease of reference, I refer to them as Andreas. They may be occasional or part-time believers. I can write about this because, in a part of my journey of faith, I've been an Andreas. If you're Andreas, even occasionally, I hope you'll read through this Section.

When I got what I wanted from the Lord, I drifted away from His path.

Then work became too demanding and my Christian life lapsed; that's assuming, of course, a pastor could agree that I'd been living my life according to the Gospel.

When life in the parish became too disappointing, I stopped helping and stayed away.

I remember a time when I was too tired to be a Christian.

I write this appeal to you to consider a faith journey because just saying, "I believe in Jesus Christ" isn't enough. This isn't my own idea—Jesus has given unequivocal advice about following Him and we'd do well to heed it.

Before you read further, let's be clear about the continuing exchange of ideas. I'm not accusing you of any wrongdoing; I can't because I don't know what's in your heart. Even if I did, I'd have no right to judge you. No one should, except the Lord, and I believe He wants to help you, notwithstanding any past or present failure to follow Him.

You do believe in the Lord's promise of salvation; otherwise, you wouldn't be reading this book. If you don't believe in Jesus Christ or in God's justice, nothing anyone says is going to change your thinking.

The service I'm providing in this Chapter is to remind you to look into your own heart to see whether you've been producing the fruit of your belief. Again this isn't my idea—this solemn requirement stems from the Word of God on which I rely in these pages.

I'm sincerely making the case that it's difficult to be and to do as a Christian on one's own. If a believer doubts or cannot accept everything about his or her faith, it's quite possible that he or she *has never been able to study the Christian teaching deeply or has never been educated in his or her faith.* This doesn't mean it's impossible to bear fruit on a solo spiritual journey. It's just tryingly tough, which leads me to the conviction that no believer should have to plan or pursue faith development on one's own.

To help you reflect on what you should consider learning, I've put together a few excerpts of the Word of God. However, I remind you that the whole content of the Faith will need to be taught by your pastor or catechist.

Please don't be offended by this Chapter. It's easy to give into pride and anger, which tend to shut our ears and, thereafter, we can't hear what God wants to say. We grow stronger when we clearly understand the love of God. Reflecting on our spiritual strengths and weaknesses helps the process to bear fruit pleasing to God. If the advice of the Word of God in this Chapter doesn't apply to you, you can sigh in relief. Continue marching on your serious journey of faith and allow the Lord to go on helping you. If the injunction does apply to you, I hope you'll take the necessary steps to allow the Lord to begin speaking to your heart.

You may say you love Jesus Christ. The Word of God tells us that to honor the Lord with lip service simply isn't enough: does your heart truly love the Lord and everything that He teaches you? (Matthew 15:8) To change your life, you should do what Jesus Christ tells you (and the rest of us included). Only then can He transform your heart on a journey of faith. The question for every believer is whether he or she is ready to cooperate with God.

To help Andreas decide, I'll share with you what I've learned about the fruit of a Christian. After reading this Chapter and finding yourself with questions or doubts, I hope you'll consult your pastor.

Does our Christian life bear fruit?

At the beginning of Part 2, in Chapter 14, I passed on an important piece of advice from the Lord in the Parable of the Sower. If we sincerely want to be faithful disciples, Jesus tells us we must have commitment, perseverance, and fortitude. Such attitudes require us to understand, embrace, and act on the Word of God.

Why do we need to commit to the Word of God? We should want to know what the Lord of heaven and earth tells us to do, and cooperate with God.

Why do we need perseverance to learn the Faith? Because there are many attractions in the world that distract our heart from discerning and accepting the Word of God.

Why do we have to show fortitude on the long journey of faith? Once we have the Word in our life, we ought to do what Christ has told us, struggle like Jacob, and bear fruit.

Jesus tells us that some of the faithful receive the Good News like the rocky ground, which prevent the Word from taking root. In this barren landscape, many believers give up when faced with trials or persecution. Other believers receive the Good News among thorns, producing no fruit because of worries about daily life, money, peer pressure, success in society, or because of other secular attractions or distractions.

Even though we've accepted the Good News in our baptism, why do some of us live our Christian life as if the Word fell on the rocky ground or among thorns? The warning that Jesus gave His audience—*they may see and see again, but not perceive; may hear and hear again, but not understand (Isaiah 6:9-10)*—is applicable to today's Christians as well. The secrets of the Kingdom of God have been made accessible to all believers: do we desire to learn these secrets and receive a wedding garment from the Lord?

You'll consider the Lord's call? This is good news! You should know that the path of a believer, beset by the attractions and distractions of the world, reveals a constant struggle with the wayward heart until the finish line. It's also a struggle to love the people in our life who don't agree with or annoy us.

Can a Christian lose the grace of baptism?

The answer to this question depends on our attitudes and priorities. As a simple rule of thumb, if we disown the Lord, then we should expect Him to do the same. (Matthew 10:33) It's a simple choice between the Savior of the World, or all that we find appealing in the world, in this present life. The world seems to offer security and happiness, but if the Lord is not first in our life, we're likely rejecting Him. If a Christian doesn't do the will of the Father, he or she could lose the grace of his or her baptism. What does the Word say about being cut off by the Lord? (Romans 11:1-6; 16-24)

First, a note of consolation is in order. Even though some people in the past killed God's prophets and broke the altars, the Lord didn't reject all the people. There was always a remnant that didn't follow false gods. They were chosen. By God's grace, they were saved.

Second, this grace is extended to every Christian today. The Word teaches us that the initial yeast prepared for bread-making is holy, and that makes the first handful of dough holy. After the dough has risen, the whole batch of bread is infused with holiness. It's the same with the olive tree planted by the Lord, which has a holy root. All the branches sharing the sap are made holy as well. These metaphors illustrate the continuing action of God's grace, which He freely gives to everyone who believes His truth in their heart!

If we've been growing on a wild tree, what would our response be if we'd been grafted on to the Lord's tree to receive the holy sap? We should, of course, respond with gratitude and humility for the undeserved gift of faith! The Word advises us also to hold firm to our faith.

We should never be proud that the natural branches were cut off for our sake. St. Paul reminds us that *we don't support the root; it is the holy root that supports all Christians.* God could be severe to us as well should we lose faith. It would also be very easy for God to graft back the natural branches if they should turn back to the Lord with all their heart.

Moving on from the metaphor of the olive tree as the true faith, we shouldn't think we're safe, just because we've been baptized. Baptism only marks the beginning of our transformation into Christians who can love. It's also possible for any Christian to show distrust, disbelief or disobedience to the Lord for a moment as Moses, Samson, David, or Solomon did. These were great men of faith who produced much sweet fruit. Yet, they displeased the Lord for a moment and were corrected.

In Chapter 21, I refer to St. Paul's Letter to the Colossians advising us that *greed is no different from worshipping a false god.* (Colossians 2:20-3:5) In this connection, has our heart:

- Grown cold?
- Unwittingly disobeyed God?
- Showed disbelief?
- Worshipped *Baals* as a result of our greed?

We shouldn't be spiritually complacent just because we go to church on Sundays or that we don't literally bend our knee to *Baal* or other graven images. Jesus has made it clear we can't have two masters in our Christian life. (Matthew 6:24) How can we detect the existence of a master in our life, other than the Lord? If we've been offering excuses for our poor faith, we need to consider the possibility of a second master whispering the convenient justifications or rationalizations in our ear. That other master is likely preventing us from placing God front and center in our daily life; such master could take the form of money, success, health, power, or a benefactor, etc. If everything *that* master says is more important or urgent than what the Lord is saying to all of us today, then Jesus isn't our master.

St. Paul cautioned us that God might be severe to any Christian breaking faith. We've also been forewarned that God could cut us off, should we allow our heart to grow cold. It's important then that we remain vigilant in following Jesus Christ, never losing sight of the will of God in our life.

Entering the narrow door and following Jesus

We need to enter by the narrow door that's Jesus Christ. The Lord has warned us that many will try to pass through and fail. Worst is the time when the door is locked. We've been told that it's not enough to be acquainted with the Lord. This advice is given by Jesus Himself. (Luke 13:22-27) It's also a mistake to think that we need no spiritual effort beyond our baptism. We're judged when we reach the end of our journey, not at the beginning. The Lord advises everyone to try their best to struggle with the faith each has been given. (Luke 21:34-36)

The Lord has made it clear that those who enter heaven will be identified by their fruit. (Matthew 7:20-25) Such believers do the will of the Father. By listening to the words of the Lord and acting on them, they're the sensible people who built their homes on the rock.

It's simply not enough for any believer to call Jesus, "Lord, Lord." Unfortunately, Andreas may think a mere declaration of faith in Jesus is enough. Andreas might believe in Jesus Christ, but does he or she truly believe in the Good News? If Andreas is converted, does the Word of God feature in his or her daily routine? Is Andreas following the Lord and doing all that He says?

Following Jesus requires a lifetime of commitment, effort, and struggle. These patterns of spiritual action prove the faith in the heart, which is why many trying to enter the narrow doorway fail. They fail to follow the Lord, when they:

- lose heart and give up the faith; or
- get waylaid by the distractions or attractions in the world; or
- neglect to act on the will of God and so fail to bear fruit.

Jesus has been clear about the fruit of faith. Ask yourself these questions:

- "Can Andreas renounce the world?"
- "Is Andreas carrying his or her cross?"
- "Is Andreas keeping the Word?"

We should also ask these questions in another way:

- "Is Andreas able to set aside at least one hour a day for prayer, studying the Word with his or her brothers and sisters, and celebrating the Eucharist regularly?"
- "Does Andreas desire the transformation of his or her heart?"
- "Is he or she happy to share the good tidings that God loves all humankind?"

Think of the Lord's mission to assume our condition of "birth, toil, and death." He then suffered terrible indignities for the sake of mankind and died a terrible, painful, shameful death. Jesus gave His life so that everyone receives a precious chance to be saved. I don't know about you, but I acknowledge my wickedness in the past for not having listened to the advice of Jesus and acting on them. In my onward journey of faith, I can't allow my faith to be tossed aside; like the swine that was washed but got dirty again, in the proverb mentioned by St. Peter. (2 Peter 2:22)

Considering this exchange of ideas, how can believers not commit, persevere, and show fortitude when our God has displayed such great love on the cross for you, for me, and for the rest of all mankind?

St. John's warning about lukewarm faith

We turn next to St. John's essential advice for Christians, especially those who are lukewarm in their faith:

> And to the angel of the church in La-odice´a write: "The words of the Amen, the faithful and true witness, the beginning of God's creation.
>
> I know your works: you are neither cold nor hot. Would that you were cold or hot! So, *because you are lukewarm*, and neither cold nor hot, I will spew you out of my mouth. For you say, *I am rich, I have prospered, and I need nothing; not knowing that you are wretched, pitiable, poor, blind, and naked. Therefore I counsel you to buy from me gold refined by fire, that you may be rich, and white garments to clothe you and to keep the shame of your nakedness from being seen, and salve to anoint your eyes, that you may see.* Those whom I love, I reprove and chasten; so be zealous and repent. *Behold, I stand at the door and knock*; if any one hears my voice and opens the door, I will come in to him and eat with him, and he with me. He who conquers, I will grant him to sit with me on my throne, as I myself conquered and sat down with my Father on his throne. He who has an ear, *let him hear* what the Spirit says to the churches." (Emphasis added) (Revelations 3:14-22)

It's easy to know where we stand with a hot or cold believer. One's an actual witness, an earnest member of the faithful. The latter denies belief with sufficient certainty. They're both free to choose. If you're neither one nor the other, how do you follow His ways and make a difference?

If Andreas can be truthful, ask yourself sincerely if there are doubts about your faith?

Do you know why you can't give more of your time and energy to follow the Lord?

Can you be a Christian without being a disciple or a follower?

Do you suppose you can be a Christian in name only—with no need to do what the Lord tells you?

I've shared the Word with you, and your Savior is knocking at your door. Do you open the door and begin the long journey of faith with the Lord?

Remember that Jesus is always inviting every believer to seek help from Him.

Keep His Word

Attending Mass every now and then, participating in occasional charitable activities, observing a fast here or a feast day there, doesn't make a Christian, one who should be committed to the *narrow path*. Jesus has spoken clearly about those whom the Father (and He) loves: "If anyone loves me he will keep my word, and my Father will love him." (John 14:23) To scrutinize the heart, do ask yourself:

- "Have you postponed your *spiritual obligations* to a later date—because your heart demands that Maslow is right—you can't be motivated for the Lord, without first settling your primary needs and wants?"
- "Do you do what you think is the minimum necessary to gain admittance into heaven i.e. attending Mass only on Sundays or helping out in parish activities?"
- "Could the real answer to a lukewarm faith lie in wanting the world as well—just like the saying about the cake—to eat it and have it too?"

The Word advises every Christian to *try our best* and *enter by the narrow door*. This door's more than the physical door of our respective churches. It's the full breadth and depth of the Faith. It's the Christian life rooted in the will of God. To keep the Word, we need to know the Word. To know the Word, we require a structured program of faith formation, which will benefit us in a community that's permanently committed to walking in faith.

How does the act of keeping the Word benefit us? We benefit when we allow the Word to teach us how to love like Jesus Christ and do what He says.

Jesus Himself is asking whether we really love Him by allowing His Word to penetrate our heart.

Hearts grown cold

If our heart has grown cold because the Lord allowed us to experience some sadness or loss, remember the wise words of Job. Whatever the Lord gives during our lifetime, Job tells us that God can also take away. (Book of Job 1:21, 2:10b)

Can we accept whatever the Lord offers, be it happiness or sorrow? This is a good example of accepting the will of God. If we're able to accept the will of God as Job did, such an attitude helps us accept the happiness or sorrow that we experience in our life. With this acknowledgment, the Lord gives us strength, but we'll need fortitude to struggle on and allow Him to deepen our faith and love. There can be a significance in suffering, but without the Word of God, our mind can only guess His will in our life and it'll be no match for the inconstant heart that grumbles and resents. The question, as always, is whether the believer will remain steadfast, struggle on and follow Jesus Christ.

If you're still having trouble with the idea of suffering, don't worry. Just read Chapter 16 again, if you hadn't started studying the Word of God regularly. Remember that all Christians need time just learning how to listen.

Unavoidable suffering

We can't avoid the suffering in this world, made possible by Adam and Eve with the sting of original sin. Those who succeed in amassing wealth or improving health don't escape suffering either. At most, they blunt a little of the pain, for a while. It's vain to think that we can escape suffering or tell God what to do with the suffering in this world.

Baldwin of Canterbury reminds us that our Lord entered our world of suffering. He completely disregarded His divinity and allowed Himself to share our pitiful condition of being born, toiling, and dying. He came down from heaven, in order to bear the greatest injustice this world could inflict on Him. Christ did this precisely to give us the Good News of God's great love. So there should be no doubt as to the full measure of our Father's love. I should reiterate that Jesus didn't come to take away, or exempt us from, suffering. (Hebrews 5:8; John 15:20) Despite our failings, Jesus thirsts very much to teach us how to love and carry our crosses in this world of disappointment and suffering.

Have you allowed your faith to *grow cold* because you know very little about the Faith?

It's possible that,

- no one communicated the love of God to Andreas; or
- you haven't yet learned the will of God; or
- no one has formed your faith; or
- on your own, you haven't learned how to love; or
- you don't even know where to begin.

If this is the state of your faith, consider the necessary journey of faith with the brothers and sisters that God will give you. You need to set aside real time and make a significant effort to learn the New Commandments. Don't fret if you're unable to love your enemy, carry your cross, or undertake the will of the Father immediately.

You certainly shouldn't follow Jesus Christ on your own—you need the communion of your brothers and sisters.

The fact we fill out a questionnaire, pass a religious test, or pay for the membership dues to a church-based group do not satisfy the tenets of our Faith. We don't learn how to love by rote or in the privacy of our room. Our heart learns by receiving from God the Word that will give us a Christian life full of self-giving, all with the help of the Lord *in His time.*

If you're the rich man in the Gospel of Matthew, (19:16-22) but recognize that you *can't buy life without end, nor avoid coming to the grave,* (Psalm 49:7-8) you should seek the help of the Lord. Consider asking the Lord in prayer, in the following terms:

- *Be away from me, Lord, for I am a sinner and imperfect. Help my poor faith.* (Mark 9:25)
- *Reveal your ways to me and teach me your right path.* (Psalm 25:4)

QUESTIONS FOR REFLECTION ON CHAPTER 19

1. Do you have priorities in your life (examinations, career, or the goal of self-sufficiency or early retirement) that you must attend to first?
2. Do you value financial literacy more than spiritual literacy?
3. What's the fruit of your faith?
4. Do you understand your faith?

20. Christian Life

What do we need beyond mere belief?

In a number of places in this book, I've been repeating what the Word said about lip service, e.g. "Lord, Lord" (Matthew 15:8; Isaiah 29:13) because that alone won't get us to heaven. (Matthew 7:21)

I've sounded the alarm because many believers might be taking their baptism for granted, or they might not know how to be and to do as a Christian.

Finally, I've drawn your attention to the Word of God that *is* asking for the fruit of our faith.

In this Chapter, I'll discuss continuing catechism, communion in a community, and daily prayer. Together, they represent the components of faith formation and Christian life, which every believer should possess to follow Jesus Christ in daily life and to produce fruit pleasing to God.

He fills the hungry with good things

Hearts shaped by transforming grace

In the opening sentences of his encyclical *Porta Fidei*, n1, Pope Emeritus Benedict encouraged all of us to set out on a journey of faith, which should last a lifetime. As a starting point, he reminded us that the "door of faith" is always open. (Acts 14:27)

When can we pass through into His Church and take possession of a life of communion with God? Crossing that threshold becomes possible when the Word of God is proclaimed and, ". . . the heart allows itself to be shaped by transforming grace."

I'm not alone in making this appeal. In the Year of Faith, the Church herself reminded everyone about the journey of faith. This wasn't a one-time opportunity to set out. We should rejoice because the *door of faith* is still open.

For whom does the *door of faith* stay open? I don't believe his Holiness was limiting his encouragement to the nonbelievers, the lapsed, and the occasional Christians who only attend Mass at baptisms, weddings, and funerals. He was referring to all Christians. The New Evangelization calls all the baptized to be re-evangelized and allow the Lord to deepen our faith. Even those who claim to know the Lord well should be evangelized anew.

A considerable journey of faith that lasts a lifetime

The idea of a considerable journey of faith isn't new. The Church tells us the process of initiation in the early Church involved a long period of instruction. Catechumens were taught in a series of preparatory rites that provided liturgical landmarks along the path of faith. Only when the catechumens had been examined over a period of time and found to have a sound foundation in their faith, were they baptized and allowed to celebrate the Christian sacraments. (CCC 1230)

For the many baptized at birth, this very abridged Christian initiation required a post-baptismal catechumenate. (CCC 1231) Infants don't understand the Faith just because they are baptized. This is why the Church provides a course of instruction during the teenage years. When the young believers reach the age of fifteen, they're presumed to have sufficiently attained intellectual and emotional development, and the Rite of Confirmation gives them the chance to make a firm commitment to the Faith.

What form should this post-baptismal catechumenate take? The spiritual education has to be tailored to the young believer's age and understanding.

Are such courses for the teenagers sufficient to teach the basic Faith? With good teachers, yes, but no matter how well the youth catechism is taught, a deeper understanding of the Faith can only begin to take shape as young believers enter adulthood.

Unfortunately, the formal catechism doesn't continue beyond the Rite of Confirmation. More importantly, even if teaching does continue, there's no assurance that the baptismal grace will flower unless the young believers join and stay with an ecclesial community for their lifetime.

I'm not aware of any systematic integration of the young believers or newly baptized adults into an ecclesial community contemplated by CCC 6, much less the integration of all the faithful into ecclesial communities. Spiritual progress depends on the continuation of faith learning—a continuing catechism needs to be available for the lifelong education of every believer's heart, best given in an ecclesial community. The fact of a crisis of faith possibly suggests the current level of catechesis for all adults is insufficient.

This was why the Second Vatican Council was inspired to restore the adult catechumenate. (CCC 1232) However, there seems to have been some confusion since Vatican II. Many think that the adult catechumenate, incorporating stages found in the Rite of Christian Initiation of Adults (RCIA), is only relevant to new adult converts! While the RCIA does include rites matching the catechumenate in the early Church, a deeper adult catechumenate should be made available for the New Evangelization of all Christians. More importantly, this adult catechism should be thorough, gradual, and lifelong.

Instead of the ". . . necessary flowering of baptismal grace in personal growth," the false freedoms offered by the modern world seduce and ensnare many of our brothers and sisters. Without a regular training of the heart, many hearts might have turned cold, lost their way, or turned away from the Lord.

In Part 2 of this book, I make a case for the Church to supply solid food in the form of faith formation to last a lifetime. I'm not proposing this post-baptismal catechumenate for just a few adults needing additional instruction. Faith development that is structured, systematic, and steady should be offered to every believer!

Why do all Christians need a lifetime of learning? Let's first consider the path taken by Jesus. Our Lord only began His ministry at the age of thirty. The Prophet Isaiah also reminds us that every believer will need to be sustained, learning the ways of the Lord after a great length of time, until he or she is spiritually ready for any mission: "He shall eat curds and honey when he knows how to refuse the evil and choose the good." (7:15)

Secondly, the Church says that the necessary catechesis develops the faith of children, young people, and adults by teaching the Christian doctrine in a systematic way. "Teaching" and "formation" as applied to the Faith have similar meanings. Thus, the long-term intention is to initiate all believers into the fullness of Christian life. (CCC 5)

What's this fullness of Christian life?

The fullness comes from following the Lord and leading a spiritual life according to the Good News. By learning God's commandments and copying His ways, we can begin to love God and one another. (1 John 2:3-6)

If a lifetime is needed, can a Christian delay his or her initiation into the Christian life? Definitely not! No Christian should postpone his or her life with Christ. The Word tells us in too many places that the people had great difficulties in following, loving and obeying the Lord. God has already shown His patience by giving everyone this favorable time of salvation, (2 Cor 6:2) which we ought to use profitably to begin our spiritual listening and learning. That we may need the whole of our life means the learning must start today or very soon. We must also remember that life is precarious, and it's possible any of us might perish tonight in a tragic state without grace. Yes, we have this time now to learn His ways, but this time is all we have. We're here for a while, then gone in a blink of an eye. Like my friend, David Marshall, who in the past two years helped scrutinize the words you've been reading; unfortunately, he didn't make it to see the publication of this book.

If we accept that more teaching and learning are needed above and beyond the initial catechism, a program of lifelong, structured faith education is the panacea to help all believers. More so, if those who have been catechized haven't got an active Christian life. St. James in his Letter teaches us that a Christian can only acquire true religion by submitting to and accepting the Word. This acceptance isn't concerned just with listening, but requires acting on the powerful words of God and obeying them. It's the difference between talk and action; lip service and true love. Only the man or woman who listens, doesn't forget, and actively puts the Word into practice will achieve happiness. (1:21-27)

For these purposes, the much-needed catechesis in the New Evangelization can't be delivered as a *refresher* or a short series of lectures to attend out of mechanical duty. Many of us will need help from the Church and a great length of time just to listen.

What's the problem with listening?

If our heart remains shut and insists we have our way or do what we please, we won't focus on God's words and take the time necessary to accept its meaning, convert, then transform. Hence, the first, important step every believer needs to take is to listen to the

Word. The second step is to reflect upon, understand, and accept what the Word says. If we fail to take the first step, the spiritual poverty in our hearts may cause us to stumble. Consequently, the failure to listen may result in neither learning nor obeying what the Word says.

How do we put the advice of St. James into practice?

The steps identified by the CCC for the formation of faith need to be offered by the Church to every believer. At each liturgical stage, those on the path should examine themselves seriously and, with the help of their pastors, continue the process of reflection, understanding, and acceptance. Once integrated into ecclesial communities, the experience of Christian living and the celebration of the sacraments should help the believers improve their spiritual listening. With grace from the Lord, faith formation will help every believer develop his or her life according to Christ.

All believers should sign up for a structured, but gradual, program of faith formation. All should aim for a complete, spiritual transformation on a faith journey. In his First Letter to the Corinthians, St. Paul describes the spiritual training every Christian should undertake during his or her life. In a sporting competition, every sportsman is trying to win. They all train intensively because, on the day of the race, it'll be their opportunity to win. So they stretch and strain their body. They make it strong. They make it obey their will. Then, during the race, they try their best, making sure they won't be disqualified. Believers should train and compete in the same way, but the lifelong competition pits our spirit against the flesh. Our spiritual race concludes at the end of our life.

What's the prize? The sportsman wins a laurel wreath, but the leaves wither. In the race for eternal life with God, the heavenly wreath that all Christians can win will never wither. (9:24-27) I believe this spiritual prize is awarded to all Christians who understand, accept, and do the will of God. God loves these Christians because they strive to love at the cost of personal goals, ridicule, and persecution.

Ecclesial movements and new communities

How are religious groups relevant to the journey of faith?

Paragraph IV.9 of the Note with pastoral recommendations for the *Year of Faith*, drawn up by the Congregation for the Doctrine of the Faith, acknowledges the role and contribution of the ecclesial movements and new communities, and invites them to collaborate with their local pastors to promote their charism. They are to contribute to the wider initiative of the Year of Faith; i.e, both to act as witnesses to their own faith and act in service to the Church. With the help and support of their pastors, it's hoped that small communities everywhere will be formed to give witness to the Lord Jesus.

What are ecclesial movements and new communities?

There are more than 50 ecclesial movements and new forms of community life. I won't list them in this book, but they're relevant to the much-needed journey of faith. When he delivered an address to the World Congress of Ecclesial Movements and New Communities on May 27, 1998, St. John Paul II gave a superb description of a "movement." He marveled at the charismatic forms of Christian experience, in particular the realities of the faith journey and the Christian witness:

> The term is often used to refer to realities that differ among themselves, sometimes even by reason of their canonical structure. If, on the one hand, that structure certainly can't exhaust or capture the wealth of forms produced by the life-giving

> creativity of Christ's Spirit, on the other, it indicates *a concrete ecclesial reality with predominantly lay membership, a faith journey* and *Christian witness* which bases its own pedagogical method on a precise charism given to the person of the founder in specific circumstances and ways.
>
> The charism's own originality, which gives life to a movement, neither claims nor could claim to add anything to the richness of the depositum fidei, safeguarded by the Church with passionate fidelity. Nonetheless, *it represents a powerful support, a moving and convincing reminder to live the Christian experience fully,* with intelligence and creativity. Therein lies the basis for finding adequate responses to the challenges and needs of ever changing times and historical circumstances.
>
> In this light, the charisms recognized by the Church are *ways to deepen one's knowledge of Christ and to give oneself more generously to him, while rooting oneself more and more deeply in communion with the entire Christian people.* For this reason they deserve attention from every member of the ecclesial community, *beginning with the Pastors* to whom the care of the particular Churches is entrusted in communion with the Vicar of Christ. *Movements can thus make a valuable contribution* to the vital dynamics of the one Church founded on Peter in the various local situations, especially in those regions where the implantatio Ecclesiae is still in its early stages or subject to many difficulties. (Emphasis added) (World Congress of Ecclesial Movements and New Communities)

Later in the Seminar on Ecclesial Movements and New Communities held on June 18, 1999, St. John Paul II recognized the need for Christian communities. These communities offered welcome, communion, and shared experience of faith. This is only possible if the pastors, as a priority, throw the doors of the parish wide open to these ecclesial movements and new communities:

"When they exercise their teaching role, *Bishops should proclaim the Gospel of Christ to people.* This is one of the principal duties of Bishops. Fortified by the Spirit they should call on men and women to believe or should strengthen them when they already have a living faith. They should expound to them the whole mystery of Christ, that is, all those truths ignorance of which means ignorance of Christ" (Christus Dominus, n. 12). *Every Pastor's concern to reach people and to speak to their hearts, their minds, their freedom and their thirst for happiness is born of Christ's own concern for man*, his compassion for those whom he compares to a flock without a shepherd (cf. Mk 6:34 and Mt 9:36), and it echoes Paul's apostolic zeal: "Woe to me if I do not preach the Gospel!" (1 Cor 9:16). In our times the challenges of the new evangelization are often presented in dramatic terms and spur the Church, in particular her Pastors, to seek new forms of missionary proclamation and action that best meet the demands of our era.

Among today's most urgent pastoral tasks, I would first like to point out the *need to care for communities in which there is a deeper awareness of the grace connected with the sacraments of Christian initiation,* which give rise to the vocation to be Gospel witnesses in all areas of life. The dramatic events of our time spur believers to the essentials of the Christian experience and message in their everyday encounters and friendships, *for a faith journey illumined by the joy of communication. Another pastoral priority, not to be underestimated, is the formation of Christian communities as authentic places of welcome for everyone,* with constant care for the specific needs of each individual. Without these communities it becomes more and more difficult to grow in faith and one gives into the temptation to reduce to a fragmentary and occasional experience precisely that faith which, on the contrary, should enliven all human experience. (Emphasis added) *(*Seminar on Ecclesial Movements and New Communities*)*

The parish as a community of communities!

In his Easter address to the Bishops of Ontario on May 4, 1999, St. John Paul II invited all priests, religious and the laity to join in the New Evangelization. He made it clear that the parish is the privileged starting place for faith and community formation:

> *Once the faithful respond to the Lord's call and seek to enter more fully into the community of faith, they must be led ever closer to Christ through the experience of worship and catechesis* of which the Synod Fathers spoke. *The privileged place for this remains the parish,* for all the great changes it is undergoing in today's urban context (cf. Ecclesia in America, n. 41). It is true that the parish needs to be adapted to meet rapidly changing circumstances; but it is also true that the parish has shown itself extraordinarily adaptable in the past and will show itself no less adaptable now.
>
> Every adaptation, however, must keep clearly in mind that it is above all the Eucharist which reveals the unchanging truth of the Christian life. This is why the liturgy is so crucial and why Bishops and priests need to do all in their power to ensure that the Church's worship, especially the Mass, is centred on the real presence of the Lord – "for the Eucharist is the Church's entire spiritual wealth" (Presbyterorum ordinis, n. 5). *This demands both a systematic catechesis of young people and adults and a great spirit of fraternity among all who gather to worship the Lord. The anonymity of the city cannot be allowed to enter our Eucharistic communities.* New ways and structures must be found to build bridges between people, so that there really is that experience of mutual acceptance and closeness which Christian fellowship requires. *It may be that this, and the catechesis which must accompany it, would be better done in smaller communities:* as the Post-Synodal Exhortation puts it, "*one way of renewing parishes, especially urgent for parishes in larger cities,*

> *might be to consider the parish as a community of communities*" (Ecclesia in America, n. 41). This will need to be done wisely, lest it lead to new forms of fragmentation; but its potential advantage is that "*in such a human context, it will be easier to gather to hear the word of God, to reflect on the range of human problems in the light of this word, and gradually to make responsible decisions inspired by the all-embracing love of Christ*" (ibid.). (Emphasis added)

What's striking about St. John Paul II's address is that there's still an urgent need for the Church to push forward on the New Evangelization. All pastors should be helping the faithful, ". . . respond to the Lord's call and seek to enter more fully into the community of faith."

In many cities around the world, modern lifestyles encourage us to become more anonymous. This affects the way we relate to each other in our parishes. Even though surrounded by people, many believers don't experience "the spirit of fraternity" in large worshipping assemblies. The pastors encourage greetings among the assembled worshippers, but these are fleeting and not designed to break through the "anonymity of the city" and help Christian fellowship to form and flower. Should we be surprised that many parishes are increasingly empty and less warm?

Let's pause a moment for reflection.

At Masses, I often find myself giving a sign of peace to an unfamiliar parishioner sitting next to me. It's easy when I've no relationship or history with this person. Even if I do make a connection, I know I'm unlikely to see him or her again unless we make specific arrangements to meet. It's different when I'm invited to give peace to a brother or sister in a small, permanent community, especially when we've been fighting. The Sign of Peace is a meaningful representation of our unity. Even so, we ought to move beyond symbolic gestures and build a fraternal community of brothers and sisters—one that's in communion with each other and the Lord. But it's difficult to love. That's why we need God's grace to learn how to love in a community committed to becoming earnest disciples of Christ. (John 13:35)

I can't shake the conclusion that chance, warm encounters during Masses don't build the communities of faith St. John Paul II hoped to form. It's therefore important that the formation of smaller communities and the deeper catechesis of the faithful begin in churches everywhere—*let the poor receive as much as they want to eat.*

We should also heed St. Paul when he discusses the life all Christians need to possess. In his Letter to the Ephesians, he tells us that pagans have no long-term motivation. Their life is aimless. Estranged from God, their hearts deny knowledge of the Lord's ways. Indeed, this often leads them to lose understanding of right and wrong, and to live an immoral life. Christians, on the other hand, live by the truth of the Word and in the love of God. This helps them grow into Christ, ". . . who is the head by whom the whole body is fitted and joined together." All believers need to strive to give up their old way of life by learning from the Lord. (4:15-16,17-24)

What other benefits do small communities offer the parish? In the same address to the Bishops in Ontario, May 4, 1999, St. John Paul II urged the formation of small communities in the hope they'll be the foundation of God's city in the barren, urban landscape, nurturing a culture of life. The problem, as he saw it, is that modern cities encourage the development of a culture of anonymity, inequality, and rootlessness. On the other hand, small communities are adept at growing more conscious of the presence of Christ. When the brothers and sisters have Christ in their heart, these communities become *the seed of the holy city, the new Jerusalem, coming down out of heaven from God.* (Revelations 21:2)

Believers shouldn't think that, on our own, we *have* the strength to give up the old way of life, speak the truth, or be kind to one's brothers and sisters. I've no doubts that believers need to lean on Christ. We keep our eyes always on the Lord (and not the leadership, works or deeds of any other person) and carry our own cross to follow the Wonder-Counselor.

How then does a believer move forward? I submit this is only possible in a community that God will give to him or her. Together with his or her brothers and sisters, the believers in this small community will all take the same step—each a spiritual building block. They need to be encouraged by their pastor and learn systematically in a program of faith formation that may well last the duration of his or her life.

So, this is my humble appeal to you. Please consider embarking on a serious journey of faith. My writing in this book can't give faith formation to you. It's for your church to provide you with solid food for the epic journey you should start today.

It's my sincere hope that you'll think about walking with Jesus Christ at this crossroad, following and not losing sight of the Lord, so He can teach you His ways through His Church.

Need for prayer

I now wish to share what I've learned about prayer because I didn't know its all-important purpose in the early part of my faith journey: I mistakenly supposed I already had an intimate relationship with God!

What is prayer?

Prayer is an essential component in the spiritual life of all Christians, but it's more than a petition for things and needs. God meets us in prayer because the process of calling the Lord, spending time with Him, and listening to the Word, is really for our benefit. It follows that all believers should be relying on daily prayer to cultivate a beneficial relationship with our Redeemer. Of the different prayers, the most important is the Lord's Prayer as taught by Jesus. In a way, it's a summary of the whole Gospel. (Tertullian, De orat. 1: PL 1, 1155, CCC) The Church teaches that prayer is God's gift. It forms a relationship of the heart, giving us a chance to look to heaven, recognize the Lord, and adore Him. It also reflects one of the mysteries of the faith because it requires the faithful to believe in its power. By praying, we're making our life conform to Christ. By celebrating it, prayer becomes the means for creating a vital and personal relationship with God. (CCC 2558)

Although we can request good things from God, the Church warns us not to let our pride make demands. The basis of our relationship with God is of humility and contrition. Man is a beggar before God. Only when we admit we don't know how to pray, are we ready to take proper possession of the gift of prayer. (CCC 2559)

The Church also bids Christians think of the act of praying as like coming to the well for a drink of water. Jesus waits by the well and seeks every believer with a spiritual thirst. The Lord too has a thirst to give us His love. Jesus expresses His desire for us to join Him in prayer. When we pray, we're joining our thirst with His: "God thirsts that we may thirst for him." (CCC 2560)

Praying from the heart

Some people pray in words, others in gestures. Some combine the two. It doesn't really matter what form we give it, so long as it's the *whole man who prays*. As to the source, scripture sometimes mentions the soul, or the spirit, or the heart. According to the Church, scripture refers to the heart in this context more than one thousand times. We should, therefore, conclude it's the heart that prays. If we turn this around, our prayers will be in vain if we don't pray from our heart. (CCC 2562)

Focus of prayer

The Church teaches us that the focus of prayer is our Lord and Savior. Through prayer, God wishes to speak to us in our wayward, broken, and poor heart. As one of the faithful, we say we believe in Jesus Christ in our heart. If so, then prayer should come easily. If we *have* difficulties praying, i.e. spending daily, quiet time with the Lord, this could be symptomatic of our heart not being near God.

In his address to the Synodal Fathers, on January 22, 1999, St. John Paul II offered this advice about prayer. He regarded prayer as the duty of every Christian to contemplate God and seek His will in everything. That way, we grow into a life in Christ and in the Spirit. Through prayer, we express our love and hope to be fully converted so that the Holy Spirit can guide all parts of our life:

> Spirituality is 'life in Christ' and 'in the Spirit', which is accepted in faith, expressed in love and inspired by hope, and so becomes the daily life of the Church community". In this sense, by spirituality, which is the goal of conversion, we mean "not a part of life, but the whole of life guided by the Holy Spirit". *Among the many elements of spirituality which all Christians must make their own, prayer holds a pre-eminent place. Prayer leads Christians "little by little to acquire a contemplative view of reality, enabling them to recognize God in every moment and in every thing; to contemplate God in every person; to seek his will in all that happens". Prayer, both personal and liturgical, is the duty of every Christian.* "Jesus Christ, the Good News of the Father, warns us that without him we can do nothing (cf. Jn 15:5). He himself, in the decisive moments of his life, before doing something, used to withdraw to an isolated place to give himself to prayer and contemplation, and he asked the Apostles to do the same". He tells his disciples without exception: "Go into your room and shut the door and pray to your Father who is in secret" (Mt 6:6). (Emphasis added) (*Ecclesia in America, 29*)

Why should a Christian include prayer as an essential part of daily life? A spiritual person gives prayer a preeminent place in his or her Christian life; i.e. accepts prayer, both personal and liturgical, as his or her duty to God. When we pray regularly in a quiet place, it becomes possible to enter a more contemplative state in which we begin to recognize God in all parts of our life. Then, we can hope to see His will in everything that happens.

If you don't understand or see the will of God in your life, it may be that you haven't been praying as you should. Have you been spending quiet time with the Lord in prayer, every day of your life?

Some confusion about prayer

This Chapter offers just a snapshot of what the Church knows about prayer. The Church has much more it wishes to teach every believer, so I'll leave it to the pastors to take up the role of teaching this. My real purpose has been to make a simple point to the brothers and sisters who might be confused. There's something wrong if the only time we seek, or communicate with, the Lord is when we're in trouble. The absence of God in my early life revealed my confusion because I thought prayer was about an asking for this or that from the Lord. Looking back, even this form of prayer misunderstood the fundamental relationship. How do I ask for gifts from someone with whom I've had little or no relationship in my day-to-day living? I'm not saying the Lord won't listen to our petitions, but when the Lord is silent, or no help is forthcoming, we should resist becoming frustrated and angry with the Lord. We should all remember the advice of St. James in his Letter about the correct purpose of praying. (4:1-9)

Those who fight inside themselves are likely to fight with those around them. That's how battles and wars begin. People want things they haven't got, and they're prepared to fight and kill to get them. It's the ultimate selfishness when people use force to get their way. Yet the reason these people don't have what they want is because they aren't praying correctly.

These people put their own desires above everything else, making friends with the world and not with God. St. James reminds us that God opposes the proud, but gives generously to the humble. If we resist the Devil and give in to God, He will come nearer to us. If we clean our hands and clear our minds, God will become our friend. We can't waver. We all need to enter into an active relationship with the Lord, grasping the Faith through the Word of God and through the teachings of His Church, all cultivated in daily prayer.

Daily prayer is spending quiet time with the Lord listening and learning and is a necessary part of our Christian life. If we don't have this Christian life, how can we say we believe in, or possess an intimate relationship with, Jesus Christ? Christians can't do this alone because we'll need the help and support of our brothers and sisters in a small community to pray and live our life according to Christ.

What if we don't know how to pray or have difficulties praying?

Well, we need to *march on*. When we're in active communion with the Lord, in a structured program of gradual faith formation, our heart becomes responsive. It won't answer with religious feelings that wilt like cut flowers, but with the enduring response a faithful Christian can (eventually) offer—a humbled, contrite heart that God will not spurn.

How do we acquire this humbled, contrite heart? We acquire this heart through *a journey of faith that lasts a lifetime*, where *the heart allows itself to be shaped by transforming grace.* (Porta Fidei, n.1)

QUESTIONS FOR REFLECTION ON CHAPTER 20

1. Do you see an adult catechism or faith formation as an irrelevant proposition?
2. What catechesis have you received and is this faith education continuing in a lifelong program?
3. Do you experience the *anonymity of the city* in your church?
4. Have you set out on a *journey that lasts a lifetime*, and allowed your heart to be *shaped by transforming grace*?
5. Are you in a Christian community with brothers and sisters taking the same step?

Section X

APPEAL TO ALL PASTORS OF SOULS

21. A Way Out of the Crisis

How should we move forward?

In this Chapter and the next, I offer my thinking on the crisis of faith and a solution for getting every believer on to the Lord's path. To help show the way, I rely on the *Catechesi Tradendae* to explain how catechesis is so important to the New Evangelization. From the clarity it offers, I'm able to propose a road map for the re-evangelization of every believer. The way forward needs to address the continuing education of every Christian heart in a setting suited for gradual and sustained learning. My small contribution acknowledges the inspiration drawn from St. John Paul II's writings and speeches.

New Evangelization

When I first heard about the New Evangelization, I mistakenly thought it was a renewal of efforts to catechize a world still without Christian hope. When I finally read St. John Paul II's Easter address to the Bishops of Ontario (on May 4, 1999), I was surprised to learn that the New Evangelization was aimed at our Christian cities and neighborhoods.

St. John Paul II cited the Synod Fathers, (Ecclesia in America, n. 21) who spoke of the need for a methodical approach to urban evangelization and specified the pastoral strategy as having three separate elements:

- catechesis;
- liturgy; and
- organization of pastoral structures.

In turn, these three elements match the ministry of the Bishop, which is to:

- teach;
- sanctify; and
- govern.

When these sets of three elements are put together, the goal is to create a greater sense of community with the parish coming together to ". . . build bridges between people . . .", ". . . which Christian fellowship requires."

When parishioners get a better understanding of the mission of Christ for everyone, the parish will be well prepared to counter the culture of anonymity, inequality, and rootlessness that's growing in many cities. Unless people come together and support each other, we can expect some believers either gradually to lose faith or to drift into sects and cults that recruit those mistakenly disenchanted with the Church.

To reinvigorate the faith and create a more profound experience of community in Christ, St. John Paul II encouraged those with faith to reach out to all who live in cities. He says this strategy is "… at the heart of *what Christ is calling us to be and to do* in the new evangelization." (emphasis added) If we sit passively in a room, people won't be motivated to join the churches. What should happen?

The new frontier in the campaign for faith is the city. Dedicated men, women, and young people need to go out in the name of Christ and invite people into the Church. For this to work, we'll need a new surge comparable to the energy that brought the faith to your country and mine centuries ago.

A new missionary heroism ought to shine as our lay urban missionaries set out. Their faith will need to be as strong as when the missionaries first ventured into unknown lands. These missionaries must be encouraged. They must not, however, be left on their own. They'll need the support of truly zealous priests who are also fired with the same missionary spirit, and who know how to kindle that spirit in others. Under the guidance of the Bishops, it's vital that seminaries and houses of formation be tasked as schools for this mission. They ought to train priests, who can inspire other Christians to become the new evangelizers the Church needs.

This New Evangelization must take place in every city, all around the world. All of us have witnessed the grave dechristianization of traditional Christian nations, societies, and neighborhoods. Even within a local church, there may be many parishioners who aren't practicing their faith. How then do we cultivate the "missionary heroism" or increase the ranks of "truly zealous priests" for this important mission?

I submit a return to first principles is needed. That is, faith formation for every believer is of paramount importance to the renewal of every parish, everywhere.

Crisis of faith

What's been done?

Pope Emeritus Benedict XVI decreed the Church would observe the Year of Faith between October 11, 2012, and November 24, 2013, to commemorate the fiftieth anniversary of Vatican II. This decree intended all the faithful to rediscover the treasured gift of faith. It was timely for the Church to revisit the grace received through the Second Vatican Council. That grace is, "… a sure compass by which to take our bearings in the century now beginning," and "… can become increasingly powerful for the ever necessary renewal of the Church." (*Porta Fidei*, n.5)

The Spirit bestowed a "great grace" on the Church through the work of the Second Vatican Council, and the Church is right to distribute the treasured gift of faith.

Why is this renewal necessary? This renewal is needed because fewer Christians recognize the need to live their life like *nomads.* Many now crown Benjamin as the unlawful king, and Mammona has *his* associates singing *his* specious songs of specie—shouldn't someone make weak sheep strong? How precious and timely is this compass to show the way in today's world where success, security, and money represent the highest hopes of the weak sheep.

I pray we won't allow the Year of Faith to pass into memory. We shouldn't think of it as a mere Jubilee event to be observed every twenty-five or fifty years. Perhaps Barbara is asking the right question—why only one night a year—and so, why only one year? Let us observe a continuing Year of Faith until all have received the fire from the Lord!

The Second Vatican Council

In his inaugural Encyclical, *Ubi Arcano,* on December 23, 1922, the late Pope Pius XI asked whether it was possible to reconvene the First Vatican Council that was interrupted in 1870. This question triggered thinking about the themes to be addressed by the Church, and materials were collected for an ecumenical council.

This process involved the service of no less than five popes over the following four decades, albeit the Second World War interrupted the hoped-for convening of the council. Finally, on October 11, 1962, the Second Vatican Council was convened. With as many as 2,625 council fathers in attendance, this council finally concluded its work three years later on December 8, 1965.

In his address on the opening of the Second Vatican Council, one of the issues highlighted by the late Pope John XXIII was the need to guard the Christian doctrine by teaching it more effectively. Why did he think no efforts should be spared to teach the Faith?

It's because we're pilgrims on this earth and should always be reminded to fix our eyes on heaven. The top-priority of Christian teaching was evident in 1962 but isn't the concern of this council still relevant today?

When he opened the Second Vatican Council, the stated intention was to ". . . let in the fresh air." His Holiness wanted to invigorate the Faith by ". . . taking into account the errors, the requirements, and the opportunities of our time, to be presented in exceptional form to all men throughout the world." This council wanted to re-invigorate the Faith and make it a better fit for the twentieth century, i.e. the Church recognized the crisis fifty years ago!

Fifty years on, the crisis of faith is deepening. It's as though the Church has switched to the narrow gauge at Port Bou, and many communities haven't crossed by reason of the wide track. Could it be that not enough has been done to spread the teachings of the Church?

Educating the believing conscience of all the faithful

As a hungry man, I write this direct appeal to all pastors of souls, everywhere in the world. Without further delay, the narrow door should be thrown wide open. Let all the hungry enter to begin the necessary, messy, and transformative journey of faith.

Why necessary? Because the Lord says so.

Why messy? Many sinners are waiting to enter the "door of faith."

Why transformative? All of us who are sinners need to learn how to love like Jesus Christ.

What's the significance of spiritual hunger? The shepherds must feed the hungry. Having eaten their spiritual fill, the sheep should be able to renounce the world, and love one another. Such strong sheep should also undertake their mission as priests, prophets, and kings to praise and worship the greatest Lover, announce the Good News with great joy and serve their neighbor. If weak sheep have forgotten how to eat, this book and the necessary work of others should help them rediscover the hunger for the Lord.

I don't have proof of the effects of modern life on spiritual hunger, but I have a theory that seems to fit the facts. We're now living through a Golden Age. The People of God have all the benefits of science and reason to improve their life. Every day, new discoveries, inventions, and ideas disrupt the old ways. Think:

- handwritten letters overtaken by instant emails; or
- sprawling music stores everywhere put out of business by ITunes.

Through the disruptive power of technology and modern life, the hearts, eyes, and ears of the faithful are now wide open.

It's therefore imperative for the Church to act quickly to educate the faithful in the love of God. If there's no effective faith formation, we're in danger of losing sheep to the seductive distractions and material temptations of the modern world. A further problem is underestimating the mischievous agents of misinformation. An incredible number of falsehoods circulate online, with the sole agenda of leading weak sheep astray.

Even though this is just a theory, the Church ought to ask why so many are losing their hunger for Christ. Remember, the crisis began more than a hundred years ago. Rather than dwelling on possible causes for the crisis, I'll leave it to others to explore.

The best starting point to tackle the crisis today is for the Church to examine what our faithful know about Jesus Christ and the will of God. Just ask the believers in an assembly these three important questions:

"What continuing faith education have you been receiving?"

"Do you accept all the teachings of Jesus Christ and His Apostles?"

"Are you able to renounce the world, carry your cross, and follow Jesus Christ?"

Is a great length of time needed?

In earlier chapters, I relied on teachings of the Church and relevant scripture to emphasize the need for a transformative journey. I'm already walking on such a journey, regularly meeting the brothers and sisters for the preparation and celebration of the Word and the Eucharist. I use the breviary for prayer every day. In obedience to the Lord's command and on assignment by my catechists, I've set out two-by-two on Sunday afternoons during Eastertide to knock on doors and announce the Good News. There *will* come a liturgical stage when the knocking on doors happens even more frequently. My faith is being examined at various liturgical milestones. There have been scrutinies at regular intervals every few years to assess my spiritual progress. I've entered the "door of faith" and am joyful to receive much-needed faith formation from the Church.

This spiritual marching must continue because I hope to achieve the *metanoia*—the profound and total conversion of my heart, soul, and strength—even if I have to spend my penultimate breath trying to attain it. Regardless the *metanoia*, I wish for my last breath to offer a final, priestly sacrifice of praises, "Alleluia, Alleluia, Alleluia."

To put it bluntly, despite my faith experience and the spiritual knowledge I've gained so far, I have to continue marching on this journey of faith because the *news of salvation* has yet to penetrate into the inmost depths of my heart. I say, "I love my Lord," but find myself not being able to love as I should. Worse, I still don't do everything that Jesus tells me to do. (cf Romans 7:15) For these reasons and speaking only for myself, I cannot consider myself a full-fledged Christian right now.

Notwithstanding my present failure to love and obey my Savior perfectly, I recognize the effectiveness of the spiritual training I've received. Hence, I beg the Church to make it the highest priority to help all who desire and need similar training of the heart. I don't have academic qualifications in theology, nor do I claim to be an authority on teachings of the Church. If I'm wrong, I *am* open to correction. Where my thoughts match the concerns and mission of the Church, this journey ought to begin for all as soon as practicable. Seeing how much time has lapsed since the Second Vatican Council, much work is needed to rescue the many sheep grown weak. I cannot imagine how the poor sheep are coping without the invaluable, lifelong training of the heart, which has been made available to a spiritual laggard like me.

I say this because it's quite possible for many to have misunderstood a simple truth: that being able to love requires the grace of God. To love as a Christian should—like Jesus Christ—might well involve a lifetime of learning, practicing, and struggling. Having said that, I want to be exceedingly clear about not postponing our Christian life to a convenient date in the indeterminate future. If I may repeat a point I made earlier: a great length of time may be needed because the commandment to love is possibly the hardest to fulfill.

The slippery slope of modern life

I possess a keen sense of the crisis of faith in our Church. I count my family, friends, colleagues, and acquaintances among the regulars, sometime, and lukewarm believers that I've written about. Some have no grasp of the Holy Trinity, or think it acceptable to skip the Eucharist, or even miss the liturgy of the Word without worrying. They also suppose our loving God will understand their hardships, take away their suffering, and always bless them with wealth and health.

Hoping for answers they want, they ask questions filled with errors.

Hoping their mistaken choices are valid, they live without the benefit of love.

Hoping their pastors will excuse their disobedience, they observe their obligations when it suits them.

Perhaps they don't know their errors or understand the dangers of their spiritual disobedience. If so, they really need faith training! My concern for these unsettled believers is real. So I make this appeal for their sake as well.

You might suppose my parish would be active and do something for those whose faith wavers. This shouldn't just be about my parish because the crisis of faith is worldwide. That's a little academic. At a local level, the church should be looking out for the interests of all the people in the community and not just those who attend Mass! Some pastors might claim there's no crisis in their parish and dismiss the idea that urgent work needs to be carried out right away.

Well, as some say, the numbers don't lie. Then again, we should heed a warning the late Fr. Alfred issued twenty-five years ago at a Sunday Mass that was bursting at the seams and spilling out into the parking lot. He said, "We must ever be stronger in our faith, brothers and sisters. Our churches may be full now, but the emptying of the churches in the West will reach our shores one day."

The churches in Singapore may not be empty today, but they're visibly less full than twenty-five years ago. Not that the numbers themselves are important. We should be mindful that numbers are real people with souls yearning for their *heavenly home*. Mere hope for their salvation is not working. Indeed, there seems a tacit conspiracy among the parishioners to sit with arms, knees, and bags thrice akimbo.

Are the parishioners trying to give the impression their parish is meaningfully occupied or has urban anonymity infected that parish? I can't say for sure. What we should acknowledge is that the Lord wishes to find faith in every Christian when He comes again.

What else is contributing to this crisis of faith?

Think of our modern life as the new serpent that tempts with a fruit from an illusory tree of secular knowledge. Like the forbidden fruit in the Garden, this fruit offers a false choice between good and evil. Where's the serpent most active? We're living in the Age of the Internet. It's supposed to be a benefit for billions of hearts and minds to be connected. This connectivity, however, does little for communion and the Christian life we ought to possess. We fritter time away instead of nourishing the soul—there's simply no time for God, not even time for our family and friends. Our mind wanders everywhere but the Lord's way.

When we look at the choices offered by modern life, there's little or no connection with the life offered by the Lord. It's very much about the I-me-my, not the other who is *Jesus Christ.* Never has the modern world been more pervasive in its influence on everyday choices: money, success, and individual happiness. These choices are touted as being good to eat and pleasing to the eye.

The secular catechesis has many teachers. Even before formal teaching starts at preschool, many infants have been coached to get ahead in life. Grandparents with best intentions egg the infants on. When education begins, the parents are anxious to add private tutors to improve their child's chances of winning and success. The children then grow up into young Christian men and women. As a young man, the Christian works his way through the education system. He finds competition increasingly more ferocious for the limited places in a school, faculty, or curriculum of his choice. No matter what he hopes for, he's in a race, hotly pursued by friend and foe. The pressure builds and the demands for reward, release, and escape grow with it. As a young woman, the Christian continues the same race against her supposed friends for the best-paying jobs. They tussle in the shadows for the corner office and membership in the restricted club. In this race for a withering wreath, winks, pats, and back-scratches are *de rigueur* for life's honors, accolades, and titles—all at stark odds with the *heavenly things.*

No matter what the gender, this race doesn't stop. Both individually and as Christian couples, they compete against the Joneses for the best homes, vacations, and seats of honor. On the Internet, radio, television, and in the glossy magazines, modern life *is* preaching incessantly to the Christian couple to postpone or cancel life-giving choices. It employs slick and sly reasoning to convince the Christian man and woman that,

- "It's your party, your life, and your body."
- "You can do whatever you please."
- "Enjoy yourself for all your hard work and the stress in your life."

When death's at the door, the weak sheep realize too late that *the city promises so much and delivers so little to so many.*

Guarding against the modern counter-catechesis

This crisis of faith has arisen because a vacuum exists. The People of God urgently need faith formation, but they aren't receiving all the Church's teachings. Indeed, how does the short period of catechesis for the young or the RCIA for adult converts stack up against the catechesis of modern life that teaches in seventy-seven clicks, day after day? Let's consider the spiritual education of the average Christian heart:

- Do we assume the faithful already possess a complete, sound understanding of the Faith?
- Do pastors unpack the week's teaching in a fifteen-minute homily to a packed hall at Mass?
- How do we help believers love one another, their neighbor, and enemy in daily living?

To answer these questions, we should ask all the sheep, "If adult faith formation isn't required, can the sheep accept the Lord's invitation?" The Lord says clearly to all the faithful, ". . . he who does not take his cross and follow me is not worthy of me. He who finds his life will lose it, and he who loses his life for my sake will find it." (Matthew 10:38-39)

If too many believers find difficulty saying, "Yes" to *lose his or her life*, doesn't this tell us quite clearly what the crisis of faith is all about? On a practical note, if few will step forward, where do we hope to find the Christians with "missionary heroism?" How are we going to raise "truly zealous priests" to undertake the New Evangelization of the cities discussed at the beginning of this Chapter?

I hope no one misunderstands me. We all need to work hard and make the best use of the opportunities in our life. Yet, for at least an hour a day in communion with the brothers and sisters, can the faithful listen to the Word of God and pray? Is the Word of God front and center in the lives of every Christian? We the faithful should struggle harder to center our life on the everlasting rock that is our God.

It's my hope that the pastors of all souls will address the need for faith formation and begin to allow the formation of lifelong communities and catechesis to be given. I'm imploring the Church to form the faithful with not just the Catechism, but also with the complete Word of God. When I refer to the Church, I make my appeal in particular to all pastors of souls everywhere—*let his fire blaze already!*

Why is knowledge of the Faith essential?

In Part 1 of this book, I recounted my early journey of faith in which I wandered about like a leaf in the wind. In Part 2, I shared the necessary path for everyone's faith journey. Looking back, my journey took me down many different paths, but let it not be so for all the brothers and sisters.

I believe there are many like me who are searching and wandering about. They're asking, ". . . who will go up for us to heaven, and bring it to us, that we may hear it and do it?" (Deuteronomy 30:11-12) In this petition, I sincerely hope the pastors of souls are able to help every Andy, Andre, and Andreas, who wish for faith formation. Such permanent training will enable believers to fully understand and embrace the complete Jesus Christ. These members of the faithful need to begin a journey of faith, with the Lord leading every believer that desires to follow Him. A program of structured faith formation should be supplied on such a journey, and faith cultivated in an ecclesial garden that causes what's sown in it to spring up.

Pope Emeritus Benedict spoke of the foundational importance of the knowledge of faith. Just as we should be able to give informed consent before surgery, so we need an adequate understanding of the full content of the Faith to say, 'Yes,' and begin collaborating with the Church. This means knowing how the mystery revealed by God can save us and give our life meaning in this world. It guides every believer to the right path and leads us to an appreciation of the mystery of God. (*Porta Fidei*, N.10)

Many of the faithful may have forgotten they're only pilgrims on this earthly journey. St. Paul tells us that many of our predecessors-in-faith died before receiving the promise they saw in the distant future. Such people think of themselves as nomads here on earth, and they're sure in their heart about their "real home." This isn't the place they came from, as it's easy to return there. They have their eyes fixed instead on heaven where God is. God isn't ashamed to love them and has founded a city for all the faithful. (Hebrews 11:13-16)

St. Paul also gives good advice regarding the focus of Christians in this world. If Christians have died with Christ, we need not let our life be limited by the dictates and desires of this world. To gain wisdom, St. Paul advises all Christians to reject the principles of this world. For instance, the faithful are obliged to give up evil desires and especially abandon greed, which is *no different from worshipping a false god.* (Colossians 2:20-3:5)

I've referred to St. Paul's teachings to show just a few examples of the knowledge of the Faith that every believer needs to learn and accept. Assuming, that is, the desire to follow Jesus Christ is in our inmost heart.

Have all believers acquired a complete knowledge of the Faith? I don't think so. It seems obvious to me that a believer should be (but isn't) asking from the Church, "I've been given the gift of faith, now teach me what it all means so I can copy and share the love of Jesus Christ."

If I'm right that the crisis of faith is simply a result of believers not receiving a complete knowledge of the Faith, then the solution is quite simple and happy. We just need to form permanent communities. Once the believers have joined their respective communities, they can take the same catechetical steps with the brothers and sisters God will give them for the lifelong journey. Then, impart all the knowledge of the Faith in a structured program allowing for gradual learning. I'm confident this solution will give believers the spiritual support all will need to develop a full and fruitful Christian life.

When more Christians are bearing fruit, all other works in the Church will become easier to do. I'm sure of this.

What's the place of the parish?

Here are two suggestions. Don't limit the experience of spiritual learning, sharing and support to the physical church building. We should also depart from the old thinking that faith needs to revolve around activities organized on Sundays or other days of obligation.

In his Post-Synodal Apostolic Exhortation on January 22, 1999, St. John Paul II spoke of the place of the parish and the leadership of the pastor. (Ecclesia in America, N.5) Parishes are useful places of first contact. They're welcoming and offer the chance for people to be initiated into the Christian faith. For this purpose, the Church not only celebrates the faith, but also teaches it.

Like the smaller, nimble *Victory* commanded by Sir John Hawkins that outmaneuvered the Spanish Galleons, the Church ought to form small, nimble communities where Christian fellowship can develop. Only in these less formal surroundings can people confidently gather to hear the Word of God. When the Word penetrates the heart, the faithful can share the difficulties they have experienced in the world (i.e. how God has acted wonderfully in their life). By giving and receiving faith, they'll gradually accept the love of Christ as central to every decision they make in life; something I too hope to achieve one day with grace from God. This is how the brothers and sisters support each other in faith and grow together in love and praise of God.

Only when there's a real collaboration between the lay people and the pastor, can the parish be renewed. The true spirit of the journeying in the desert shall begin with the Lord leading every one of these small communities.

Let's turn to the next and most important Chapter and consider a good way to help the faithful rediscover their baptism.

QUESTIONS FOR REFLECTION ON CHAPTER 21

1. Do you recognize secular disruptions in your life whose counter-catechesis is rapidly changing the way you think about your faith?
2. How does the systematic secular counter-catechesis compare with the systematic catechesis of your heart by the Church?
3. Are you conditioned by the struggle for money, success, and individual happiness that you're losing the conditioned struggle to follow Jesus Christ and what He tells you to do?

22. Road Map from St. John Paul II

Here is the path

On October 16, 1979, St. John Paul II made a crucial apostolic appeal called the *Catechesi Tradendae*. In this document, he continued the work of his predecessors and reminded the Church that catechesis remained important in its mission to educate and build up the Body of Christ. I won't repeat his entire appeal, but will highlight certain passages to emphasize:

- the essential need for continuing adult catechism;
- the mission of catechesis;
- the roles and responsibilities of the principal responsibles for catechesis; and
- the place of the family at the heart of the Church's renewal.

If you want to read what St. John Paul II actually said, relevant extracts can be found in the Appendix.

To begin, he exhorted the Church to give priority to catechesis over its other works and undertakings because it would produce more spectacular results in two ways:

- strengthening the internal life of the Church as a community of believers; and
- promoting the external work of a missionary Church.

To achieve the hoped-for spectacular results, St. John Paul II was clear about the priority of catechism, believing the Church shouldn't spare any "effort, toil or material means" to organize the catechesis and train qualified people. He felt the Church should have no problem offering its best resources to adult catechesis.

St. John Paul II said, ". . . an attitude of faith always has reference to the faithfulness of God, who never fails to respond." (*Catechesi Tradendae*, 15; Appendix-1) What does this phrase mean?

It means simply that the Church needs to give faith formation its top priority because this is what the Lord commanded. (Matthew 28:20) When this happens, we can certainly hope for the Lord to respond with graces, which every collaborator will need in the necessary mission of re-evangelization and renewal.

Why do adults need deeper catechesis?

St. John Paul II said the Church had recognized the central problem of adult catechesis. Namely, that few adults continue the spiritual training of their heart. If the Church is to be serious about giving witness to the world, it must be able to depend on the adult Christians because they have ". . . the greatest responsibilities and the capacity to live the Christian message in its fully developed form."

St. John Paul II isn't saying that the clergy or the religious are evading their responsibilities in giving witness. Rather, the adult believers are the faces, voices, arms, and legs of the Church in the world we live in. The Church will continue to struggle without the direct and knowledgeable participation of all adult Christians in their day-to-day living.

Indeed, the urgent need for deeper, adult catechesis is made more pressing by the crisis of faith.

For a moment, let's think only about the next generation of children. The world of young people is governed by adults. If young believers are to grow in the faith and give witness to it, they ought to receive catechesis from adults who are obliged to deepen and strengthen the faith of the young believers in their care.

This means that the faith of adult Christians should also be continually enlightened, stimulated, and renewed. For such catechesis to be effective, it needs to be permanent. What's more important, it shouldn't stop at the threshold of maturity. As children grow into adults, catechesis continues to be necessary as they join other adults in the community to serve the Lord. (*Catechesi Tradendae*, 43; Appendix-2)

If the Church can't depend on the participation of adult Christians, how else will it provide catechesis to every other adult and young believer needing deeper and lifelong catechism?

What are the effects of inadequate catechism?

To understand the effects of poor catechism, think about how we learn a new language at school (or learn any skill for that matter). It begins with the basics of grammar, then we add simple vocabulary. So long as we only use the new language during school lessons, the little we learn is quickly lost. To be able to write and speak fluently, regular practice in and outside the classroom is required. Only then can one improve and grow more sophisticated in the way that the language is used.

Needless to say, even though one may have mastered the language, it can still be lost through failure or neglect to improve or upgrade the skills.

Similarly, a baptized Christian may have remained a *catechumen* because he or she didn't receive a thorough or continuing education of his or her heart. Firstly, there may have been no attempt by the believers to continue spiritual learning, practice, and struggle in adult life. Secondly, we ought to count the numbers of Christians without a permanent community in which to sustain the life according to Christ. It's my thinking that the Church will have to create an immense number of small communities for the New Evangelization. Then, we need to consider the absence of the Word and prayer in daily living, so much so that Christ is practically absent in between masses or church activities on Sundays. It's imperative hence to help every believer build up his or her Christian life that's either irregular or inactive at the moment.

Depending on the circumstances and experiences of each diocese and parish, the pastoral missionary effort could be directed at those believers who:

- were born and raised in places that weren't Christian and so didn't have a chance to study Christian teachings deeply;
- only had the opportunity to learn something suited their age when they were young. As adults and having now drifted away from religion, their knowledge of the Faith remains incomplete and undeveloped;
- received religious education that was either not well taught or learned; and
- may have been born in a Christian area or country, but have never received any teaching in the Faith. (*Catechesi Tradendae*, 44; Appendix-3)

My main hypothesis in this book is that *inadequate faith formation of most, if not all, Christians is the likely root of the crisis.* I won't repeat what I said about identifying adequate faith formation. Instead, I invite the pastors of souls to ask what the hearts of their sheepfold say about following Jesus Christ, carrying their crosses, and becoming disciples who can love. (Matthew 10:38-39)

How is catechesis different from the initial conversion?

My reading of St. John Paul II's exhortation in *Catechesi Tradendae* tells me to make a proper distinction between catechesis and the initial conversion. The initial conversion affects a person receiving the gift of faith, who then unreservedly accepts Jesus Christ as his or her Savior. Catechesis, on the other hand, aims to deepen the initial proclamation of faith and help a convert become a disciple by learning, copying, and reproducing the complete Jesus Christ.

St. John Paul II also advised the Church to ". . . allow for the fact that the initial evangelization hasn't taken place." Catechesis is more than just teaching the Faith. It needs to accept that a good number of believers remain on the threshold of, and haven't entered the door of, faith. Being on the threshold implies that the believers are Christians in name, but haven't yet committed their whole lives to Jesus Christ. This probably explains why these Christians say they believe in Jesus Christ, but find themselves unable to obey the Lord's commandments.

Some believers may pick and choose what they wish to obey, and even challenge the tenets of Faith or its application in today's world of science and enlightenment. They may also be unwilling to carry their cross of suffering to follow Jesus Christ. Such attitudes and conduct don't square with their profession of faith.

Just telling the believers to do the right thing or do better won't help them deepen their faith.

What's needed is a thorough re-evangelization program to open the hearts of all believers (regardless whether they have yet to commit), convert them so they fully accept the Faith, and prepare them to be devoted followers of Christ. Which examples did St. John Paul II offer to identify the believers ". . . that are still on the threshold of faith?"

- Some children were baptized in infancy and are attending catechesis in the parish without receiving any other initiation into the faith. They often have no explicit personal attachment to Jesus Christ. They only have the capacity to believe placed within them by baptism and the presence of the Holy Spirit. Sadly, they may quickly lose their way as a result of opposition stemming from their non-Christian family background or a secular education that's opposed to faith.

- Some children, who haven't been baptized, receive catechesis at a later age.
- Then we come to the pre-adolescents and adolescents, who have been baptized and received ordinary catechesis, but remain hesitant about committing their whole lives to Jesus Christ. Many of these young believers may even resist religious education in the name of their freedom.
- Finally, even adults aren't safe from the temptation to doubt and abandon their faith. This is often the effect of their unbelieving surroundings. (*Catechesi Tradendae*, 19; Appendix-4)

Andy, Andre, and Andreas will need re-evangelization to accept the complete Jesus Christ. This is especially so if the baptism of the believers didn't lead to an *experience of Christian living, celebrations of the sacraments, an integration into the ecclesial community, and the apostolic and missionary witnessing.* (CCC 6)

What's the spiritual motivation for adult catechesis?

St. John Paul II advised us that the adult catechesis not only helps all Christians develop their faith thoroughly, but it also prepares them as witnesses of Christ. We all need complete knowledge of our Savior, so we can share with nonbelievers and hesitant Christians our precious hope in God's desire to save everyone. (*Catechesi Tradendae*, 25; Appendix-5)

If we don't want to or can't share our hope in the Good News, doesn't this speak volumes about our acceptance of Jesus as our Lord and Savior? If a reason for not sharing the great love of God is a poor grasp of the Good News, shouldn't it be clear that many of us need deeper catechesis? Every believer needs to train to prepare for the mission that Christ gave to *every* one of His sheep.

In my early years, I feared questions and avoided discussing the Faith with other believers. I skirted my obligation to bear witness for fear of saying the wrong thing. Even in the first steps of my faith journey, I hesitated to be an actual disciple. This was because my faith formation wasn't sufficiently rooted. Speaking for myself only, I'm a believer who needs continuing catechesis to deepen and mature the faith I've acquired from the Lord through His Church. I must learn the complete Jesus Christ to be His witness and share the incredible Good News of God's great love!

What kind of "Yes" did we say to Jesus Christ?

Being a Christian means saying "Yes" to Jesus Christ, but what does this involve?

- At the first level, it requires the Christian to surrender to the Word of God, i.e. to rely on it in everyday life.
- The "Yes" a Christian says should progress toward the second level. There's much to learn and understand, so the Christian must persevere and acquire a deeper and more complete acceptance of the Word of God. (*Catechesi Tradendae*, 20; Appendix-6)

St. John Paul II has helped me to understand that these two levels of "Yes" are similar to the idea of the two-stage healing described in Mark 8:22-26. At the first instance of surrendering to the Word of God, what I saw was only a *dim reflection* because my initial knowledge of the Word of God was imperfect. (1 Corinthians 13:12) The Lord may give me the grace to experience the second level if I make a sincere commitment to learn from Him.

When I reach the second level, I'll have a real hope of acquiring the profound meaning of the Word of God so that I *shall know as fully as I am known*. This thorough understanding is needed to help me live a new life according to Christ and love as the Lord has commanded me.

Every believer should be given the opportunity to say, "Yes!", to Jesus Christ at both the first and second levels.

How does a Christian deepen the faith?

St. John Paul II reminds all of us that whoever follows Jesus Christ should try to deepen his or her faith, in communion with brothers and sisters taking the same steps. If catechesis is given to a catechumen without such a community and the accompanying Christian life, there's a risk the catechesis will be unfruitful. (*Catechesi Tradendae*, 24; Appendix-7)

Why did St. John Paul II think there was a risk of catechesis being unfruitful?

Catechesis shouldn't be packaged as a series of lectures, after which the students are left to their own devices. If the believers retreat to their respective spaces or even church ministries unsuited to faith formation, they are less likely to find opportunities to practice their emerging faith. Without the communion of brothers and sisters taking the *same steps*, these faithful (though instructed) are being allowed to drift away from grace. We should be particularly concerned with those hailing from unbelieving and prejudiced backgrounds, which might tempt any Christian to doubt. None of us should be left on our own to pursue faith development. Each community should be accompanied by shepherds monitoring and supervising the structured faith formation of the brothers and sisters.

A small community should be like a phalanx—a military tactic of old. This ancient battle formation was very strong because the well-trained soldiers moved and fought closely together as one unit. Applying this thinking to small permanent faith communities, Christians marching on the journey of faith should be in spiritual formation with their own community of brothers and sisters. The faith of each will be stronger and reinforce progress, whereas a solitary believer in a large, impersonal parish may well lose his or her way. This idea supplies a spiritual ideal, which is that every small community of faith should march in lockstep with the church, producing a community of communities at the local level.

How do we test this proposition? When a Christian learns the commandment to love but isn't given the opportunity to practice what's been learned, how does he or she deepen the understanding of love in this *new* language of the cross? How does he or she learn to forgive an unkind brother or pray for a sister who persecutes him? If there's no community of like-minded brothers, can we expect those without faith to understand this Christian's practice or expression of love? The world outside may pour scorn at the mercy the Christian is learning to offer and call him, "fool." Without spiritual encouragement from his brothers and sisters, he or she might be tempted to abandon the teachings of Jesus Christ after a few attempts, bungled or otherwise. Even another believer at a different stage of the journey might not appreciate the depth of the faith expression of other Christians with mature faith; e.g. death of self (ego), missionary zeal, or renouncing the world. I'm on, or near to, the mark in thinking that a Christian not marching seriously or not marching at the same pace might just misunderstand, be scandalized, or be scared away.

Here's the $64,000 question: if a Christian is unable to learn how to love his brothers and sisters, how can anyone expect this believer to love a neighbor or even an enemy outside the community?

It should be easy to see why the mission of faith formation was important to St. John Paul II. It enables the formation of permanent communities of faith, which will provide catechesis to all the brothers and sisters. In the long journey, the small community of faith should nurture the life that each ought to be living according to the Gospel; i.e. practice and grow the faith (or spiritually skydive with Jesus Christ).

An ecclesial community isn't formed as an end in itself: it isn't inward looking, with spiritual activities solely for the benefit of its members. It's also not merely about membership (being a Christian isn't judged by mechanically ticking boxes and collecting points for attendance or performing parish activities).

What I understand St. John Paul II to mean is that there's a spectrum of fruit, benefits, and purposes that a community may produce. Families within each community can be taught to give catechesis to their children. Once the faith has aroused a brother or sister to proclaim the Good News, he or she can't do this on his or her own. All evangelizing Christians should set out two-by-two and always at the instruction of the Church. They should be fully mindful of their duty to share the Good News, the amazing love of God. I should add that this duty isn't anything onerous, but one that's borne out of grateful love for God and necessary love for neighbor—*Caritas Christi urget nos!* (2 Corinthians 5:14)

The possibilities for the flowering of community life are numerous and good, but they need to be united with the Church. An ecclesial community should remain together on a lifelong journey of faith pursuing the Word of God to the finish line.

Are church groups exempt?

The answer is that they shouldn't be. The Church draws great comfort from the flourishing number of youth groups, living by the Gospel, and making Jesus Christ known. They fit a broader pattern of Christian action, charitable, prayer, and meditation groups. As if in springtime, these groups are a source of great hope for the Church of tomorrow, being exceptional occasions for:

- meeting others;
- being blessed with riches of friendship and solidarity among the young;

- joy and enthusiasm; and
- a chance to reflect on events and facts.

St. John Paul II, however, implored the young people who belong to these groups not to avoid serious study of Christian doctrine. If they do, they'll be in danger; a danger that has, unfortunately, proved only too real—of disappointing their members and the Church as well. (*Catechesi Tradendae*, 47; Appendix-8) His advice was also directed at the leaders of these groups, and the priests who devote the best part of their ministry to them.

A lifelong study of the Faith will strengthen the mission and objectives of these church groups. It goes without saying that all of us need prayer and the Word in our daily life. Ministry life and other parish activities are faith-centric when they're grounded with prayer and the Word. Yes, daily prayer will deepen our relationship with God. It's through the Word of God that all of us convert, transform and bear fruit. The living Word—the Teacher—the Gardener will prune Christians who seek Him. They'll seek the Lord, praise Him, and spread the Gospel—*long life to their hearts!*

Who has the responsibility for lifelong catechesis?

In *Catechesi Tradendae*, 16 (Appendix-9), St. John Paul II accepted that Church members have different responsibilities, depending on their individual missions. The chief responsibility for fostering, guiding, and coordinating catecheses falls to the pastors. Teachers, the various ministers of the Church, catechists, and the organizers of social communications have very precise responsibilities to educate the believing conscience, all of which enhances the life of the Church and its role in society. Building for the future, parents also have a unique responsibility as the primary catechists to their children.

Who has the primary responsibility for catecheses?

St. John Paul II emphasized the role of the Bishops. They have a special mission within their Churches. Together with the Pope, they're the ones primarily responsible for catecheses throughout the Church.

This despite the fact their ministry as Bishops is daily growing more complex and overwhelming. They have a thousand matters demanding their attention: from training to being actively present in communities, celebrating the sacraments, universal concern for human advancement, and the defense of human rights.

Why should Bishops give catechesis top priority?

Bishops assume the chief management of catechesis by surrounding themselves with competent and trustworthy assistants. When Bishops personally transmit the doctrine of life to their flocks, it'll bring about and maintain a real passion for catechesis in that diocese. The path and direction that any bishop sets for his diocese should contemplate a collaborative, as opposed to a top-down process. If the message is clear, everyone should understand the way to proceed. Those responsible for the catechetical process (e.g. priest, parent, catechist, etc.) play a role as important as the Bishop's and the sheep ask for spiritual food without being rejected.

It seems as if I might be saying something extraordinary, but I'm not. A bishop can't possibly teach every individual in a diocese. Everyone needs to cooperate, participate, and collaborate. But when Bishops lead the charge, teaching, lifelong learning, and Christian life will be seen as vital to the faith!

Once catecheses in local parishes are done well, every other mission will become easier. Although Bishops have the thankless task of identifying deviation and correcting error, they'll also have the joy and consolation of seeing their churches flourish because catechesis is given to the flock as the Lord commanded. (*Catechesi Tradendae*, 16; Appendix-10)

Who are the instructors in the Faith?

St. John Paul II identified the important role of priests as the immediate assistants of the Bishops. They're called "instructors in the faith" and are expected to devote their best efforts to grow the faith of local communities. Whether they are:

- in charge of a parish;
- chaplains to institutions of learning;
- responsible for pastoral activity at any level; or
- leaders of communities, especially youth groups;

the Church expects all pastors to be well trained for catechesis and to organize a structured catechetical effort. The deacons and other ministers may be available to assist in producing an environment in which every believer can receive catechesis. All pastors have the duty to provide for it. We should never lament, ". . . the children beg for food, but no one gives to them." (*Catechesi Tradendae*, 64; Appendix-11)

What if there aren't enough priests?

Many religious institutions were created to give Christian education to children and young people. Throughout history, religious men and women have been deeply committed to the Church's catechetical activity, doing particularly useful work.

At a time when the Church needs the religious and pastors to work closely, St. John Paul II urged the religious to make themselves available for the benefit of the Church. (*Catechesi Tradendae*, 65; Appendix-12) He called on the religious with catechetical and evangelical charisms to help in the New Evangelization—this is the solution to the majority of priests who are presently overstretched in their busy parishes.

The vital importance of the family in catechesis

According to the Second Vatican Council, the family's role in faith education is special and irreplaceable. Christian families serve as indispensable branches that spring, nurture, and support new shoots of faith. Parents are the primary caregivers. They're primarily responsible for the health and growth of their children, and every aspect of their education. St. John Paul II advised parents that they aren't just potential teachers, but they're also the primary role models of faith. The parents begin the education of their children in the faith by living a complete, Christian life.

Earlier in Chapter 6, I discussed how primary caregivers play a critical role in the safety and welfare of children in their care. It's the same thinking here. Parents play a vital, spiritually essential role in the faith formation of their children because they *are* the primary teachers of the Faith; catechism teachers and pastors play the supporting, albeit specialized, roles. Who make the ultimate decisions in every aspect of the children's lives, if not the parents (or other caregivers such as guardians)?

The catechesis given by parents is more effective during the course of family events in the faith, when:

- receiving the sacraments;
- celebrating the great liturgical feasts;
- welcoming the birth of a child; or
- dealing with a death in the family;

if care is taken to explain the Christian meaning of these events. That is, however, not enough.

Within the setting of family life, Christian parents should follow and repeat faith teaching received elsewhere, on a regular (if not daily) basis. By repeating these truths about the main questions of faith and Christian life in their actions and words, they'll help their children grow in faith and love. This does, of course, depend on the family setting being full of love and respect. The parents themselves benefit from their efforts because, in faith transmission within the family, they give and receive faith themselves.

Family catechesis, therefore, precedes, accompanies, and enriches all other forms of catechesis. The family is "the church of the home" and it possesses the potential to offer life-giving catechesis to children and young people. The homes complement the parish and the small communities as additional places that welcome and initiate new spiritual shoots into the Christian life.

In other words, there can't be too great an effort for Christian parents to prepare for this ministry of being their own children's catechists and to carry it out with tireless zeal. The catechesis they give within the family home is priceless. These aren't my ideas; they *are* the apostolic appeals of St. John Paul II. (*Catechesi Tradendae*, 62-68; Appendix-13)

Parents can ask for help from specialists, but they shouldn't relinquish or delegate their primary responsibility. Although they can turn to the church for catechetical help, it remains their paramount duty to explain the Faith to their children and cultivate a home that welcomes Jesus Christ.

If families haven't been the priority of re-evangelization efforts, should we be surprised by the crisis of faith? From the perspective of the parish, the church can't afford to provide one-off training to parents and leave them to manage on their own. Every Christian family needs to be at the center of the New Evangelization. There should be regular monitoring and follow-up on a continuing basis, and this is best done in the context of a permanent community of brothers and sisters taking the same steps.

A shovel-ready proposal

The venues of the church and the family home

I believe the New Evangelization should begin with the parish as the center for faith formation, but the development of faith should *not* depend on a particular location. Why? Because the special and indispensable role of families in nurturing the children in their care makes all activities inside and outside the home "multitudinous branches," which can serve the parish as additional places of spiritual welcome, study, and worship. Yes, as families did in the days of the early Church. This solves the logistical problem of time and venue. Sadly, no matter how hard we might try, it's very difficult to persuade every parishioner to attend church for faith learning at the same time.

Taking membership in a community in and of itself won't suffice to deepen one's faith. Everyone should be making efforts to:

- leave New Egypt;
- walk regularly on a journey of faith through the many meetings for faith learning, progression, and transformation;
- meet Jesus Christ in the celebrations;
- spend quiet time in daily prayer with the Lord; and
- climb the mountain of God steadily—all of us are sinners, and all need the grace of the Eternal-Father straightaway!

Faith formation and community development happen best through personal interaction, communal experiences, and spiritual growth. There's no place in the New Evangelization for distance-learning models on the web or by email.

Following the example of the Holy Family of Nazareth, each committed family becomes a basic community of faith. The family becomes a vital building block of faith formation when it joins the small community of like-minded brothers and sisters. Each of these lifelong faith communities belongs to the parish, which St. John Paul II described as the community of communities. These small communities strike me as the *Ekklesia* referred to frequently in the Greek Old Testament for the assembly of the Chosen People before God.

So when I tell my mother I'm going to church, it doesn't mean just the parish building. We should move away from the old thinking of the parish as the only faith destination.

In a barren, urban landscape, the community of communities and all its branches need to be the local beacon of spiritual light, hope, and love.

Allow for a gradual transformation

Faith formation can't simply be packaged as a series of lectures run once a week for the sake of convenience nor should we aspire anxiously to teach the entire Faith within a short period. The Church should never indulge those who claim to have little time to spare. We shouldn't set a time limit, target or Key Performance Indicator for the New Evangelization to bear fruit in any preset period. Instead, the re-evangelization efforts should take place gradually, albeit on frequent, regular days other than Sundays or days of obligation. We should be mindful that faith formation will need to be like the learning and practice of any talent, art, or skill; but always anticipating the track record of the rebellious heart.

Can we honestly say there's no time for the Lord? It's like saying we recognize the Lord has come down from the highest heaven to humble earth, then died on the cross to communicate God's great love, but we simply have no time beyond Mass or church activities on Sunday:

- "I have important business, a project deadline or critical homework, which require my urgent attention," or
- "*. . . because He is too far away . . . maybe God isn't keeping track of everything I do . . .*"; (Job 22:13) or
- "God should understand my priorities."

Are these our responses to the Lover of us all? How do we respond to the Redeemer against whom every sinner has sinned, yet He persists in His thirst to save all of us and give life beyond measure?

The serious questions can be put another way: is it possible to quickly teach love, renouncing oneself, and the carrying of one's cross? I personally don't think so. Faith formation has to be a lifelong journey concerned with rediscovering our baptism, the two levels of "Yes," and the *metanoia*. It requires the lifelong commitment of believers, who are seeking the help and grace of God.

A baptized Christian with an immature faith might find it disturbing to join a community of believers who have reached an advanced stage of the spiritual journey. Separate communities are needed to support those taking steps at later starting times. Communities shouldn't be geographical or grouped around similar age groups, interests, or even ethnic formations. When St. Paul made references to *Jew, Greek, slave, free, male or female*, he was talking about an inclusive community. Such inclusiveness means groups of repentant believers should be mixed across ages and social backgrounds, and not just people with similar interests or profiles the majority can be comfortable with. This gives everyone the opportunity to learn how to love every other *Jew, Greek, slave, free, male or female* within the community, during a faith journey likely to last a lifetime.

We also shouldn't exclude tax collectors and prostitutes who believe in the way of righteousness. (Matthew 21:32)

I submit that the only requirement for membership is the sinner turning to the Lord for gradual healing and transformation by taking small steps—the Lord was quite clear about the sick and healthy. For many, the journey of faith will be like climbing a high mountain with thousands of steps, with possibilities of regressing at the various stops. Each step needs to be taken carefully. Progress ought to be constant, sure and steady, with the Spirit accompanying all the brothers and sisters *by day in the form of a pillar of cloud to show them the way, and by night in the form of a pillar of fire to give them light.*

When the brothers and sisters in the community are able to say sincerely and unequivocally, "We love each other," these disciples will have fulfilled an all-important commandment of our Lord Jesus Christ. (John 13:34-35) From this fruit, nonbelievers will gradually, and finally, recognize the love of God in this world.

What's the first step moving forward?

All I've written so far appears promising on paper, but even if we confess the crisis of faith, how do we take the first step forward together? What's the practical solution for the New Evangelization?

To borrow a construction term, this book's proposal needs to be shovel-ready.

St. John Paul II has identified the Bishops as chief managers of faith formation. In this connection, they need to declare the re-evangelization, continuing catechesis, and faith formation as the pressing, paramount mission of the Church. Then, they must open the doors *wide* in their dioceses and marshal the best resources as chief managers of each local New Evangelization. Then it's for the pastors, as assistants of the Bishops, to be the primary instructors of faith and sowers of small, permanent faith communities. This is a major outreach effort so every priest will need help and assistance.

Given the diminishing number of priests, there's a clear need to ask the religious institutes, associations of the faithful, ecclesial movements, and new communities to help. Not just any group, but those specifically blessed with the gifts of catechesis and evangelization. The Church should draw up a list of the Aquila, Priscilla, Aristarchus, the cousin of Barnabus, Epaphras, Jesus Justus, Luke, Onesimus, Philemon, and Tychicus that are permitted to assist bishops and priests in every diocese and parish, all around the world. This list will also need to approve the content of catechesis and faith formation, which shall be supplied by these evangelizers—unleash these Christians who are yearning to do the will of God!

The catechesis should be delivered in intimate communities of faith, where Christian fellowship and faith experience may be shared, nurtured, and come to flower. Once this list of evangelizers is drawn up, the doors should open and the outreach should begin everywhere.

The foregoing action plan makes this proposal shovel-ready.

What if many of the faithful are simply not hungry?

It doesn't matter if this idea of faith formation seems strange, faddish, or merely curious to the majority. We must accept the possibility that many poor believers have forgotten how to eat. They might continue their spiritual routine as before and remain content with spiritual milk. After all, the Lord Himself was prescient about the small numbers when he said, ". . . many are called, but few are chosen." (Matthew 22:14) Efforts shouldn't be spared to re-evangelize all hesitant Christians nonetheless, especially those still "on the threshold of faith."

There's no greater joy in prodigally wasting our time, energy, and effort for the sake of the Good News!

The new missionary outreach will be fruitful even if only a pitiful handful responds to the call for a serious journey of faith. The initial focus should be on the Christians who are hungry for Christ: *let the poor receive as much as they want to eat!*

I wouldn't be surprised that some may even run away or rebel, once this small handful taking the first, hesitating steps learns the actual extent of Christian life. The Lord is clear about the narrow path, and the rebellion of the people in the desert also offers many lessons. The small numbers taking up their crosses and following Christ will only prove the truth of God's boundless love, immeasurable mercy and timeless faithfulness recorded in the Bible, and the epic struggle for a believer to remain faithful to the Lord's commandments for life and love. For this reason, any plan of New Evangelization might have to provide for at least three generations to restore the Christian life of a family currently struggling in unbelieving surroundings.

People need to be free in their choice to follow the Lord. From my faith journey, I went far off the beaten path because I was free to say *No* to Fr. Alfred's spiritual help.

To counter this *No*, weak sheep and the People of God will, of course, fare better if the shepherds offer a clear direction for the faith journey to be necessarily undertaken by the entire Church. The direction will be even clearer if the bishops personally lead the march in a small community of faith, with the cross borne high for his brothers and sisters to follow in lockstep, if possible. That's just a faint dream of the future, but who knows how the wind will blow?

Then again, who can say that the flags of the churches everywhere won't dance, won't whirl and won't wave with the wind?

For now, the pastors of souls need only ask if there are ten at least willing to say, "Yes," and be salt and light. We don't need five hundred, but larger numbers would be helpful. Twelve frightened, simple men were moved by the Lord to set out and they *have* faithfully made disciples of the nations. Imagine what the Paraclete *can* do for the New Evangelization (should the Church *ask* for help to be sent) with just ten frightened, but spiritually formed Christians in each parish, in each city, all over the world!

QUESTIONS FOR REFLECTION ON CHAPTER 22

1. Are you a sinner?
2. Can you love?
3. Are you able to commit your whole life to Jesus Christ? If not, will you seek faith formation to help you make this commitment and maintain the Christian struggle?
4. What do you think of the proposition that "a Christian needs most of his lifetime to learn how to love?"
5. What do you think of the thinking that information, opinions, and attitudes in the fast changing world pretty much overwhelm the initial faith education that you've received?
6. Have you come across prejudices against the Faith in your home, workplace, or village? Do you feel as if you need to hide or suppress your Christian identity?
7. Besides the catechesis received in your teens or in the RCIA, what other faith training are you receiving on a regular basis?
8. Do you teach your children the Faith regularly?

Conclusion

Take Courage

"See, I have set before you this day life and good, death and evil. If you *obey the commandments of the Lord your God* which I command you this day, *by loving the Lord your God, by walking in his ways*, and *by keeping his commandments* and his statutes and his ordinances, then you shall live and multiply, and the Lord your God will bless you in the land which you are entering to take possession of it. But if your heart turns away, and you won't hear, but are drawn away to worship other gods and serve them, I declare to you this day, that you shall perish; you shall not live long in the land which you are going over the Jordan to enter and possess. I call heaven and earth to witness against you this day, that I have set before you life and death, blessing and curse; therefore choose life, that you and your descendants may live, loving the Lord your God, obeying his voice, and cleaving to him; for that means life to you and length of days, that you may dwell in the land which the Lord swore to your fathers, to Abraham, to Isaac, and to Jacob, to give them. (Emphasis added)"

—(Deuteronomy 30:15-20)

Awesome beyond

The message in these pages isn't new. Many others before me have spoken about the necessary journey of faith. I only did a bit of research, dusted old memory files, and retold the message in the only way I knew how. Someone else will come again on another day to tell this message because too many still won't attend the Lord's wedding feast. There are many more without a wedding garment. In far too many places, a great multitude has yet to receive His wedding invitations. I've been laboring to earn a *denarius* to repeat this simple message.

Are you free to reject this message? Yes, you've always been free.

Are there are other routes? Yes, there should be.

Whatever path you choose, it has to lead you through the narrow door and more importantly, beyond and clear of the threshold of faith. Such other route will have to help you follow Jesus Christ in your everyday moments and do the will of God.

If you've read this book and now long to encounter Jesus Christ our Lord, I hope you'll accept the message—on the threshold of your heart at the very least. Think of Mary. She welcomed the Word *into* her heart and said *Yes* to the Lord despite her many difficulties and heartaches, then gave birth to the Wonder-Counselor, Mighty-God, Eternal-Father, Prince-of-Peace. In a similar way, the same grace can fall on you. Speak to your pastor and find out if you should say, "Yes!", to the Word of God and follow Jesus. May the Good News grow inside you and be born in your life!

This is the Christmas message that all of us celebrate in the present tense. It isn't just a commercial carol or a pleasant sounding song about a miraculous child born two thousand years ago. In truth, it's a timeless invitation from the Savior of the World. Christ shall be born in us, then our faith grows and matures in an intimate community, not unlike the Holy Family of Nazareth!

I'm sure the Lord loves you and is waiting for you to say *Yes* today. Begin the journey out of New Egypt and allow the Lord to lead you to the awesome beyond. That first and every other day of your faith journey promise to be as spectacular and full of wonder as our Lord is.

Trust in the Lord

I give thanks to and praise the Lord for meeting me, walking with me, and guiding me on His path all this time. In my faith journey so far, I've encountered Jesus, my Savior. I regret (but won't despair) not recognizing this when I was younger.

He wishes to walk with you too. Jesus brings good tidings to His people and has planted His Spirit in you and me. The Lord loves me as He surely loves you; each of us as we are—warts and all. When we're all united in His ways, you and I are in Him, as He is in us—we *can* be one.

There are many saints, of course, who have shown great love for the Lord, renounced the world and carried their crosses in unity with Him.

Even so, saints were sinners too!

The only One who has fulfilled the *Shema*, the Law, and all of the heavenly above is Jesus Christ. I'm certain it's my God who makes me holy. This despite being a man full of sin, who has yet to achieve *metanoia*. He makes you holy too and will help you with the transformation of your heart. All you have to do is *ask* Jesus Christ.

From my history, I recognize the thirst of my Lord to help me become a Christian. The day I become a Christian is that very day when I can love as my Lord loves me. It's on that selfsame day when I must renew my baptism in the waters of the Jordan. In the Preface, I referred to the observations by St. John Paul II about believers remaining on the "threshold of faith" and being "catechumens." Given what I know about my incomplete faith formation, I'm forced to regard myself as a kind of catechumen for now. I need Jesus Christ to continue teaching me love until I *get it* in my heart.

In this light, I accept that the Devil may accuse me of my sins and my pitiful struggle to sin no more. The Accuser may confound me with more ways to stumble than I can anticipate. Hence, the best way forward is to keep close to the Lord in the holy journey, as Abraham and many others did in their time. I know there'll be days without water, so I must be careful at Meribah. I must remain in communion with my brothers and sisters, pastors, catechists, and the Church. The Beguiler must not fool me with his choice of death.

A Nathan will also come tell me that I'm a sinner. In reply, I must ask the Lord for strength to confess my sin without defending or excusing myself. For so much is revealed to me already that, as I venture farther out on the spiritual trail, I'll only acknowledge more of my sins; many more than I could have recognized at the start of my journey.

Anticipating the extent of my sins can only be great news. Why should I take courage as a sinner? Because the more honest I *am* about the extent of my failings, the easier it *is* for my Lord to do the work of transformation in me. Yes, O happy fault! As long as I want to learn from Jesus on this holy journey, I'm confident of His grace and not stress about my sins.

Do I sound like a convert? How can it be? There are still thorns, chaff, and darnel caught in my flesh. I'm a convert only because I've accepted His promise of salvation on the threshold of my heart. In following Jesus Christ, I do my best to cooperate with His Spirit, listen to the Word, and allow the Gospel to penetrate my heart, little by little. And no matter what happens, my Savior has advised me to keep my faith until my last breath.

Yes, this is the low bar of *the easy yoke and light burden* that the Lord sets for me. Faith formation is the Lord doing His work in my heart (and yours if you want to). Hoping for the Lord's salvation means I commit, persevere, and make every effort to cooperate with the Lord to transform my heart, soul, and strength—for God, nothing is impossible.

When you put this book down, I hope you too will consider walking with the Lord and don't look at me (or anyone else). Look only to the Lord, for Adam mostly disappoints.

March on!

This memorial of the Lord in my life's journey ends for now. Though I was searching for Jesus Christ in the least of His brothers, I now recognize my understanding of the Faith has been quite inadequate. I wasn't ready to follow Jesus Christ when I was baptized and confirmed. For a long time, I wasn't prepared to do what the Lord told me, despite doing service in the parish. Spending much of my life searching, I've come to learn that my Lord has been with me. He hasn't given up on helping me. So I'm confident Jesus will continue to lead me to the place of rest and get me *ready* to love.

Throughout my life, I suffered abuse, dark suffering, and much grief. All of which I accept were a necessary part of my spiritual journey and conversion, even though the suffering remains a sore segment of my memory. Nevertheless, my Lord is bigger than my history, as was His companionship and help in the dark days of my journey. My suffering has strengthened the seed of faith implanted in me—God has been faithful indeed.

I didn't share the story of my abuse, suffering, and grief to win your sympathy. Such abuse should never happen to anyone, let alone a child or other vulnerable person. I shared my account with you hoping we can all acknowledge that the world we live in is full of the free (and sometimes wrong) choices men and women make. In this world, cruel acts of nature also occur randomly, and damage or destroy our lives in one way or another. My soul reaches out especially to anyone who has suffered abuse and oppression of any kind. No one should have to endure any torment, both of the mind and the body. Children should be protected and kept safe. Adults should be shown dignity in their workplaces and societies.

Speaking only for myself, I accept my history and should seek reconciliation with every one of my abusers and tormentors who couldn't or wouldn't understand me. I also beg the Lord to give consolation to all who have suffered similarly and the grace to forgive.

Life's also precarious. You and I could have been taken today (just like my friend, David Marshall), and our plans for tomorrow come to nothing. With this realization in mind, I urge you to make full use of the Lord's patience *today*, beg for His mercy and receive His help.

My faith experience has helped me learn the most important sign of faith: the cross, which also stands for the love of my God. Through my growing desire to love Him, I'm entering the cross with the necessary love for my neighbor and enemy. When everything I held dear in my married life was torn apart, I was ashamed of this failure. In those distressing times, the sign of love seemed mangled to me. I reveal this suffering now because I realize, not belatedly, my *broken* sign has a beauty. Its beauty is faintly similar to the infinitely illuminating sign of the cross—the sign of a love that seems shameful, defeated, and rejected to those who have no faith. My Lord gave me the eyes of faith, so I can now plainly see the cross in my life and the uplifting meaning of Christian love.

I hope my history can be of some help to a brother or sister who is trying to save a troubled marriage or one, who is like me, also left with a *broken* sign. Remember, such a sign isn't broken at all because our Lord has risen. He will help each one of us, crushed (but not broken) as we are in our individual ways, and all of us will rise with Him. All we need to do is carry our cross, march on a journey of faith, and let Him lead us.

Our Lord has promised a share in His triumph over death. Remember also: Baptism signals only the beginning of, and not the completion of, our new life in Christ. We have a share in His victory if we remain together in Jesus Christ—*let our Savior be the theme of our praise in the Great Assembly!*

Though many of the early Christians were frightened, persecuted, and martyred, the Lord remained faithful to them and made them disciples of the nations. Countless Christians in the preceding twenty centuries then kept and passed on the faith all over the world, and some have even glorified the Lord by their life. His water is sure, (Isaiah 33:16) and our hope in the Lord will never be shamed. (Psalm 25:2) On my faith journey, I have no doubt the Lord will teach me how to love, if only I will let Him speak to my heart, as I hope you will too.

So I've resolved to remain faithful to my promises. My hope in the Lord's promise of salvation has to be steady. I must try harder to listen to the Word, and do what Jesus tells me. That means getting ready to lay down my life and spend it for the love of Jesus—as a follower of Christ should.

In this book, I've shared my history and recounted how I was like a *Fourth Wise Man* searching for Jesus Christ. I haven't reached the gates of Jerusalem yet, but this Artaban has found the path to follow the Savior of the World. I hope the pastors of souls will continue to form my faith, tiny steps by tiny steps, so my faith may eventually mature. Yes, I want to become like the man in 1 Corinthians 13:12, with all my unformed ways left behind.

I'll march on.

I *will* follow my Teacher.

Trusting that my Lord will train me gradually and progressively through His Church, I hope to love as He loves me.

Reader, I hope you'll consider departing from New Egypt. The Lord beckons all of us to start walking in the spiritual desert, where He thirsts to speak to all our hearts. Will you receive as much as you need to eat? I'm convinced that, in this journey of faith, He will help all of us recognize who we really are, (1 John 3:1) and the original purpose of our life.

Will you march on?

Postscript

Dear reader, I've shared with you the precious memory of my journey of faith. It began when I was twelve, and it continues with grace from the Lord of Mercy. I believe some of you, if not all, hope to begin a similar journey of faith. The lesson I want to share with you from my experience is that you don't have to search for Him. The Savior of the World will come to you. All you need to do is say, "Yes."

With your *Yes*, your pastor of faith can help you begin a lifelong, spiritual journey with the Lord. Faith formation will benefit you as a believer, one who desires to love as He loves, but it should be more than Sunday worship and activities in the parish. Your Christian life needs to spread its wings beyond functional service in a ministry, trying to read the Bible in your room, or saying occasional prayers on your own. What the Word tells us is that Christ needs to be the center of every moment in our life, with a spiritual life lived in communion with the Body of Christ that He gives to all of us.

Trust in the Lord, who thirsts to give you life; not take it away!

On such a journey, the Lord will teach you His ways, so you can begin sharing in His priestly, prophetic, and royal office. The best part of the journey is that you need only ask the Lord for help, for He will do the real work of change, not you; certainly not me! The second excellent part is that you qualify to begin this spiritual journey if you're a sinner willing to carry your cross and follow Him. Don't worry about your failure to love or fight your sins on your own. Moving forward today, you need only walk earnestly with the Lord leading all of us.

For the most part, I spend about an hour a day. Can you spare at least an hour a day to allow Jesus to form your faith and penetrate your inmost heart?

So how does one begin this marching? Make an appointment with your pastor and have a good heart-to-heart talk about the questions and thoughts raised in this book. If a faith journey isn't available for any reason in your parish, don't worry. While you wait for the "door of faith" to let you enter, light a candle at your church at 7 pm *every* Saturday, which is the time after the first Vespers of the Sunday in question. Then, in prayer, make your desire known to Jesus, "Lord, I'm a sinner, and I need your help to begin following you."

I anticipate that the "instructors in the faith" or catechists might need time to reach you, so I urge you to be patient. While you're waiting, learn how to pray—not the saying of many words and wishes—you know what the Lord says about these.

I recommend you use the Breviary, which contains prayers for the Liturgy of the Hours said throughout the day, for every day in a given week and for the appropriate seasons. You can, of course, use any other prayer book that helps you spend quiet, daily time with the Lord, contemplating His will for you. If you should lapse in praying, don't fret. Say your regrets to the Lord, pick yourself up (again and again, and yet again), and continue spending quiet time with the Lord.

For if our Father so loved the world that He allowed His son to be humiliated, hurt and killed for the sake of every sinner, then His Love is definitely greater than the sum of our collective sins, failings, and wickedness. That said, you must never fail to turn back to the Lord and ask for His spiritual help. In your prayers or on your journey, you should neither give up nor doubt the Lord, for I'm confident that His help is sure and it's coming to you; if only you'll say *Yes*.

While you're waiting for your marching to begin and your heart urges you to help in the New Evangelization, why not start something small by passing your copy of this book to your family members, friends, or neighbors who are (or were) believers in our Savior? If, however, the message has aroused your faith in any meaningful way, share the proposal of re-evangelization with your family, friends and the whole world!

Jesus has commanded each and every Christian to announce His Good News: may we never tire of echoing our encounter or experience with the Eternal-Father!

Bibliography

Mere Christianity by C.S. Lewis

Cathechism of the Catholic Church, courtesy of http://www.vatican.va

Constitution On The Sacred Liturgy **Sacrosanctum Concilium** Solemnly Promulgated By His Holiness Pope Paul VI on December 4, 1963, Courtesy Of *http://www.vatican.va*

The Matrix by Lana Wachowski and Andrew Paul Wachowski

The Story of the Other Wise Man by Henry Van Dyke

Triple Time by Philip Larkin

Dogmatic Constitution on the Church **Lumen Gentium** solemnly promulgated by His Holiness Pope Paul VI on November 21, 1964, Courtesy Of *http://www.vatican.va*

Apostolic Constitution **Paenitemini** of the Supreme Pontiff Paul VI on Fast and Abstinence, courtesy of http://www.vatican.va

Apostolic Letter "*Motu Proprio Data*" **Porta Fidei** of the Supreme Pontiff Benedict XVI for the Indiction of the Year of Faith, courtesy of *http://www.vatican.va*

Congregation For The Doctrine Of The Faith **Note With Pastoral Recommendations For The Year Of Faith**

Message of St. John Paul II for the **World Congress of Ecclesial Movements and New Communities** on May 27, 1998, courtesy of http://www.vatican.va

Message of St. John Paul II to the Participants in the **Seminar on Ecclesial Movements and New Communities** on June 18, 1999, courtesy of http://www.vatican.va

St. John Paul II, in his **Easter address on May 4, 1999 to the Bishops of Ontario,** © *L'Osservatore Romano*, Editorial and Management Offices, Via del Pellegrino, 00120, Vatican City, Europe, digitally provided as item 1041, courtesy of CatholicCulture.org

Post-Synodal Apostolic Exhortation **Ecclesia In America** of St. John Paul II to The Bishops, Priests And Deacons, Men and Women Religious, and All The Lay Faithful on the Encounter with the Living Jesus Christ: The Way To Conversion, Communion And Solidarity In America, given on January 22, 1999, courtesy of http://www.vatican.va

Apostolic Exhortation **Catechesi Tradendae** of St. John Paul II on Catechesis In Our Time, given on January 22, 1999, courtesy of *http://www.vatican.va*

The Nature and Scope of Sexual Abuse of Minors by Catholic Priests and Deacons in the United States 1950-2002, A Research Study conducted by John Jay College of Criminal Justice, 2004

A Grief Observed by C.S. Lewis

The Secret Thoughts of an Unlikely Convert, An English Professor's Journey Into Christian Faith by Rosaria Champagne Butterfield

United States Conference of Catholic Bishops website *http://www.usccb.org* web articles on "New Evangelization"

Appendix: Extracts of the Apostolic Exhortation Catechesi Tradendae Of St. John Paul II On Catechesis In Our Time

Appendix-1: Here is the path

The more the Church, whether on the local or the universal level, gives catechesis *priority* over other works and undertakings the results of which would be more spectacular, the more she *finds in catechesis a strengthening of her internal life as a community of believers and of her external activity as a missionary Church* . . . She is bidden to offer catechesis her best resources in people and energy, *without sparing effort, toil or material means*, in order to organize it better and to train qualified personnel. *This is no mere human calculation; it is an attitude of faith*. And an attitude of faith always has reference to the faithfulness of God, who never fails to respond. (Emphasis added) (Catechesi Tradendae, 15)

Appendix-2: Why do adults need deeper catechesis?

. . . *I can't fail to emphasize now one of the most constant concerns* of the synod fathers, a concern imposed with vigor and urgency by present experiences throughout the world: I am referring to the *central problem of the catechesis of adults.* This is the principal form of catechesis, because it is addressed to persons who have the greatest responsibilities and the capacity to live the Christian message in its fully developed form. *The Christian community can't carry out a permanent catechesis without the direct and skilled participation of adults, whether as receivers or as promoters of catechetical activity.* The world, in which the young are called to live and to give witness to the faith which catechesis seeks to deepen and strengthen, is governed by adults. The faith of these adults too should continually be enlightened, stimulated and renewed, so that it may pervade the temporal realities in their charge. Thus, for catechesis to be effective, it must be permanent, and it would be quite useless if it stopped short at the threshold of maturity, since catechesis, admittedly under another form, *proves no less necessary for adults.* (Emphasis added) (Catechesi Tradendae, 43)

Appendix-3: What are the effects of inadequate catechism?

Among the adults who need catechesis, our pastoral missionary concern is directed to those who were born and reared in areas not yet Christianized, and who *have never been able to study deeply the Christian teaching* that the circumstances of life have at a certain moment caused them to come across. It is also *directed to those who in childhood received a catechesis suited to their age but who later drifted away from all religious practice and as adults find themselves with religious knowledge of a rather childish kind.* It is likewise directed to those who feel the effects of *a catechesis received early in life but badly imparted or badly assimilated.* It is directed to those who, although they were born in a Christian country or in sociologically Christian surroundings, *have never been educated in their faith* and, as adult are really catechumens. (Emphasis added) (Catechesi Tradendae, 44)

Appendix-4: How is catechesis different from the initial conversion?

The specific character of catechesis, as distinct from the initial conversion - bringing proclamation of the Gospel, *has the twofold objective of maturing the initial faith and of educating the true disciple of Christ* by means of a deeper and more systematic knowledge of the person and the message of our Lord Jesus Christ.

But in catechetical practice, this model order *must allow for the fact that the initial evangelization has often not taken place.* A certain number of children baptized in infancy come for catechesis in the parish without receiving any other initiation into the faith and still without any explicit personal attachment to Jesus Christ; they only have the capacity to believe placed within them by baptism and the presence of the Holy Spirit; and *opposition is quickly created by the prejudices of their non-Christian family background or of the positivist spirit of their education.* In addition, there are other children who haven't been baptized and whose parents agree only at a later date to religious education: for practical reasons, the catechumenal stage of these children will often be carried out largely in the course of the ordinary catechesis. Again, many pre-adolescents and adolescents who have been baptized and been given a systematic catechesis and the sacraments *still remain hesitant for a long time about committing their whole lives to Jesus Christ* - if, moreover, they don't attempt to avoid religious education in the name of their freedom. Finally, *even adults aren't safe from temptations to doubt or to abandon their faith, especially as a result of their unbelieving surroundings. This means that "catechesis" must often concern itself not only with nourishing and teaching the faith, but also with arousing it unceasingly with the help of grace*, with opening the heart, with converting, and with preparing total adherence to Jesus Christ on the part of those *who are still on the threshold of faith.* This concern will in part decide the tone, the language and the method of catechesis. (Emphasis added) (Catechesi Tradendae, 19)

Appendix-5: What's the spiritual motivation for adult catechesis?

. . . In the final analysis, *catechesis is necessary both for the maturation of the faith of Christians and for their witness in the world*: It is aimed at bringing Christians to "attain to the unity of the faith and of the knowledge of the Son of God, to mature manhood, to the measure of the stature of the fullness of Christ"; *it is also aimed at making them prepared to make a defense to anyone who calls them to account for the hope that is in them.* (Emphasis added) (Catechesi Tradendae, 25)

Appendix-6: What kind of 'Yes' did we say to Jesus Christ?

It is true that being a Christian means saying "yes" to Jesus Christ, but let us remember that this "yes" has two levels: It consists in surrendering to the word of God and relying on it, but it also means, at a later stage, endeavoring to know better—and better the profound meaning of this word. (Catechesi Tradendae, 20)

Appendix-7: How does a Christian deepen the faith?

A person who has given adherence to Jesus Christ by faith and is endeavoring to consolidate that faith by catechesis *needs to live in communion with those who have taken the same step.* Catechesis runs the risk of becoming barren if no community of faith and Christian life takes the catechumen in at a certain stage of his catechesis. *That is why the ecclesial community at all levels has a twofold responsibility with regard to catechesis: it has the responsibility of providing for the training of its members, but it also has the responsibility of welcoming them into an environment where they can live as fully as possible what they have learned.*

Catechesis is likewise open to missionary dynamism. *If catechesis is done well, Christians will be eager to bear witness to their faith, to hand it on to their children, to make it known to others, and to serve the human community in every way. . .* (Emphasis added) (Catechesi Tradendae, 24)

Appendix-8: Are church groups exempt?

I may also mention the youth groups that, under varying names and forms but always with the purpose of making Jesus Christ known and of living by the Gospel, are in some areas multiplying and flourishing in a sort of springtime that is very comforting for the Church. These include Catholic action groups, charitable groups, prayer groups and Christian meditation groups. These groups are a source of great hope for the Church of tomorrow. But, in the name of Jesus, I exhort the young people who belong to them, their leaders, and the priests who devote the best part of their ministry to them: no matter what it costs, don't allow these groups-which are exceptional occasions for meeting others, and which are blessed with such riches of friendship and solidarity among the young, of joy and enthusiasm, of reflection on events and facts—*don't allow them to lack serious study of Christian doctrine.* If they do, they will be in danger—a danger that has unfortunately proved only too real—of disappointing their members and also the Church. (Emphasis added) (Catechesi Tradendae, 47)

Appendix-9: Who has the responsibility for lifelong catechesis?

. . . the Church's members have different responsibilities, derived from each one's mission. Because of their charge, *pastors have, at differing levels, the chief responsibility for fostering, guiding and coordinating catechesis* . . . On another level, *parents have a unique responsibility.* Teachers, the various ministers of the Church, catechists, and also organizers of social communications, *all have in various degrees very precise responsibilities in this education of the believing conscience, an edu-*

cation that is important for the life of the Church and affects the life of society as such . . . (Emphasis added) (Catechesi Tradendae, 16)

Appendix-10: Who has the primary responsibility for catecheses?

Dearly beloved brothers, you have here a special mission within your Churches: *You are beyond all others the ones primarily responsible for catechesis*, the catechists par excellence. Together with the Pope, in the spirit of episcopal collegiality, you too have charge of catechesis throughout the Church. Accept therefore what I say to you from my heart.

I know that your ministry as Bishops is growing daily more complex and overwhelming. A thousand duties call you: from the training of new priests to being actively present within the lay communities, from the living, worthy celebration of the sacraments and acts of worship to concern for human advancement and the defense of human rights. *But let the concern to foster active and effective catechesis yield to no other care whatever in any way.* This concern will lead you to transmit personally to your faithful the doctrine of life. But it should also lead you to take on in your diocese, in accordance with the plans of the episcopal conference to which you belong, the chief management of catechesis, while at the same time surrounding yourselves with competent and trustworthy assistants. *Your principal role will be to bring about and maintain in your Churches a real passion for catechesis*, a passion embodied in a pertinent and effective organization, putting into operation the necessary personnel, means and equipment, and also financial resources. You can be sure that if catechesis is done well in your local Churches, everything else will be easier to do. And needless to say, although your zeal must sometimes impose upon you the thankless task of denouncing deviations and correcting errors, it will much more often win for you the joy and consolation of seeing your Churches flourishing because catechesis is given in them as the Lord wishes. (Emphasis added) (Catechesi Tradendae, 16)

Appendix-11: Who are the instructors in the Faith?

For your part, priests, here you have a field in which you are the immediate assistants of your Bishops. The Council has called you "*instructors in the faith*"; there is no better way for you to be such instructors than by devoting your best efforts to the growth of your communities in the faith. Whether you are in charge of a parish, or are chaplains to primary or secondary schools or universities, or have responsibility for pastoral activity at any level, or are leaders of large or small communities, especially youth groups, the Church expects you to neglect nothing with a view to a well-organized and well-oriented catechetical effort. *The deacons and other ministers that you may have the good fortune to have with you are your natural assistants in this. All believers have a right to catechesis; all pastors have the duty to provide it.* I shall always ask civil leaders to respect the freedom of catechetical teaching; but with all my strength I beg you, ministers of Jesus Christ: Don't, for lack of zeal or because of some unfortunate preconceived idea, leave the faithful without catechesis. *Let it not be said that "the children beg for food, but no one gives to them."* (Emphasis added) (Catechesi Tradendae, 64)

Appendix-12: What if there aren't enough priests?

Many religious institutes for men and women came into being for the purpose of giving Christian education to children and young people, especially the most abandoned. Throughout history, men and women religious have been deeply committed to the Church's catechetical activity, doing particularly apposite and effective work. At a time when it is desired that the links between religious and pastors should be accentuated and consequently *the active presence of religious communities and their members in the pastoral projects of the local Churches*, I wholeheartedly exhort you, *whose religious consecration should make you even more readily available for the Church's service*, to prepare as well as possible for the task of catechesis according to the differing vocations of your institutes and the missions entrusted to you, and to carry this concern everywhere. Let the communities dedicate as much as possible of what ability and means they have to the specific work of catechesis. (Emphasis added) (Catechesi Tradendae, 65)

Appendix-13: The vital importance of the family in catechesis

The family's catechetical activity has a special character, which is in a sense irreplaceable. This special character has been rightly stressed by the Church, particularly by the Second Vatican Council. *Education in the faith by parents, which should begin from the children's tenderest age*, is already being given when the members of a family help each other to grow in faith through the witness of their Christian lives, a witness that is often without words but which perseveres throughout a day-to-day life lived in accordance with the Gospel. This catechesis is more incisive when, in the course of family events (such as the reception of the sacraments, the celebration of great liturgical feasts, the birth of a child, a bereavement) *care is taken to explain in the home the Christian or religious content of these events. But that isn't enough: Christian parents must strive to follow and repeat, within the setting of family life, the more methodical teaching received elsewhere.* The fact that these truths about the main questions of faith and Christian living are thus repeated within a family setting impregnated with love and respect will often make it possible to influence the children in a decisive way for life. The parents themselves profit from the effort that this demands of them, *for in a catechetical dialogue of this sort each individual both receives and gives.*

Family catechesis therefore precedes, accompanies and enriches all other forms of catechesis. Furthermore, in places where anti- religious legislation endeavors even to prevent education in the faith, and in places where widespread unbelief or invasive secularism makes real religious growth practically impossible, "*the church of the home*" *remains the one place where children and young people can receive an authentic catechesis. Thus there can't be too great an effort on the part of Christian parents to prepare for this ministry of being their own children's catechists* and to carry it out with tireless zeal. *Encouragement must also be given to the individuals or institutions that, through person-to-person contacts, through meetings, and through all kinds of pedagogical means, help parents to perform their task: The service they are doing to catechesis is beyond price.* (Emphasis added) (Catechesi Tradendae, 62-68)

www.ingramcontent.com/pod-product-compliance
Lightning Source LLC
LaVergne TN
LVHW011320080426
835513LV00006B/130